Cosmopo

David Held

COSMOPOLITANISM

Ideals and Realities

polity

First published in 2010 by Polity Press

Polity Press
65 Bridge Street
Cambridge CB2 1UR, UK

Polity Press
350 Main Street
Malden, MA 02148, USA

ISBN-13: 978-0-7456-4835-4
ISBN-13: 978-0-7456-4836-1(pb)

A catalogue record for this book is available from the British Library.

Typeset in 11 on 14 pt Sabon
by Toppan Best-set Premedia Limited
Printed and bound in Great Britain by MPG Books Group Limited, Bodmin, Cornwall

The publisher has used its best endeavours to ensure that the URLs for external websites referred to in this book are correct and active at the time of going to press. However, the publisher has no responsibility for the websites and can make no guarantee that a site will remain live or that the content is or will remain appropriate.

Every effort has been made to trace all copyright holders, but if any have been inadvertently overlooked the publisher will be pleased to include any necessary credits in any subsequent reprint or edition.

For further information on Polity, visit our website: www.politybooks.com

Contents

Preface   ix

**Introduction: Changing Forms of
Global Order**   1
Towards a multipolar world   2
The paradox of our times   4
Economic liberalism and international
    market integration   5
Security   7
The impact of the global financial crisis   12
Shared problems and collective threats   13
A cosmopolitan approach   14
Democratic public law and sovereignty   17
Summary of the book ahead   20

1 **Cosmopolitanism: Ideas, Realities and Deficits**   27
Globalization   28
The global governance complex   31
Globalization and democracy: Five
    disjunctures   35

v

Contents

Cosmopolitanism: Ideas and trajectories   39
Cosmopolitan realities   50
Addressing the institutional deficit:
    Reframing the market   59

2 **Principles of Cosmopolitan Order**   67
Cosmopolitan principles   69
Thick or thin cosmopolitanism?   75
Cosmopolitan justifications   81
From cosmopolitan principles to
    cosmopolitan law   92

3 **Cosmopolitan Law and Institutional
Requirements**   93
The idea of cosmopolitan law   97
Institutional requirements   103
In sum   112
Political openings   115

4 **Violence, Law and Justice in a Global Age**   117
Reframing human activity: International
    law, rights and responsibilities   120
9/11, war and justice   128
Islam, the Kantian heritage and double
    standards   137
Concluding reflections   141

5 **Reframing Global Governance: Apocalypse
Soon or Reform!**   143
The paradox of our times   143
Why be concerned with global
    challenges?   146

Contents

Deep drivers and governance challenges   149
Global governance: Contemporary
    surface trends   157
Problems and dilemmas of global
    problem-solving   160
Strengthening global governance   165
Global governance and the democratic
    question   172
Multilevel citizenship, multilayered
    democracy   177

6 **Parallel Worlds: The Governance of**
  Global Risks in Finance, Security and
  the Environment   **184**
Global governance and the paradox of
    our times   185
The global governance of finance   188
The global governance of security   195
The global governance of the environment   198
Conclusion: Crisis, politicization and
    reform   202

7 **Democracy, Climate Change and Global**
  Governance   **208**
Democracy I: The democratic nation-state
    and climate change   209
Democracy II: Global governance and
    climate change   220
The policy debate: Squaring the circle?   224
The political elements of a democratic
    global deal   230
Democracy and the policy menu ahead   234

Contents

Afterword   **239**

Acknowledgements   253

List of Abbreviations   255

Notes   259

References   268

Index   292

Preface

The arguments in this volume have evolved over the past decade. Throughout this period three key terms have defined my intellectual preoccupations: democracy, globalization and cosmopolitanism. Each of these refers to a set of ideas as well as social processes which have shaped, and continue to shape, our lives.

Democracy, from ancient cities to contemporary political systems, has been the most powerful of all political ideas, expressing, as it does, the yearning for self-determination and all the achievements and limitations of the actual processes involved. From cities to nation-states, democracy has become associated with the aspiration of people to rule themselves in their own community, and with the gains and frustrations associated with this. Democracy has set itself against arbitrary rule in all its forms and yet has only incompletely achieved its core objective.

Globalization defines a set of processes which are reshaping the organization of human activity, stretching political, economic, social and communicative networks across regions and continents. Power is no longer simply articulated in particular geographic sites and locations, but is spread and diffused across the world in such a way that what occurs in one place can have ramifications across many others. If democracy expresses the idea of self-government within a delimited space, the local and national territory, globalization refers to activities and systems of interaction which create what I call overlapping communities of fate – the interlinking of the fortunes of cities and countries.

Democracy and globalization pull in different directions, or so it seems. Democracy pulls towards the self-organization of activity in delimited territories, and globalization pulls towards the creation of new dense forms of transborder interaction, raising the question of how these can be brought under democratic control and rendered accountable. If all our key political ideas and mechanisms have been developed with reference to particular communities and spaces, how can they be reinvented to embrace a global age?

Clues to an answer to this question can be found in the third term: cosmopolitanism. Cosmopolitanism elaborates a concern with the equal moral status of each and every human being and creates a bedrock of interest in what it is that human beings have in common, independently of their particular familial, ethical, national and religious affiliations. It does not deny the historical, sociological and political significance of these kinds of identity, but argues that they can obscure what it is that all people share – the bundle of needs, desires, anxieties and passions that define us all as members of the same species. Human life can come to an end for diverse reasons, but these have common roots: hunger, illness, loneliness and so on. Human life cannot be sustained without satisfying basic needs whether these be physical, psychological or social.

We need to understand the latter if we are to grasp the proper limits to human diversity, limits which specify necessary conditions for human activity, whether it is found in families, groups or nation-states. These limits articulate necessary boundaries which no human activity should cross – boundaries concerning violence, arbitrary decision-making, the nature and scope of power, among other pressing concerns.

If democracy is about self-determination, globalization about transborder processes and cosmopolitanism about universal principles which must shape and limit all human activity, together they help us understand that the fate of humankind can no longer be disclosed merely by examining self-enclosed political and moral communities, and that the principles of democracy and cosmopolitanism need to be protected and nurtured across all human spheres – local, national, regional and global. If some of the most powerful processes and forces in the world are to be brought under the sphere of influence of public deliberation and democratic accountability, then we need to articulate the changing basis of communities and the interconnection among them. This is both an empirical challenge and a political one.

These concerns do not generate a simple aspiration for one global community, democratically organized on cosmopolitan principles. Rather, it suggests the necessity to recognize the multilevel and multilayered nature of human associations in which we already live, and to find new procedures and mechanisms to ensure that they are bound together by common principles and democratic processes which allow for democracy to flourish, from cities to global networks, in the context of a shared commitment to boundaries which define necessary limits on human action, whether these are political, economic, social or environmental. This volume addresses this overriding concern.

The chapters that follow were all written initially as essays. The dates of their original publication can be found in the acknowledgements. They all have been substantially rewritten for this book in order to develop arguments where relevant, to minimize overlap, to avoid repetition and to change examples if the originals now seem out of date or anachronistic. Chapter 4, 'Violence, Law and Justice in a Global Age' (written in November 2001), has been least altered because it is my attempt to make sense of 9/11 and the military response that followed, and because I think the arguments and examples are still valid despite the passage of some years. Reworked, the chapters constitute an account of my thinking about democracy, globalization and cosmopolitanism – their changing rationale and relevance to life in a global age.

Of the many people who have influenced this book, I would particularly like to acknowledge my co-authors of chapter 6, Kevin Young, and of chapter 7, Angus Fane Hervey. Neither chapter would have the shape or detail they have without their contribution. Pietro Maffettone has been indispensable in helping to compile and edit the book, as has Charlie Roger, whose eye for detail has been immensely valuable.

David Held
January 2010

Introduction: Changing Forms of Global Order

Until recently, the West has, by and large, determined the rules of the game on the global stage. During the last century, Western countries presided over a shift in world power – from control via territory to control via the creation of governance structures created in the post-1945 era. From the United Nations Charter and the formation of the Bretton-Woods institutions to the Rio Declaration on the environment and the creation of the World Trade Organisation, international agreements have invariably served to entrench a well-established international power structure. The division of the globe into powerful nation-states, with distinctive sets of geopolitical interests, and reflecting the international power structure of 1945, is still embedded in the articles and statutes of leading intergovernmental organizations, such as the IMF and the World Bank. Voting rights are distributed largely in relation to individual financial contributions, and geo-economic strength is integrated into decision-making procedures.

1

The result has been susceptibility of the major international governmental organizations (IGOs) to the agendas of the most powerful states, partiality in enforcement operations (or lack of them altogether), their continued dependency on financial support from a few major states, and weaknesses in the policing of global collective action problems. This has been dominance based on a 'club' model of global governance and legitimacy. Policy at the international level has been decided by a core set of powerful countries, above all the 'G1', G5 and G7, with the rest largely excluded from the decision-making process.

Towards a multipolar world

Today, however, that picture is changing. The trajectory of Western dominance has come to a clear halt with the failure of dominant elements of Western global policy over the past few decades. The West can no longer rule through power or example alone. At the same time, Asia is on the ascent. Over the last half-century, East and Southeast Asia has more than doubled its share of world GDP and increased per capita income at an average growth rate almost two and a half times that in the rest of the world (Quah, 2008). In the last two decades alone, emerging Asian economies have experienced an average growth rate of almost 8 per cent – 3 times the rate in the rich world (*Economist*, 2009).

As a result, Asia has been both a stabilizing influence on and a steady contributor to world economic growth.

Introduction: Changing Forms of Global Order

According to the IMF, China alone accounted for around a third of global economic growth in 2008, more than any other nation, and its economy was the only one of the world's 10 biggest which expanded in the wake of the financial crisis (IMF, 2009). Other Asian economies have bounced back from the financial crisis far more quickly than anyone expected. As an article in the *New York Times* (2009) points out, the United States has always led the way out of major global economic crises, but this time the catalyst came from China and the rest of Asia. These countries are no longer simply beholden to the US and other Western countries as recipients of their exports, and this decoupling has to some extent allowed Asian economies to recover more quickly. Boosted by increased consumer spending and massive government-led investment, the region as a whole grew by more than 5 per cent in 2009 – at a time when the old G7 contracted by over 3.5 per cent. Simply put, we are seeing a fundamental rebalancing of the world economy, with the centre of gravity shifting noticeably to the East.

The trajectory of change is towards a multipolar world, where the West no longer holds a premium on geopolitical or economic power. Moreover, different discourses and concepts of governance have emerged to challenge the old Western orthodoxy of multilateralism and the post-war order. At the same time, complex global processes, from the ecological to the financial, connect the fate of communities to each other across the world in new ways, requiring effective, accountable and inclusive problem-solving capacity. How this capacity can be ensured is another matter.

Introduction: Changing Forms of Global Order

The paradox of our times

What I call the paradox of our times refers to the fact that the collective issues we must grapple with are of growing cross-border extensity and intensity, yet the means for addressing these are weak and incomplete. While there is a variety of reasons for the persistence of these problems, at the most basic level the persistence of this paradox remains a problem of governance.

We face three core sets of problems – those concerned with (i) sharing our planet (climate change, biodiversity and ecosystem losses, water deficits); (ii) sustaining our humanity (poverty, conflict prevention, global infectious diseases); and (iii) developing our rulebook (nuclear proliferation, toxic waste disposal, intellectual property rights, genetic research rules, trade rules, finance and tax rules) (Rischard, 2002). In our increasingly interconnected world, these global problems cannot be solved by any one nation-state acting alone. They call for collective and collaborative action – something that the nations of the world have not been good at, and which they need to be better at if these pressing issues are to be adequately resolved. Yet, the evidence is wanting that we are getting better at building appropriate governance capacity.

One significant problem is that a growing number of issues span both the domestic and the international domains. The institutional fragmentation and competition between states can lead to these global issues being addressed in an ad hoc and dissonant manner. A second problem is that even when the global dimension of a problem is acknowledged, there is often no clear division of labour among the myriad of international institutions that seek to address it: their functions often overlap, their mandates conflict and their objectives often become blurred. A third problem is that the existing system of global governance suffers from severe deficits of accountability and inclusion. This problem is especially relevant in regard to how less economically powerful states and, hence, their entire populations are marginalized or excluded from decision-making.

Economic liberalism and international market integration

For the past two to three decades, the agenda of economic liberalization and global market integration – the Washington Consensus, as it is sometimes called – has been the mantra of many leading economic powers and international financial institutions (see Held, 2004). The thrust of the Washington Consensus was to promote this view and to adapt the public domain – local, national and global – to market-leading institutions and processes (see chapters 5 and 6). It thus bears a heavy burden of responsibility for the common political resistance or unwillingness to address significant areas of market failure, including:

- the problem of externalities, such as the environmental degradation exacerbated by current forms of economic growth;
- the inadequate development of non-market social factors, which alone can provide an effective balance

between 'competition' and 'cooperation' and thus ensure an adequate supply of essential public goods, such as education, effective transportation and sound health;

- the underemployment or unemployment of productive resources in the context of the demonstrable existence of urgent and unmet need; and
- global macroeconomic imbalances and a poor regulatory framework – policies that led to the financial crisis.

Today, there are strong grounds for doubting that the standard liberal economic approach delivers on promised goods and that global market integration is the indispensable condition of development. The implementation of such policies by the World Bank, the IMF and leading economic powers has often led to counter-productive results at national and global levels. The countries that have benefited most from globalization are those that have not played by the rules of the standard liberal market approach, including China, India and Vietnam.

Leaving markets alone to resolve problems of resource generation and allocation neglects the deep roots of many economic and political difficulties, such as the vast asymmetries of life chances within and between nation-states, the erosion of the economic fortunes of some countries in sectors like agriculture and textiles while these sectors enjoy protection and assistance in others, the emergence of global financial flows which can rapidly destabilize national economies, and the development of serious transnational problems involving the global commons.

The financial crisis is a case in point. High levels of consumer spending in the West, fuelled by easy access to credit, underwritten by high rates of savings in exporting countries in the East (especially China) and aided by China's fixed exchange rate and the accumulation of reserves in sovereign wealth funds, created a global liquidity overflow. The resulting asset bubbles and excess leverage which eventually caused the crisis were, however, not due to these factors alone. The key fault-line can be traced to a 'light touch' regulatory system that encouraged risk-taking and allowed money to be diverted into very specific areas: mortgage securitization and off-balance sheet activity (Blundell-Wignall et al., 2008). The fallout, when it came, was devastating – and while many financial institutions have emerged relatively unscathed, the damage to Western economies has been huge. The financial crisis has to be understood as part of the structural weakness of the Anglo-American model of capitalism – a model which recently sought to reshape the post-war welfare state through privatization and deregulation in the name of promoting economic efficiency and market success (Lim, 2008).

Security

From the period following the Second World War until 1989, the nature of national security was shaped decisively by the contest between the United States and the

Soviet Union. The dominance of these world powers, and the operation of alliances like NATO and the Warsaw Pact, constrained decision-making for many states in the post-war years. In the post-Cold War world of the 1990s and the 2000s, the constraints upon state security policy have not been eradicated so much as reconfigured. Instead of bipolarity, the global system now exhibits characteristics of a multipolar distribution of political-economic power. Within this more complex structure, the strategic and foreign policy options confronting an individual state are still significantly defined by its location in the global power hierarchy. But there is much more uncertainty and indeterminacy in the system.

The war against Iraq in 2003 gave priority to a narrow security agenda which was at the heart of the post-9/11 American security doctrine of unilateral and pre-emptive war. This agenda contradicted most of the core tenets of international politics and international agreements since 1945, and had many serious implications. Among them was a return to an old realist understanding of international relations, in which states rightly pursue their national interests unencumbered by attempts to establish internationally recognized limits (such as self-defence or collective security) on their ambitions. But if this 'freedom' is granted to the US, why not also to Russia, China, India, Pakistan, North Korea, Iran and so on? It cannot be consistently argued that all states bar one should accept limits on their self-defined goals. The flaws of international law and multilateralism can either be addressed or taken as an excuse for the further weakening of international institutions and legal arrangements. In either event, America's unilateralist moment proved to be short-lived – Iraq and Afghanistan have subsequently revealed the dangers of such a strategy. The US and its allies generalized the wrong warfare model – the Cold War model – onto an era of fragmented, complicated conflicts, and stalled at best, lost at worse.

Most armed forces of the world – military/air/navy – are still developed on a model of nation-states at war with one another, based on the organizational principle of conflicting geopolitical state interests. And global military spending, fuelled by such preconceptions, has been on a sustained upward trend. Total global military expenditure in 2008 is estimated to have reached $1.464 trillion, representing an increase of 4 per cent in real terms compared to 2007, and of 45 per cent over the 10-year period 1999–2008 (SIPRI, 2009: 179). To put this in perspective, the total is:

- 2.4 per cent of global GDP, or $217 for every person on the planet;
- 13 times the total spent on all types of development aid;
- 700 times the total amount spent on global health programs;
- roughly the same as the combined total GDP of every country in Africa;
- only the total cost of the financial crisis, eight times as large, dwarfs it.

The United States accounts for the majority of the global increase – representing 58 per cent of the global increase since the turn of the century, largely due to the wars in Iraq and Afghanistan, which have cost around a trillion dollars thus far (ibid.: 185). However, the US is far from the only country to pursue such a determined course of militarization. China and Russia have both nearly tripled their military expenditure, while other regional powers – such as Algeria, Brazil, India, Iran, Israel, South Korea and Saudi Arabia – have also made substantial contributions to the total increase. Of the five permanent members of the UN Security Council, only France has held its spending relatively steady, with a rise of just 3.5 per cent in the first decade of the twenty-first century. The effects of the global financial crisis – in particular, growing government budget deficits and the economic stimulus packages that are aimed at countering the crisis – seem to have had little impact so far on military spending, with most countries, including the US and China, remaining committed to further increases in the years ahead.

Yet, according to the 2009 SIPRI yearbook, the most comprehensive open-source account of developments in global conflicts and security, of the 16 major armed conflicts that were active in 15 locations around the world in 2008, not one was a major interstate conflict (ibid.: 69).

Militaries remain organized on a national, rather than regional or multilateral basis, with vast duplication, overlap and waste of resources. In countries like the UK and the US, spending levels are now far in excess of any plausible *defensive* needs, and are no longer justified on such grounds. With the exception perhaps of the US and China, no country is capable of acting independently in major conflicts or of intervening against regimes that threaten global peace and security. There is something quite baroque about existing armaments, defence positions and tactics (Kaldor, 1982, 2007). Against this background, the way we conduct military spending looks increasingly anachronistic. It bears pointing out that total global spending on multilateral operations such as peacekeeping forces was $8.2 billion, or 0.56 per cent of total global military expenditures (SIPRI, 2010).

Learning has been slow, but now some of the world's most senior military figures have taken up the challenge and are changing the way warfare is conceived. In a speech at Chatham House, the new head of the British Army, General Sir David Richards, warned that traditional methods and forms of warfare are becoming redundant (*Guardian*, 2009). According to Richards, globalization is increasing the likelihood of conflict with non-state and failed state actors, and reducing the likelihood of state-on-state warfare. Despite the use of impressive amounts of traditional combat power, the US and NATO, 'the most powerful military alliance in the history of the world', has failed to impress or deter opponents with recourse to asymmetric tactics and technology (ibid.). Similarly, General Stanley McChrystal, formerly NATO's most senior commander in Afghanistan, has warned that the West's military strategy is failing, and that a new approach is necessary. He is reported to have said that the initiative may have been handed to the Taliban by NATO forces charging like bulls at 'matador' insurgents and haemorrhaging with each thrust of the sword (*Independent*, 2009).

What might such an approach look like? For a start, armed forces of the future will have to deal with new types of weapons systems and methods of warfare. According to General Richards, the lexicon of today is 'non-kinetic effects teams, counter-IED, information dominance, counter-piracy, and cyber attack and defence' (*Guardian*, 2009). Armed forces of the future will need to be relevant to emerging security challenges and the increasingly sophisticated adversaries they face. Moreover, General David Petraeus, until recently head of the US Central Command, and the man who oversaw the 2007 and 2008 'surge' in Iraq, has pointed out that new techniques of warfare are not enough. He stresses the importance of a more comprehensive approach to conflict. By this he means that while the traditional military approach to high ground, bridge crossings and key infrastructure remains valid to varying degrees 'the terrain that matters most is the human terrain' (2010: 116). He emphasizes that 'we have to understand the people, their culture, their social structures, and how systems to support them are supposed to work – and how they do work. And our most important tasks have to be to secure and to serve the people, as well as to respect them and to facilitate the provision of basic services, the establishment of local governance, and the revival of local economies' (ibid.).

The impact of the global financial crisis

The financial crisis and its after-effects are a particular instance of both of the themes discussed so far – the end of the Washington Consensus and the decline of interstate conflict. It will put further pressure on budgets, and put in sharp relief trade-offs on public expenditure. Of course, such trade-offs are nothing new. The issue is less about the contraction of available money as it is about a shift in public priorities. Security threats are in the process of being downgraded, and at the top of the agenda are now unemployment, finance and low carbon growth, as well as ring-fenced domains such as health services. In short, a time is rapidly approaching when defence budgets will not only taper off as war supplements disappear, but will also compete against ballooning mandatory spending programmes for fewer and fewer tax resources – all, of course, amidst an uncertain path to recovery in the US and Europe.

The financial crisis has also resulted in the emergence of the G20 as the new de facto governance coalition of powerful states – with the US and China at the forefront of all negotiations. While both countries still acknowledge the significance of multilateralism, the shift from the G1, G5 and G8 to the G2 and the G20 reflects the changing balance of power in the world.

Shared problems and collective threats

Today, there is a newfound recognition that global problems cannot be solved by any one nation-state acting alone, nor by states just fighting their corner in regional blocs. As demands on the state have increased, a whole series of policy problems have arisen which cannot be adequately resolved without cooperation with other states and non-state actors. There is a growing recognition that individual states are no longer the only appropriate political units for either resolving key policy problems or managing a broad range of public functions.

The policy packages that have largely set the global agenda – in economics and security – have been discredited. The Washington Consensus and Washington security doctrines have dug their own graves. The most successful developing countries in the world are successful because they have not followed the Washington Consensus agenda, and the conflicts that have most successfully been diffused are ones that have benefited from concentrated multilateral support and a human security agenda. The future of organized force in countries like the UK is through regional and international organizations. Cooperation between states is still important, if not more so, but what has changed is the rationale, which is now deeper and more complex. The old threat was the 'other'; the new threat is shared problems and collective threats. Here are clear clues as to how to proceed in the future. We need to follow these clues and learn from the mistakes of the past if democracy, effective governance and a renewed multilateral order are to be advanced.

Or, to sum up, realism is dead; long live cosmopolitanism!

A cosmopolitan approach

Just as there is not one form of liberalism or one single way to conceptualize democracy, there is not one unified or monolithic understanding of cosmopolitanism (see Brown and Held, 2010: Introduction). The first sustained use of the term 'cosmopolitan' can be traced to the Stoics. Their main aspiration was to replace the primacy of the individual's relation to the polis with the idea of the cosmos as encompassing the whole of humanity in an ideal of universal belonging. A second significant meaning can be dated back to the Enlightenment. Kant connected the idea of cosmopolitanism with the standpoint of public reason. An individual's entitlement to enter the realm of public reason is mirrored in the right to free membership in the global community of argument. A third and more recent understanding of cosmopolitanism involves three key elements: (i) egalitarian individualism, (ii) reciprocal recognition, and (iii) impartialist reasoning (see Barry, 1999; Pogge, 1994a; Beitz, 1979). The first element simply states that individuals are the 'ultimate units of moral concern'. The second implies that the equal moral worth of persons should be recognized by all. Finally, the third mandates that each person's claims are to enjoy impartial consideration in public deliberation and argument.

The specific model of cosmopolitanism I defend draws on elements of all three of these accounts. It recognizes each person as an autonomous moral agent entitled to equal dignity and consideration. The acknowledgement of each person as the ultimate unit of moral focus does not deny the importance of local affiliations (Pogge, 1994b). Rather, it is a way of setting limits to what the latter can entail. The model also promotes a way of translating individual agency into collective political enterprises. It sets down consent, deliberation

15

and collective decision-making as the essential mechanisms for the creation and development of cosmopolitan institutions and forms of governance. These are vital for non-coercive, legitimate political processes. Finally, the model identifies the prevention of 'serious harm' and 'sustainability' as the main instruments to prioritize urgent need and resource conservation. The latter function as tools for the orientation of public decision-making in critical cases (for further discussion of these principles, see chapter 2).

While my account aims at being universal, it tries to address cultural and political specificity seriously. Universal moral principles play a defining role, yet the hermeneutical necessity of interpreting their precise meaning in the local settings in which they operate is recognized. It is in the intersection of principle and pluralism – in the space where the former creates the conditions for the latter, and the latter elucidates the former – that regulative cosmopolitan principles and democracy conjoin. I call this a layered cosmopolitan approach (see chapters 2 and 3).

Every moral and political outlook calls for justification. The historical and geographical origin of cosmopolitanism in the West should not per se disqualify its reach; origin and validity are separate issues (see Weale, 1998). Two fundamental metaprinciples bear the justificatory weight of my account. They are the metaprinciple of autonomy (MPA) and the metaprinciple of impartialist reasoning (MPIR). I see these two principles as organizing notions of ethical discourse. The MPA represents a crystallization of the historical process that understands citizens in democracies as free and equal

16

individuals entitled to moral autonomy and political self-determination. The MPIR characterizes the basic philosophical interpretation of reciprocity when it comes to the elaboration of political and moral principles that all should be able to endorse and adopt. The two meta-principles constitute side-constraints on the elaboration of my cosmopolitan account and form the basis of its justificatory shape and force.

Democratic public law and sovereignty

At the core of the transition from cosmopolitan principles to the real world of politics lies the entrenchment of these principles in what I call 'democratic public law' – the precondition of a cosmopolitan order. This involves a redefinition of the idea of sovereignty as it has been commonly developed in international relations. From terrorism to climate change, from global economic turmoil to the financial crisis, the nation-state and the international governance structures are often ineffective and lacking in accountability and democratic legitimacy. Yet, if we learn the lessons of past policy failures and the limits of current institutional developments, the way ahead is not unclear.

At the heart of democratic public law lies the protection of certain fundamental human interests in self-determination and autonomy. As I have argued elsewhere, what is crucial to the goal of democratic autonomy is the ability of democratic public law to address different spheres of power (Held, 1995: 189ff.). Democratic public law needs to address all obstacles to citizens' ability to fully participate in the democratic process. If citizens are to make effective use of their democratic rights, to paraphrase the late John Rawls, all sources of important influence over the vital aspects of their lives must be within reach of their decision-making abilities (Rawls, 1971). Yet, today more than ever, the elusive fit between those who make decisions and those whose vital interests are affected by those decisions cannot be assumed to exist at the national level. In a world of complex interdependences, the actual prospects of people depend more on forces that are external (rather than internal) to the nation-state. Put simply, by concentrating on the state alone, irrespective of the circumstances in which the latter operates, there is a risk of focusing on the wrong level of analysis and governance.

The entrenchment of democratic public law at the global level requires a revision of the traditional under-standing of sovereignty. In the classic model of sover-eignty the state has effective and untrammelled power over a unified territory. Following the Second World War, and the creation of the human rights regime, the classic model of sovereignty was challenged by what I call the liberal model of sovereignty. At its core, the liberal model of sovereignty recasts the relationship between the state and its citizens. It anchors the state's legitimacy to the protection of basic human rights which become the essentials of political legitimacy. But the current state of global political relations mandates a further revision. The liberal model of sovereignty needs to be replaced by what I call a cosmopolitan model of sovereignty. The latter recasts the attribution of legitimate political power altogether. Cosmopolitan sovereignty challenges the very idea of fixed borders and territories governed by states alone. It sees sovereignty as the networked realms of public authority shaped and delimited by an overarching cosmopolitan legal framework (see chapter 3). In this model bounded political communities lose their role as the sole centre of legitimate political power. Democratic politics and decision-making are thought of as part of a wider framework of political interaction in which legitimate decision-making is conducted in different loci of power within and outside the nation-state.

The bottom line is that we can no longer ignore our common problems and destiny. We need a framework of political and moral interaction in order to coexist and cooperate in the resolution of our shared (and pressing) problems. From ecological disasters to financial meltdowns, there is no other solution but to find a common solution. If this is correct, then a cosmopolitan approach is not a form of Western yearning for a form of ideological dominance or imperial control. Rather, it is a framework of ideas and principles that can guide us towards the governance of the challenges we face. Cosmopolitanism is, contrary to popular criticism, the triumph of difference and local affiliations. Insofar as a cosmopolitan institutional project aims at the entrenchment of law-governed relations, it creates the requirements for political autonomy that each person and group needs in order to foster its ideas of the good life. Without such a framework, solutions will not be adopted on the basis of deliberation and law, but on the basis of power and economic strength. A world without cosmopolitan principles is not a world in which communal differences are entrenched and valued for their own sake, but rather a world in which power (in its different manifestations) drives the resolution of what I have called the pressing issues of our time.

Summary of the book ahead

Chapter 1 addresses the relationship between globalization, governance, democracy and social justice. Globalization is presented as the stretching and intensification of social, political and economic activities across political frontiers and geographic borders. Such phenomena in turn highlight the alteration of the meaning of democracy and accountability at the national level. After recalling the genesis of contemporary meanings of cosmopolitan principles, the chapter goes on to argue that many of the main tenets of cosmopolitanism are at the core of the human rights-driven expansion of international institutions after the Second World War. While this is part of what can be called 'cosmopolitan realities', it is also important to recognize that the current global order has crucially omitted to address many key sources of power, including market forces and the provision of effective mechanisms for the monitoring and regulation of the economic domain. The solution lies in the reframing of market forces according to cosmopolitan standards in order to establish fair conditions for economic cooperation and competition.

The second chapter introduces the principles that underpin my conception of cosmopolitan order. The

chapter develops the idea of a layered form of cosmopolitanism as the conceptual space occupied by eight
key principles of cosmopolitan order. A layered account
of cosmopolitanism remains faithful to its foundations
in the moral equality of all individuals while recognizing
the necessity to include cultural specificity in the interpretation and implementation of cosmopolitan prescrip-
tions and ideals. After developing the basic tenets of the
justification of my cosmopolitan account, the chapter
goes on to introduce the idea of cosmopolitan law as
distinct from the law of states and international law.
Cosmopolitan law, following Kant, is seen as the best
representation of persons' equal moral standing and
dignity. The process of entrenchment of cosmopolitan
law requires the redefinition of classic ideas of sovereignty and the repositioning of legitimate political
authority away from the borders of the nation-state
alone.

The third chapter starts by providing an account of
the contemporary context of cosmopolitanism. From
9/11 to the war in Iraq, from self-determination to cultural clashes, recent years seem to speak of a constant
decline of cosmopolitan ideals in global politics. But the
picture is not that bleak. From the foundations of the
UN charter to international human rights agreements
and treaties (not to mention the establishment of the
EU), major developments of international law reject the
idea of moral particularists that geographical and political origins determine the content of people's rights and
moral standing. What remains at stake, though, is
exactly what form of cosmopolitanism is embodied
in such practices and regimes. The chapter offers an

analysis of this question. In so doing, it provides an account of the structure of cosmopolitanism as well as of its institutional requirements. It concludes by focusing on the political openings that may exist for the deepening hold of the cosmopolitan project.

The fourth chapter takes up the challenge of interpreting 9/11 and its implications. The first part of the chapter argues that the current international legal order already contains the idea that there are moral limits to legitimate state and non-state action. From human rights regimes to international tribunals, one of the basic tenets of international law is the recognition that certain crimes cannot go unpunished, no matter what their source of inspiration or the authority by which they were originated. In this context, it can be seen that existing legal international instruments make acts of terrorism such as the ones perpetrated on 9/11 a common international concern. These instruments should form the basis of a more diversified range of responses to international terrorism. Traditional forms of warfare are typically options that will contribute to the erosion of consent without reaching appreciable results. An effective response calls for the reconstitution of international legitimacy and a human security approach. The latter implies primarily addressing the main sources of global insecurity such as unemployment, inadequate housing, schooling and health. Finally, the chapter rejects the idea that the universal standards mandated by a cosmopolitan account are an outsider's challenge to Islam. Like all major cultures, Islam can find, internally, the resources to meet cosmopolitan ideas and aspirations.

Chapter 5 takes up the task of addressing what I refer to as the paradox of our times: the inconsistency between the global nature of many of our pressing problems (from climate change to nuclear proliferation and global poverty) and contemporary forms of governance rooted in the nation-state. Four reasons are central if we want to understand why we should care about solving such collective action problems: solidarity, social justice, democracy and policy effectiveness. Subsequently, the deep drivers of globalization and the challenges to governance are presented in terms of what I call the emergent system of structural global vulnerability. The latter, combined with the Washington Consensus and the Washington security doctrines, explains our current inability to come to terms with our shared problems. Trends in global governance are assessed and the crucial structural fragilities of the post-1945 institutional order are exposed. The rest of the chapter deals in some detail with the implications of the approach adopted for democracy and citizenship. It argues in favour of a revision of traditional conceptions of state power and prerogatives and in favour of a new model of cosmopolitan citizenship involving the development of both independent political authority and administrative capacity at regional and global levels.

Chapter 6 offers an analysis of the drivers and consequences of the current financial crisis. The analysis tries to address the often overlooked implication of the crisis for global governance issues. The basic idea put forward is that the current financial turmoil should be understood as a symptom (rather than an issue-specific calamity) of broader deficiencies in global governance. The basic characteristics of contemporary global governance, and associated shortcomings, are outlined. Structural similarities are found in the three policy domains of finance, security and the environment. From a global governance perspective, all three signal the current difficulties in managing global risks associated with human interdependence. Each of these policy domains suffers from what can be called a 'capacity problem' – existing institutions which address the global nature of risk are not fit for purpose. They also suffer, to varying degrees, from a 'responsibility problem' – the generation of risks, and the costs borne by their realization, are not commensurate with the nature and form of their governance. Yet, the attention recently received by global financial governance issues shows the potential effectiveness of focused politicized efforts in order to attain significant reform.

Finally, chapter 7 deals with the role of democracy in responding to the pressing challenge of climate change. The structural features of democratic problems in addressing climate change are analysed. The latter include what I label short-termism, self-referring decision-making and weak multilateralism. While there are reasons to qualify such structural constraints, all of them contribute to democracies' weaknesses in addressing global collective action problems. Furthermore, the chapter argues that existing efforts to address global climate change suffer from familiar deficits in the current system of global governance. While a number of individual international environmental agreements exist, they are often both poorly coordinated and weakly enforced. The overall picture is rather bleak; current efforts to tackle climate change not only lack in effectiveness, but are also deficient along the democratic faultlines of inclusiveness and accountability. In the rest of the chapter different practical solutions for solving climate change are assessed. Despite vigorous debate surrounding the ideal bundle of policies required (and how they should or should not be implemented), there is considerable overlap on what the political elements of a global deal might look like. At the most general level, the latter should be broadly inclusive, multifaceted, multilayered and sustainable. Furthermore, at the core of any successful response lies the necessity of protecting entrepreneurialism and innovation, while at the same time enhancing institutional capacity and planning. The prospects of democracies in this respect are mixed. While some democratic polities perform poorly, the countries that have the best records in reducing carbon emissions are all democratic ones.

This book focuses, in sum, on the principles of cosmopolitanism and the challenges of entrenching its standards in political life, from the global to the local level. Cosmopolitanism is an ethical approach to political life which champions self-determination and freedom from domination and arbitrary power. Its principles and standards, embedded in democratic public law, provide a framework for cultural diversity and individual difference to flourish in a public life marked by deliberation and argument, bounded by legitimate rules and mechanisms of conflict resolution. Stepping-stones exist to the development of this cosmopolitan order. The failure of leading global policies in economics and security in recent times are not just a cause of concern, but also a learning opportunity that beckons. How far this opportunity can be grasped remains to be seen, as the Afterword to this book emphasizes. Yet, there are many good reasons to deepen the hold of cosmopolitan principles on our collective life. This book explains why.

1

Cosmopolitanism: Ideas, Realities and Deficits

The struggle over the accountability of the global economic order has been intense. Violence in Seattle, Prague, Genoa and elsewhere marked a new level of conflict about globalization, democracy and social justice. The issues which have been raised are clearly fundamental, concerned as they are with the nature of free markets, the relation between corporate and public agendas, and with the type and scope of political intervention in economic life. These matters are complex and extremely challenging, although they are not new to political debate and political analysis. What is new is the way the issues are framed, disseminated and fought over in transnational and global contexts.

In this chapter I want to draw out some of the concerns underlying these controversies by reflecting on the changing nature and form of global processes, networks and connections, and on the meaning and significance today of cosmopolitan ideas and theories. The chapter has six parts. It begins with sections on globalization and global governance and then, in the third section, traces their relevance for the locus and home of democracy, accountability and social justice. Against this background, the meaning of cosmopolitanism is set out in philosophical and institutional terms, in the fourth and fifth sections, respectively. The argument is made that not only is cosmopolitanism increasingly important to politics and human welfare, but that it ought also to be embraced further in thinking about the proper form of globalization and global governance. A final section explores some basic gaps between cosmopolitan principles and institutions that need to be overcome if cosmopolitanism is to extend its purchase on governance structures and, thus, on the conditions for greater accountability, democracy and social justice in global politics.

Globalization

Globalization has become the 'big idea' of our times, even though it is frequently employed in such a way that it lacks precise definition. Moreover, it is so often used in political debate that it is in danger of becoming devoid of analytical value. Nonetheless, if the term is properly formulated, it does capture important elements of change in the contemporary world which can be usefully specified further.

Globalization can best be understood if it is conceived as a spatial phenomenon, lying on a continuum with 'the local' at one end and 'the global' at the other. It implies a shift in the spatial form of human organization and activity to transcontinental or interregional patterns of activity, interaction, and the exercise of power (Held et al., 1999). Today, globalization embraces at least four distinct types of change. First, it involves a stretching of social, political and economic activities across political frontiers, regions and continents. But if these are something other than occasional or random, then something else is suggested: intensification. Thus, second, globalization is marked by the growing magnitude of networks and flows of trade, investment, finance, culture and so on. Third, globalization can be linked to a speeding up of global interactions and processes, as the evolution of worldwide systems of transport and communication increases the velocity of the diffusion of ideas, goods, information, capital and people. And, fourth, it involves the deepening impact of global interactions and processes such that the effects of distant events can be highly significant elsewhere and even the most local developments can come to have enormous global consequences. In this particular sense, the boundaries between domestic matters and global affairs become fuzzy. In short, globalization can be thought of as the widening, intensifying, speeding up and growing impact of worldwide interconnectedness.

Globalization is made up of the accumulation of links across the world's major regions and across many domains of activity. It can be related to many factors, including the rapid expansion of the world economy. International trade has grown to unprecedented levels, both absolutely and relatively in relation to national income. Although the global financial crisis of 2008–9 has reversed trade growth in many places, the indications are that it will recover in many sectors. In comparison with the late nineteenth century – an era of rapid trade growth – export levels today (measured as a share of GDP) are much greater for OECD states. As barriers to trade have fallen across the world, global markets have emerged for many goods and, increasingly, services (ibid.: ch. 3).

The growing extensity, intensity and speed of trade have led to the increasing enmeshment of national economies with each other. Key elements of the production process are being sliced up, dispersed and located in different countries, especially in developing and emerging economies. Thus, not only do countries increasingly consume goods from abroad, but their own production processes are significantly dependent on components produced overseas. Economic activity in any one country is, accordingly, strongly affected by economic activity in other countries. Alongside transnational production networks, the power of global finance has become central to economic globalization. World financial flows have grown exponentially, especially since the 1970s. Trillions of dollars worth of financial transactions are carried out weekly across the globe. Most countries today are incorporated into rapidly growing global financial markets, although the nature of their access to these markets is markedly unequal.

Processes of economic globalization have not, however, occurred in an empty political space; there has been a shift in the nature and form of political organization as well. The sovereign state now lies at the intersection of a vast array of international regimes and organizations that have been established to manage whole areas of transnational activity (trade, financial

30

flows, risk management and so on) and collective policy problems. The rapid growth of transnational issues has spawned layers of governance both within and across political boundaries. This has resulted in the transformation of aspects of territorially based political decision-making, the development of regional and global organizations and institutions, and the emergence of regional and global law.

The global governance complex

Global governance today has some of the characteristics of a multilayered, multidimensional and multi-actor system (see Held and McGrew, 2002a: 78–84). It is multilayered insofar as the development and implementation of global policies can involve a process of political coordination between suprastate, transnational, national and often substate agencies. Attempts to combat AIDS/HIV, for instance, involve the coordinated efforts of global, regional, national and local agencies. It is multidimensional insofar as the engagement and configuration of agencies often differs from sector to sector and issue to issue, giving rise to significantly differentiated political patterns. The politics of, for example, global financial regulation is different in significant ways from the politics of global trade regulation. Further, many of the agencies of, and participants in, the global governance complex are no longer purely intergovernmental bodies. There is involvement by representatives of transnational civil society, from Greenpeace to the Make Poverty History campaign and an array of NGOs;

the corporate sector, from BP to the International Chamber of Commerce and other trade or industrial associations; and mixed public–private organizations, such as the International Organization of Security Commissions (IOSCO). Accordingly, global governance is a multi-actor complex insofar as diverse agencies participate in the development of global public policy. Of course, this broad pluralistic conception of global governance does not presume that all states or interests have an equal voice in, let alone an equal influence over, its agenda or programmes – not at all.

Another important feature of the formulation and implementation of global public policy is that it occurs within an expanding array of different kinds of networks: transgovernmental networks, such as the Financial Action Task Force (FATF); trisectoral networks involving public, corporate and NGO groups, such as the World Commission on Dams Forum; and transnational networks, such as the International Accounting Standards Board (IASB) (McGrew, 2002; Slaughter, 2004). These networks – which can be ad hoc or institutional – have become increasingly important in coordinating the work of experts and administrators within governments, international organizations and the corporate and NGO sectors. They function to set policy agendas, disseminate information, formulate rules and establish and implement policy programmes, from the money-laundering measures of the FATF to global initiatives to counter AIDS. While many of these networks have a clear policy and administrative function, they have also become mechanisms through which civil society and corporate interests can become embedded in the global policy process (examples include the Global Water Partnership and the Global Alliance for Vaccines and Immunization). In part, the growth of these networks is a response to the overload and politicization of multilateral bodies, but it is also an outcome of the growing technical complexity of global policy issues and the communications revolution.

To this complex pattern of global governance and rule-making can be added the new configurations of regional governance. The EU has taken Europe from the edge of catastrophe in two world wars to a world in which sovereignty is pooled across a growing number of areas of common concern. For all its flaws, it is, judged in the context of the history of states, a remarkable political formation. In addition, there has been a significant acceleration in regional relations beyond Europe: in the Americas, in Asia-Pacific and, to a lesser degree, in Africa. While the forms taken by these regional governance structures are very different from the model of the EU, they have nonetheless had significant consequences for political power, particularly in the Asia-Pacific, which has seen the formation of ASEAN, APEC, ARF, PBEC and many other groupings (see Payne, 2003). Furthermore, as regionalism has deepened, so interregional diplomacy has intensified as old and new regional groups seek to consolidate their relations with each other. In this respect, regionalism has not been a barrier to globalization; it has been a building block for it (see Hettne, 1997).

At the core of all these developments is the reconfiguration of aspects of political power since 1945. While many states retain the ultimate legal claim to effective supremacy over what occurs within their own territories, this claim has to be understood in relation to the expanding jurisdiction of institutions of global and regional governance, and the constraints of, as well as the obligations derived from, new and changing forms of international regulation. This is especially evident in the European Union, but it is also evident in the operation of IGOs such as the WTO (Moore, 2003). Moreover, even where sovereignty still seems intact, states by no means retain sole command of what transpires within their own territorial boundaries. Complex global systems, from the financial to the ecological, connect the fate of communities in one locale to the fate of communities in distant regions of the world. There has, in other words, been a transformation or an 'unbundling' of the relationship between sovereignty, territoriality and political outcomes (see Ruggie, 1993).

This unbundling involves a plurality of actors, a variety of political processes, and diverse levels of co-ordination and operation. Specifically, it includes:

- different forms of intergovernmental arrangements embodying various levels of legalization, types of instruments utilized and responsiveness to stakeholders;
- an increasing number of public agencies, for example central bankers, maintaining links with similar agencies in other countries and, thus, forming transgovernmental networks for the management of various global issues;
- diverse business actors (i.e. firms, their associations and organizations such as international chambers of

commerce) establishing their own transnational regulatory mechanisms to manage issues of common concern;

- NGOs and transnational advocacy networks (i.e. leading actors in global civil society) playing a role in various domains of global governance and at various stages of the global public policymaking process;
- public bodies, business actors and NGOs collaborating in many issue areas in order to provide novel approaches to social problems through multistakeholder networks.

There is nothing inevitable, it should be stressed, about these trends and developments. While they are highly significant to understand the nature and form of global politics, they are contingent upon many factors, and could be halted or even reversed by protracted global conflicts or cataclysmic events. Although these bodies and networks lack the kind of centralized, coordinated political programme that is associated with national governance, it would be a mistake to overlook the expanding jurisdiction and scope of global policymaking, most especially, the substantial range of issues it touches on and its growing intrusion into the domestic affairs of states.

Globalization and democracy: Five disjunctures

The world is no longer made up of relatively 'discrete civilizations' or 'discrete political communities'

(Fernández-Armesto, 1995: ch. 1); rather, it is a world of overlapping communities of fate, where the fates of nations are significantly entwined. Political communities are enmeshed and entrenched in complex structures of overlapping forces, processes and networks. During the period in which the nation-state was being forged – and the territorially bounded conception of democracy was consolidated – the idea of a close mesh between geography, political power and democracy could be assumed. It seemed compelling that political power, sovereignty, democracy and citizenship were simply and appropriately bounded by a delimited territorial space. These links were by and large taken for granted, and generally unexplained in modern political theory (Held, 1995). Globalization and changes in the nature and form of global governance raise issues concerning the proper scope of democracy, or democratic jurisdiction, given that the relation between decision-makers and decision-takers is not necessarily symmetrical or congruent with respect to the territory.

The changing relation between globalization and the modern nation-state can be characterized by five disjunctures. All indicate an increase in the extensity, intensity, velocity and impact of globalization. And all suggest important questions about the evolving character of the democratic political community in particular.

First, the idea of a self-determining national collectivity – which delimits and shapes a community of fate – can no longer be simply located within the borders of a single nation-state. Many of the most fundamental, economic, social, cultural and environmental forces and processes that determine the nature of the political good and political outcomes now lie – in terms of their operation and dynamics – beyond the reach of individual polities. The current concern about genetic engineering and its possible regulation is a case in point.

Second, it can no longer be presupposed that the locus of effective political power is synonymous with national governments and the nation-state; national states and national governments are now embedded in complex networks of political power at regional and global levels (see Keohane, 1995, 2001; Rosenau, 1997, 1998). In other words, political power is shared and negotiated among diverse forces and agencies at many levels, from the local to the global. The link between effective government, self-government and a bounded territory is being broken.

Third, while significant concentrations of power are found, of course, in many states, these are frequently embedded in, and articulated with, new and changing forms of political capacity. The power and operations of national government are altering, although not all in one direction. The entitlement of states to rule within circumscribed territories – their sovereignty – is not on the edge of collapse, but the practical nature of this entitlement – the actual capacity of states to rule – is changing its shape (Held et al., 1999: Conclusion; Held, 2004). A new regime of government and governance is emerging which is displacing traditional conceptions of state power as an indivisible, territorially exclusive form of public power.

Fourth, the nurturing and enhancement of the public good increasingly requires coordinated multilateral action (e.g. to ensure security or to prevent global recessions). At the same time, the resolution of transboundary issues (e.g. responsibility for carbon omissions) may often impose significant domestic adjustments. In this respect, political and social agents are witnessing a shift in the operation and dynamics of state power and political authority. This has become most apparent as states have become locked into regional and global regimes and associations. The context of national politics has been transformed by the diffusion of political authority and the growth of multilayered governance (see Nye and Donahue, 2000).

Fifth, the distinctions between domestic and foreign affairs, internal political issues and external questions are no longer clear-cut. Governments face issues, such as the international drugs trade, AIDS, terrorism, the use of non-renewable resources, the management of nuclear waste, the spread of weapons of mass destruction, and climate change, which cannot meaningfully be categorized in these terms. Moreover, issues like the location and investment strategy of MNCs, the regulation of global financial markets, the threats to the tax base of individual countries in the context of a global division of labour and the absence of capital controls all pose questions about the continued value of some of the central instruments of national economic policy. In fact, in nearly all major areas of policy, the enmeshment of national political communities in regional and global flows and processes involves them in intensive transboundary coordination and regulation.

In the context of these complex transformations, the meaning of accountability and democracy at the national level is altering. In circumstances where transnational actors and forces cut across the boundaries of national communities in diverse ways, where powerful international organizations and agencies make decisions for vast groups of people across diverse borders, and where the capacities of large companies can dwarf those of many states, the questions of who should be accountable to whom, and on what basis, do not easily resolve themselves. The mesh between geography, political power and democracy is challenged by the intensification of regional and global relations.

Cosmopolitanism: Ideas and trajectories

The problems and dilemmas of contemporary national politics, just described, can be referred to, following Jeremy Waldron, as the 'circumstances of cosmopolitanism' (2000: 236–9); that is, the background conditions and presuppositions which inform and motivate the case for a cosmopolitan framework of accountability and regulation. Not only are we 'unavoidably side by side' (as Kant put it), but the degrees of mutual interconnectedness and vulnerability are rapidly growing. The new circumstances of cosmopolitanism give us little choice but to consider the possibility of a common framework of standards and political action, given shape and form by a common framework of institutional arrangements (Held, 1995: Part III).

How should cosmopolitanism be understood in this context? There are three broad accounts of cosmopolitanism, previously mentioned, which are important to bear in mind and which contribute to its contemporary meaning (for a more detailed historical narrative, see Brown and Held, 2010: Introduction). The first was explored by the Stoics, who where the first to refer explicitly to themselves as cosmopolitans, seeking to replace the central role of the polis in ancient political thought with that of the cosmos in which humankind could live in harmony (Horstmann, 1976). The Stoics developed this thought by emphasizing that we inhabit two worlds – one that is local and assigned to us by birth and another that is 'truly great and truly common' (Seneca). Each person lives in both a local community and a wider community of human ideals, aspirations and argument. The basis of the latter lies in what is fundamental to all – the equal worth of reason and humanity in every person (Nussbaum, 1997: 30, 43). Allegiance is owed, first and foremost, to the moral realm of all humanity, not to the contingent groupings of nation, ethnicity and class. Deliberations and problem-solving should focus on what is common to all persons as citizens of reason and the world; collective problems can be better dealt with if approached from this perspective, rather than from the point of view of sectional groupings. Such a position does not require that individuals give up local concerns and affiliations to family, friends and fellow countrymen; it implies, instead, that they must acknowledge these as morally contingent and that their most important duties are to humanity as a whole and its overall developmental requirements.

The basic idea of classical cosmopolitanism involves the notion that each person is 'a citizen of the world' and owes a duty, above all, 'to the worldwide community of human beings' (Nussbaum, 1996: 4). While

there are many difficulties with this classical formulation (for instance, its link to a teleological view of
nature – see Nussbaum, 1997), the main point of the
Stoics contained a most significant idea: 'that they
were, in the first instance, human beings living in a
world of human beings and only incidentally members
of polities' (Barry, 1999: 36). The boundaries of polities
are understood to be historically arbitrary, and most
often the result of coercion and violence. Borders obscure
the common circumstances of humankind and, thus,
could not have the moral significance frequently ascribed
to them (Pogge, 1994a: 198). The individual belongs
to the wider world of humanity; moral worth cannot
be specified by the yardstick of a single political
community.

The second conception of cosmopolitanism was introduced in the eighteenth century when the term *weltbürger* (world citizen) became one of the key terms of
the Enlightenment. The most important contribution to
this body of thought can be found in Kant's writings
(above all, 1970: 41–53, 54–60, 93–130). Kant linked
the idea of cosmopolitanism to an innovative conception of 'the public use of reason', and explored the ways
in which this conception of reason can generate a critical vantage point from which to scrutinize civil society
(see Schmidt, 1998: 419–27). Building on a definition
of enlightenment as the escape from dogma and unvindicated authority, Kant measured its advance in terms
of the removal of constraints on 'the public use of
reason'. As one commentator eloquently remarked,
Kant grounds reason 'in the repudiation of principles
that preclude the possibility of open-ended interaction

and communication. . . . The principles of reason are those that can secure the possibility of intersubjectivity' (O'Neill, 1990: 194). Locked into the roles, practices and organizations of civil society, people, Kant argued, do not have the opportunity to explore fully the nature and limits of existing rules, prejudices and beliefs. But people are also, if only potentially, members of a 'cosmopolitan society', and as members of this society they can 'enjoy a right to the free and unrestricted public use of their reason' (Schmidt, 1998: 424). Individuals can step out of their entrenched positions in civil and political life and enter a sphere of reason free of 'dictatorial authority' – which Kant associated (rather uncritically) with the world of writers, readers and intellectuals – and can, from this vantage point, examine the one-sidedness, partiality and limits of everyday knowledge, understanding and regulations. In this context, individuals can learn to think of themselves as participants in a dialogue – a critical process of communication – in which they can come to an understanding with others about the nature and appropriateness of the demands made upon them (cf. Arendt, 1961: 220–1).

Kant conceived of participation in a cosmopolitan (*weltbürgerlich*), rather than a civil (*bürgerlich*), society as an entitlement – an entitlement to enter the world of open, uncoerced dialogue – and he adapted this idea in his formulation of what he called 'cosmopolitan right' (1970: 105–8). Cosmopolitan right connoted the capacity to present oneself and be heard within and across political communities; it was the right to enter dialogue without artificial constraint and delimitation. He emphasized that this right extended to the circumstances which allow people to enjoy an exchange of ideas (and goods) with the inhabitants of other countries, but that it did not extend as far as the right to permanent settlement or to citizenship in their homelands (ibid.).

Cosmopolitan right, thus understood, transcends the particular claims of nations and states and extends to all in the 'universal community'. It connotes a right and duty which must be accepted if people are to learn to tolerate one another's company and to coexist peacefully. It is the condition of cooperative relations and of just conduct. These arguments also lead Kant to make a striking rejection of colonialism: 'the inhospitable conduct of the civilized states of our continent, especially the commercial states' and 'the injustice they display in visiting foreign countries and peoples (which in their case is the same as conquering them)' (ibid.: 105–6). Cosmopolitan right is a 'necessary complement' to the codes of existing national and international law, the basis on which cultural, religious and political dogmas can be tested in order to help construct a cosmopolitan order – where all relationships, political and social, should be bound by a willingness to enter into dialogue and interaction constrained only by elementary principles of reason, impartiality and the possibility of intersubjective agreement (see Held, 1995: 266ff; McCarthy, 1999). In this sense, individuals can be citizens of the world as well as of existing states; citizenship can become an attribute not just of national communities, but of a universal system of 'cosmo-political' governance in which the freedom of each person underpins the freedom of all others (Kant, 1970: 47–53, 128–30).

The third conception of cosmopolitanism is more recent and is expounded in the work of Beitz, Pogge and Barry, among others (see, in particular, Beitz, 1979, 1994, 1998; Pogge, 1989, 1994b; and Barry, 1998a, 1999, although they by no means agree on many matters: see, for instance, Miller, 1998). In certain respects, this work seems to explicate, and offer a compelling elucidation of, the classical conception of belonging to the human community, first and foremost, and the Kantian conception of subjecting all beliefs, relations and practices to the test of whether or not they allow open-ended interaction, uncoerced agreement and impartial judgement. This third conception of cosmopolitanism involves three key elements, noted earlier in the Introduction. The first is that the ultimate units of moral concern are individual human beings, not states or other particular forms of human association. Humankind belongs to a single moral realm in which each person is regarded as equally worthy of respect and consideration (Beitz, 1994, 1998; Pogge, 1994b). This element can be referred to as the principle of individualist moral egalitarianism or, simply, egalitarian individualism. To think of people as having equal moral value is to make a general claim about the basic units of the world comprising persons as free and equal beings (see Kuper, 2000). This broad position runs counter to the view of moral particularists that belonging to a given community limits and determines the moral worth of individuals and the nature of their autonomy. It does so because, to paraphrase (and adapt) Bruce Ackerman, there is no nation without a woman who insists on equal liberties, no society without a man who denies the need for deference, and no country without a person who does not yearn for a predictable pattern of meals to help sustain his or her life projects (1994: 382–3). The principle of egalitarian individualism is the basis for articulating the equal worth and liberty of all humans, wherever they were born or brought up. Its concern is with the irreducible moral status of each and every person – the acknowledgement of which links directly to the possibility of self-determination and the capacity to make independent choices.

The second element emphasizes that the status of equal worth should be acknowledged by everyone. It is an attribute of every living person, and the basis on which each person ought to constitute their relations with others (Pogge, 1994b: 89f.). Each person has an equal stake in this universal ethical realm and is, accordingly, required to respect all other people's status as a basic unit of moral interest (ibid.: 90). This second element of contemporary cosmopolitanism can be called the principle of reciprocal recognition. To be satisfactorily entrenched in everyday life, it necessitates that all people enjoy an equality of status with respect to the basic decision-making institutions of their communities. Agreed judgement about rules, laws and policies should ideally follow from the 'force of the better argument' and public debate – not from the intrusive outcome of non-discursive elements and forces (Habermas, 1973; Held, 1995: ch.7). If people are marginalized or fall outside this framework, they suffer disadvantage not primarily because they have less than others in this instance, but because they can participate less in the processes and institutions that shape their lives. It is their 'impaired agency' that becomes the focus of concern (Doyal and Gough, 1991: 95–6; see Raz, 1986: 227–40).

The third element of contemporary cosmopolitanism stresses that equality of status and reciprocal recognition requires that each person should enjoy the impartial treatment of their claims; that is, treatment based on principles upon which all could act. Accordingly, cosmopolitanism is a moral frame of reference for specifying rules and principles that can be universally shared; and, concomitantly, it rejects as unjust all those practices, rules and institutions anchored to principles not all could adopt (O'Neill, 1991). At issue is the establishment of principles and rules that nobody, motivated to establish an uncoerced and informed agreement, could reasonably reject (see Barry, 1989; cf. Scanlon, 1998).

To test the generalizability of claims and interests involves 'reasoning from the point of view of others' (Benhabib, 1992: 9–10, 121–47). Attempts to focus on this 'social point of view' find their most rigorous explication in Rawls's original position, Habermas's ideal speech situation and Barry's formulation of impartialist reasoning (Rawls, 1971; Habermas, 1973, 1996; Barry, 1989, 1995). These formulations have in common a concern to conceptualize an impartial moral standpoint from which to assess routine forms of practical reasoning. The concern is not overambitious. As one commentator aptly explained:

> All the impartiality thesis says is that, if and when one
> raises questions regarding fundamental moral stan-

dards, the court of appeal that one addresses is a court in which no particular individual, group, or country has special standing. Before the court, declaring 'I like it', 'it serves my country', and the like, is not decisive; principles must be defensible to anyone looking at the matter apart from his or her special attachments, from a larger, human perspective. (Hill, 1987: 132, quoted in Barry, 1998b: 226–7)

This social, open-ended moral perspective is a device for focusing our thoughts, and a basis for testing the inter-subjective validity of our conceptions of the good. It offers a way of exploring principles, norms and rules that might reasonably command agreement (cf. Nussbaum, 1997: 29–36). Impartialist reasoning is a frame of reference for specifying rules and principles that can be universally shared. In order to meet this standard, a number of particular tests can be pursued, including an assessment of whether all points of view have been taken into consideration; whether there are individuals in a position to impose on others in such a manner as would be unacceptable to the latter, or to the originator of the action (or inaction), if the roles were reversed; and whether all parties would be equally prepared to accept the outcome as fair and reasonable, irrespective of the social positions they might occupy now or in the future (see Barry, 1989: 372, 362–3).

Impartialist reasoning will not produce a simple deductive proof of the ideal set of principles and conditions which can overcome the deficiencies of the global economy or global political order; nor can it produce a deductive proof of the best or only moral principles that should guide institutional formation. Rather, it should be thought of as a heuristic device to test candidate principles of moral worth, democracy and justice and their forms of justification (see Kelly, 1998: 1–8). These tests are concerned with a process of reasonable rejectability in a theoretical dialogue that is always open to fresh challenge and new questions and, hence, in a hermeneutic sense, can never be complete (Gadamer, 1975). But to acknowledge this is not to say that the theoretical conversation is 'toothless', either with respect to principles or the conditions of their entrenchment.

One 'biting' principle is the principle of the avoidance of serious harm and the amelioration of urgent need. This is a principle for allocating priority to the most vital cases of need and, where possible, trumping other, less urgent, public priorities until such a time as all human beings enjoy the status of equal moral value, reciprocal recognition, and have the means to participate in their respective political communities and in the overlapping communities of fate which shape their needs and welfare. A social provision which falls short of this can be referred to as a situation of manifest 'harm' in that the recognition of, and potential for, active agency will not have been achieved for all individuals or groups; that is to say, some people would not have adequate access to effectively resourced capacities which they might make use of in particular circumstances (see Sen, 1999). This practical and participative conception of agency denotes, in principle, an 'attainable' target – because the measure of optimum participation, and the related conception of harm, can be conceived directly in terms of the 'highest standard' presently achieved in a political community (see Doyal and Gough, 1991: 169). But attainable participative levels are not the same thing as the most pressing levels of vulnerability, defined by the most urgent need. It is only too clear that within many, if not all, countries, certain needs, particularly concerning health, education and welfare, are not universally met (Held and McGrew, 2000: chs. 31, 32, 37). The 'harm' that follows from a failure to meet such needs can be denoted as 'serious harm', marked, as it often is, by immediate, life-and-death consequences. Accordingly, if the requirements specified by the principle of the avoidance of serious harm are to be met, public policy ought to be focused, in the first instance, on the prevention of such conditions; that is, on the eradication of severe harm inflicted on people 'against their will' and 'without their consent' (Barry, 1998b: 231, 207).[1]

I take cosmopolitanism ultimately to connote the ethical and political space which sets out the terms of reference for the recognition of people's equal moral worth, their active agency and what is required for their autonomy and development (see Held, 2003). It builds on principles that all could reasonably assent to in defending basic ideas which emphasize equal dignity, equal respect, the priority of vital needs and so on. On the other hand, this cosmopolitan point of view must also recognize that the meaning of these cannot be specified once and for all. That is to say, the connotation of these basic ideas cannot be separated from the hermeneutic complexity of traditions, with their unique temporal and cultural structures. The meaning of cosmopolitan regulative principles cannot be elucidated independently of an ongoing discussion in public life

(Habermas, 1996). Accordingly, there can be no adequate specification of equal liberty, rights and vital interests without a corresponding institutionalization of 'the public use of reason' in uncoerced national and transnational forms of public dialogue and debate (McCarthy, 1999). The institutionalization of cosmopolitan principles requires the entrenchment of accessible and open public fora.

Cosmopolitan realities

After more than 200 years of nationalism, sustained nation-state formation and intensive geopolitics, cosmopolitan principles and political positions could be thought of as being out of place. Yet, in certain respects, cosmopolitanism defines a set of norms and legal frameworks in the here and now – and not in some remote future. Cosmopolitanism is already embedded in rule systems and institutions which have transformed the sovereign states system in a number of important respects. States have been the initiators of, and have been pressed into, the creation of rights and duties, powers and constraints, and regimes and organizations which impinge on and react back upon them. These transformations go to the heart of the privileged moral and legal position once claimed on behalf of states.

In the first instance, the principle of universal belonging and the relativization of the polity as an independent source of rights and obligations, as expounded by the Stoics, find echoes today in the international realm. In a number of international treaties and customary rules, it is what people share – as human beings *simpliciter*

(Benhabib, 2000) and as creatures in a common, global habitat – that has guided the foundation and formulation of certain governing principles, norms and rules. However tentative and fragile its entrenchment might be, the emerging regional and universal regulatory order takes what all human beings have in common (the human rights regime) and their ecosystems (the environmental regimes) as a starting point (Crawford and Marks, 1998; Weller, 1997). Human beings are recognized as active members of the world whose political structures may, or may fail to, contribute to their well-being. This is a view of the public sphere which some classical thinkers might have recognized. Of course, against this, the continuing powerful place of state sovereignty in international law and regulation, the central role of great powers and the complexity of the global governance system would mean that such thinkers would certainly need a helping hand in tracing universal tendencies (see Held, 2002b).

Second, the Kantian concern with membership, both of national communities and of a wider cosmopolitan order, constituted by the unrestricted use of public reason and universal hospitality (cosmopolitan right), finds expression in a number of articles of the International Bill of Human Rights, and in regional human rights agreements. Those of particular relevance have sought to entrench a common structure of rights and duties in relation to self-determination and the democratic principle (see article 21 of the UD, and article 25 of the CCPR); full liberty of conscience, thought, speech and the press (see, for example, articles 18 and 19 of the UD, and articles 18 and 19 of the

CCPR); participation in educational, cultural and scientific realms (see, for instance, article 27 of the UD, and article 15 of the CESCR); freedom of movement and travel (article 13 of the UD, article 12 of the CCPR); and freedom to seek asylum from persecution (article 14 of the UD).

For Kant, cosmopolitan society was the realm of critical reason, in which all were, in principle, free to enter; republican national polities, on the one side, and the possibility of a universal dialogue across borders, on the other, were its essential preconditions. However, despite political and legal progress in this direction, we see now that an enlightened public life is even harder to achieve than Kant thought. Even though liberal democracy has spread to most regions of the world, many democracies are still best described as 'partial' (marked by some accountability of government to citizens through elections, but with curtailed and limited election procedures, rights and associational autonomy); they are far from 'full' liberal democracies (with accountable governments, open deliberative processes, free and fair competitive elections, civil and political rights, associational autonomy and so on) (see Potter et al., 1997). Accountable government, alongside freedom of speech, association and movement, remain fragile achievements or simply unattained in many counties and regions. But even if the Kantian conditions were fully met, they would still not adequately specify the conditions of a 'cosmopolitan society'; and this for three reasons.

First, formal commitments to allow each person to become part of a cosmopolitan society take no account of the complexity of power, power relations and inequality which turn 'the free realm of reason' all too often into a market-driven sphere, marked by massive inequalities of access, distribution and outcome (see Held and McGrew, 2000: Parts III and V; Held and Kaya, 2007). For example, new information and communication systems are helping to establish a global communication system, while, at one and the same time, creating new divisions between the informed, connected and isolated (UNDP, 1999; Held and McGrew, 2007b). International rules and procedures do not address the gulf between assigned rights and effective power or opportunities. Second, participants in a cosmopolitan society of reason can find themselves entering a world of discourse often shaped by sectional interests, private priorities or particular substantive commitments. Existing forms of international law do not address the disjuncture between every person's right to participate in diverse deliberative fora and the *modus operandi* of these, which can all too often marginalize the concerns and interests of the least powerful. The diverse and often eccentric voting systems of IGOs is a case in point; for example, the operations of the Bretton Woods institutions are heavily weighted in favour of leading industrialized states, while the WTO rules require a wider consensus. Third, the Kantian conception of cosmopolitan right is too weak to underpin the free movement of people and ideas. For universal hospitality, even when guaranteed, is too limited a notion to clarify the dilemmas and proper treatment of, for instance, refugees and asylum seekers (see Benhabib, 2000). In a world where goods and services have greater opportunity for mobility than people (see Held et al., 1999: chs. 3 and 6), cosmopolitan right alone will not open sufficient doors to strangers and aliens in need of entry, sanctuary or membership in another country.

Finally, the principles of egalitarian individualism, reciprocal recognition and impartialist reasoning – the principles that I earlier referred to as leading elements of contemporary cosmopolitanism – find direct expression in significant post-Second World War legal and institutional initiatives and in some of the new regulatory forms of regional and global governance (Held, 2002b). To begin with, the 1948 UN Declaration of Human Rights and the subsequent 1966 Covenants of rights raised the principle of egalitarian individualism to a universal reference point: the requirement that each person be treated with equal concern and respect, irrespective of the state in which they were born or brought up, is the central plank of the human rights worldview (see UN, 1988). In addition, the formal recognition in the UN Declaration of all people as persons with 'equal and inalienable rights', and as 'the foundation of freedom, justice and peace in the world', marked a turning point in the development of cosmopolitan legal thinking. Single persons are recognized as subjects of international law and, in principle, the ultimate source of political authority (see Weller, 1997; Crawford and Marks, 1998; Held, 2002b). Moreover, the diverse range of rights found in the International Bill and regarded as integral to human dignity and autonomy – from protection against slavery, torture and other degrading practices to education and participation in cultural, economic and political life (irrespective of race, gender or religious affiliation) – constitute the basis of a cosmopolitan orientation to politics and human welfare. Human rights entitlements can trump, in principle, the particular claims of national polities; they set down universal standards against which the strengths and limitations of individual political communities can be judged.

The cosmopolitan commitment to the equal worth of all human beings finds reinforcement in the acknowledgement of the necessity of a minimum of civilized conduct and of specific limits to violence found in the laws of war and weapons diffusion; in the commitment to the principles of the Nuremberg and Tokyo war crimes tribunals (1945–6, 1946–8), the Torture Convention (1984) and the statutes of the International Criminal Court (1998), which outlaw genocide, war crimes and crimes against humanity; in the growing recognition of democracy as the fundamental standard of political legitimacy, which finds entrenchment in the International Bill of Human Rights and regional treaties; in the development of new codes of conduct for IGOs and INGOs concerning the transparency and accountability of their activities; and in the unprecedented flurry of regional and global initiatives, regimes, institutions, networks and treaties seeking to tackle climate change, ozone depletion, the pollution of oceans and rivers, and nuclear risks, among many other factors (for a survey, see Held, 2002b; also see chapter 7).

Cosmopolitan ideas are, in short, at the centre of significant post-Second World War legal and political developments. The idea that human well-being is not defined by geographical or cultural location, that national or ethnic or gendered boundaries should not determine the limits of rights or responsibilities for the satisfaction of basic human needs, and that all human beings require equal respect and concern are notions embedded in aspects of contemporary regional and global legal and political thinking, and in some forms of transnational governance (Beitz, 1994: 127; see Held et al., 1999: ch. 1 and Conclusion). There has been a significant shift in emphasis, as one observer has noted, 'in the character and goals of international society: away from minimalist goals of co-existence towards the creation of rules and institutions that embody notions of shared responsibilities, that impinge heavily on the domestic organization of states, that invest individuals and groups within states with rights and duties, and that seek to embody some notion of the planetary good' (Hurrell, 1995: 139).

Yet, while there may be cosmopolitan elements in existing international law, these have, of course, by no means generated a new deep-rooted structure of cosmopolitan accountability and regulation. The principle of egalitarian individualism may be widely recognized, but it scarcely structures much political and economic policy, North, South, East or West. The principle of universal recognition informs the notion of human rights and other legal initiatives such as the 'common heritage of humankind' – embedded in the Law of the Sea (1982) – but it is not at the heart of the politics of sovereign states or corporate colossi; the principle of impartial moral reasoning might be appealed to justify limits on the actions of states or IGOs, but it is, at best, only an incidental part of the institutional dynamics that have created such chronic political problems as the externalities (or cross-border spill-over effects) generated by many national economic and energy policies, overlapping communities of fate in areas as diverse as security and the environment, and the global polarization of power, wealth and income.

This should not be a surprise. In the first instance, the global legal and political initiatives of 1948 onward, referred to above, do not just curtail sovereignty; they clearly also support and underpin it in diverse ways. From the UN Charter to the Rio Declaration on the environment, international agreements have often served to entrench, and accommodate themselves to, the sovereign international power structure. The division of the globe into powerful nation-states, with distinctive sets of geopolitical interests, has often been built into the articles and statutes of IGOs (see Held, 1995: chs. 5 and 6). The 'sovereign rights of states' are frequently affirmed alongside more cosmopolitan leanings. Moreover, while a case can be made that cosmopolitan principles are part of 'the working creed' of officials in some United Nations agencies such as UNICEF, UNESCO and the WHO, and NGOs such as Amnesty International, Save the Children and Greenpeace, they can scarcely be said to be constitutive of the conceptual world of most modern politicians, democratic or otherwise (Barry, 1999: 34–5; cf. Held and McGrew, 2000: 31–9).

Second, the cosmopolitan reach of contemporary regional and global law rarely comes with a commitment to establish institutions with the resources and clout to make declared cosmopolitan intentions and objectives effective. The susceptibility of the UN to the agendas of the most powerful states, the partiality of many of its enforcement operations (or the lack of them altogether), the underfunding of its organizations, its continued dependency on financial support from a few major states, the weaknesses of the policing of many environmental regimes (regional and global) are all indicative of the disjuncture between cosmopolitan aspirations and their partial and one-sided application.

Finally, the focus of cosmopolitan political initiatives since 1945 has been on the domain of the political. These efforts have only had a tangential impact on the regulation of economic power and market mechanisms. The emphasis has been on checking the abuse of political power, not economic power. Cosmopolitan international politics has developed few, if any, systematic means to address forms of economic domination. Its conceptual resources and leading ideas do not suggest or push towards the pursuit of self-determination and autonomy in the economic domain; they do not seek the entrenchment of democratic rights and obligations outside the sphere of the political. Issues concerning corporate power, corporate governance and flourishing economic inequalities have to be brought back into the centre of cosmopolitan practice if this lacuna – at the heart of the struggle over globalization today – is to be addressed. Cosmopolitan theory, with its emphasis on illegitimate and unacceptable structures of power and vital need, has to be reconnected to cosmopolitan institution-building.[2]

Addressing the institutional deficit: Reframing the market

The impact of developing cosmopolitan standards is highly differentiated and uneven across the world's regions. This creates moral and competitive problems for socioeconomic agents and institutions of economic governance, and generates a conundrum: how to uphold cosmopolitan standards and values without eroding sound economic practice and legitimate corporate interests? Outside a cosmopolitan framework there is, I think, no escape from this conundrum.

Onora O'Neill has argued that, in the context of political turbulence, i.e., against the background of rogue states or imploding polities, corporations can find that they are 'the primary agents of justice'; that is, the primary agents with responsibility for maintaining and sustaining cosmopolitan standards and virtues (2000: 192–3). She holds that both states and companies can be judged by the principles and standards they claim to uphold; and that such a judgement today must be made in relation to the principles and standards which are already developing as the universal basis of action – as a result of the spread of democratic values, human rights agreements, environmental regimes and so on. This already provides a tough matrix of social requirements even before the cosmopolitan thinker presses it further.

There is much in this position to affirm: the particular culture and practices of companies matter; the difference between a responsible or irresponsible corporation with respect, for example, to pollution is of great significance; and the involvement of companies in the infrastructural development of local communities can be of marked import. Nonetheless, corporations can find themselves extremely vulnerable to shifting competitive circumstances if they bear the burdens and costs of certain environmental or social standards alone. Accordingly, business men and women object less to political regulation and social reform per se than to the intrusion of regulatory mechanisms that upset 'the rules of the game' in some particular place or country only. Stringent environmental conditions, tough equal opportunity requirements, high labour standards, more accommodating working hours, for example, are particularly objectionable to companies if they handicap their competitive edge in relation to enterprises from areas not subject to similar constraints. Under such circumstances, companies will be all too tempted to do what they can to resist such standards or depart for more 'hospitable shores'; and this will be perfectly rational from their economic and moral point of view.

Thus, if economic interaction is to be entrenched in such a way as to allow markets to flourish within the constraints of cosmopolitan principles and processes, the rules of the game will have to be transformed systematically, at regional and global levels (e.g. at the level of the EU and the WTO). This target for political and economic change provides a potentially fruitful focus, I believe, for both corporate interests and social movements concerned with widespread poverty, social standards and environmental degradation. What are the institutional and procedural implications of these considerations? The requirements of the cosmopolitan framework of accountability and regulation are many and various; there are legal, political, economic and cultural preconditions. But I focus in this chapter on the economic (see Held, 2002b, 2003).

The market system is highly indeterminate – often generating costly or damaging externalities with regard to health, welfare, income distribution or the environment. The 'anti-globalization' protestors or global social justice movements are at their clearest and most articulate on these issues. These challenges can only be adequately addressed, and market economies can only function in a manner fully commensurate with cosmopolitan principles and virtues, if the market system is reframed. This should not be taken, as it all too often is, as an argument for either abandoning or undermining the market system – not at all. The market system has distinct advantages, as Hayek among others has emphasized, over all known alternative economic systems as an effective mechanism to coordinate the knowledgeable decisions of producers and consumers over extended territories (Hayek, 1976). But it is an argument for restructuring – or 'reframing', as I prefer to put it – the market itself. A bridge has to be built between international economic law and human rights law, between commercial law and environmental law, between state sovereignty and transnational law, and between cosmopolitan principles and cosmopolitan practices (see Chinkin, 1998). Precedents exist in, for instance, the Social Chapter of the Maastricht Agreement or in the attempt to attach labour and environmental conditions to the NAFTA regime, for the pursuit of this objective.

This position generates a rationale for a politics of intervention in economic life, not to control and regulate markets per se, but to provide the basis for reforming and regulating those forms of power which compromise, disrupt or undermine fair and sustainable conditions for economic cooperation and competition – the necessary background conditions of the particular choices of human agents in a world of overlapping communities of fate. What is required is not only the firm enactment of existing human rights and environmental agreements and the clear articulation of these with the ethical codes of particular industries (where they exist or can be developed), but also the introduction of new terms of reference into the ground rules or basic laws of the free market system.

At stake, ultimately, are two interrelated sets of transformations. The first is the entrenchment of revised rules, codes and procedures – concerning health, child labour, trade union activity, environmental protection, stakeholder consultation and corporate governance, among other matters – in the articles of association and terms of reference of economic organizations and trading agencies. The key groups and associations of the economic domain would have to adopt, within their very *modus operandi*, a structure of rules, procedures and practices compatible with cosmopolitan social requirements, if the latter are to prevail. The second set of transformations concerns the institutionalization of cosmopolitan principles as the basis of rightful public authority, at local, national, regional and global levels.

Recognizing the complex structures of an interconnected world, cosmopolitanism views certain issues as appropriate for delimited (spatially demarcated) political spheres (the city, state or region), while it sees others – such as the environment, genetic engineering, the terms of trade and financial stability – as requiring new, more extensive, regional and global institutions to address them (see chapters 2 and 3).

Only by introducing new rules, standards and mechanisms of accountability throughout the global economic system, as a supplement and complement to collective agreements and measures in national and regional contexts, can an enduring settlement be created between business interests, regulatory capacity and cosmopolitan concerns (cf. Lipietz, 1992: 119–24). While the advocacy of such a position clearly raises enormous political, diplomatic and technical difficulties, and would need a substantial period to pursue and, of course, implement, this is a challenge that cannot be avoided if people's equal interest in cosmopolitan principles and outcomes is to be adequately protected.

There are many possible objections to such a position. Among these is the pressing cultural concern that the standards and values being projected are those of Western origin which, concomitantly, mask sectional interests – to the advantage, for example, of entrenched corporate and labour interests in the developed world. This point is often made in relation to ILO standards vis-à-vis child labour, freedom to join trade unions, equal pay for men and women for work of equal value. However, this concern, in my judgement, is misplaced and hits the wrong target.

Cosmopolitanism: Ideas, Realities and Deficits

In the first instance, dissent about the value of ideas such as equal consideration, equal liberty and human rights is often related to the experience of Western imperialism and colonization. The way in which these ideas have been traditionally understood in the West – that is, the way in which they have been tied to political and civil rights, above all, and not, for example, to the satisfaction of fundamental human need – has fuelled the view that the language of liberty and democracy is the discourse of Western dominance, especially in those countries which were deeply affected by the Western empires of the nineteenth and twentieth centuries. There are many good historical reasons why such language provokes scepticism. Understandable as they are, however, these reasons are insufficient to provide a well-justified critique: it is a mistake to throw out the language of equal worth and self-determination because of its contingent association with the historical configurations of Western power. The origins of principles should not be confused with their validity (Weale, 1998).

A distinction must be made between those political discourses which obscure or underpin particular interests and power systems and those which seek explicitly to test the generalizability of claims and interests, and to render power, whether it be political, economic or cultural, accountable (see above, 'Globalization and democracy: Five disjunctures'). The framework of cosmopolitan principles and values is sound, preoccupied, as it is, with the equal liberty and development possibilities of all human beings, but it cannot be implemented plausibly without addressing the most pressing cases of economic suffering and harm. Without this commitment, the advocacy of cosmopolitan standards can descend into high-mindedness, which fails to pursue the socioeconomic changes that are a necessary part of such an allegiance.

At a minimum, this means linking the progressive implementation of a cosmopolitan regulative framework with efforts to reduce the economic vulnerability of many developing countries by eliminating debt, reversing the outflow of capital assets from the poorest countries to the richest, and creating new economic facilities at organizations like the World Bank, the IMF and the UN for development purposes. In addition, if such measures were combined with a (Tobin) tax on the turnover of financial markets, and/or a consumption tax on energy usage and/or a shift of priorities from military expenditure to the alleviation of severe need, then the developmental context of Western and Northern nation-states could begin to accommodate those nations struggling for survival and minimum welfare (for a fuller account of these proposals, see Held, 1995: ch. 11; 2004; Giddens and Hutton, 2000: 213ff.; Held et al., 2005; also see chapters 4–7).

Improbable? Unrealistic? Two points should be made in this regard. First, elements of a cosmopolitan covenant have already been set down as political authority and new forms of governance are diffused 'below', 'above' and 'alongside' the nation-state, and as new forms of international law, from the law of war to human rights law and environmental regimes, begin to establish universal standards. Second, these standards can be built upon, locking cosmopolitan principles into economic life, in developed and developing countries.

To meet the requirements of impartialist reasoning, they have, of course, to be pressed much further. The intense battles about globalization in recent years have helped create an environment in which questions about these matters can be pursued in the public domain. Entrenched geopolitical and economic interests are more likely to respond to a mix of pressure and argument, rather than to argument alone. But globalization protestors need to understand the complexity of the issues they are seeking to address, the diversity of legitimate viewpoints (the difference, for example, between those who object to unbridled free trade and the positions of many developing countries seeking greater access to developed markets), and the extraordinary complexity of institutional solutions. In the end, whether cosmopolitan rules and regulations can be pursued successfully in the long term remains to be seen. But one thing is certain: the modern territorial state was not built in a generation, and one should not expect major and equally significant transformations – in this case to a multilevel, multilayered cosmopolitan polity – to take less time.

2

Principles of
Cosmopolitan Order

Cosmopolitanism is concerned to disclose the ethical, cultural and legal basis of political order in a world where political communities and states matter, but not only and exclusively.[1] In circumstances where the trajectories of each and every country are tightly entwined, the partiality, one-sidedness and limitedness of 'reasons of state' need to be recognized. While states are hugely important vehicles to aid the delivery of effective public recognition, equal liberty and social justice, they should not be thought of as ontologically privileged. They can be judged by how far they deliver these public goods and how far they fail; for the history of states is marked, of course, not just by phases of bad leadership and corruption, but also by the most brutal episodes. A cosmopolitanism relevant to our global age must take this as a starting point, and build an ethically sound and politically robust conception of the proper basis of political community and of the relations among communities.

Two classic accounts of cosmopolitanism, as previously noted, bear on its contemporary meaning (see chapter 1). The first was set out by the Stoics; they sought to replace the central role of the polis in ancient political thought with that of the cosmos in which humankind might live together in harmony (Horstmann, 1976). The second was introduced in the eighteenth century when the term *weltbürger* (world citizen) became one of the elements of Enlightenment thought. The key contribution here can be found in Kant's work (above all, 1970: 41–53, 54–60, 93–130). Kant linked the idea of cosmopolitanism to an innovative conception of 'the public use of reason', and assessed its advance in relation to the removal of constraints upon such reason. He conceived of participation in a cosmopolitan (*weltbürgerlich*) society as an entitlement to enter a world of open, uncoerced dialogue – and he adapted this idea in his formulation of what he called 'cosmopolitan right' (ibid.: 105–8). Cosmopolitan right connotes the capacity to present oneself and be heard within and across political communities; it is the right to enter dialogue without artificial constraint and delimitation of power.

Contemporary conceptions of cosmopolitanism draw on aspects of these ideas and mould them in new directions (see, in particular, Beitz, 1979, 1994, 1998; Pogge, 1989, 1994a, 1994b; and Barry, 1998a, 1999). In the sections that follow, I also draw on some of these notions and use them as a basis to set out the contours of a comprehensive account of the principles of cosmopolitanism – their nature, status, justification and political implications. I begin by stating the principles and explain how they cluster into three types. I then go on to explore their standing and scope. In providing this account, I build substantially on the arguments of chapter 1, creating a new framework for cosmopolitan thinking.

Cosmopolitan principles

Cosmopolitan values can be expressed formally in terms of a set of principles (see Held, 2002b; 2004). These are principles which can be universally shared, and can form the basis for the protection and nurturing of each person's equal significance in 'the moral realm' of humanity. Eight principles are paramount. They are the principles of: (i) equal worth and dignity; (ii) active agency; (iii) personal responsibility and accountability; (iv) consent; (v) collective decision-making about public matters through voting procedures; (vi) inclusiveness and subsidiarity; (vii) avoidance of serious harm; and (viii) sustainability. The meaning of these principles needs unpacking in order that their nature and implications can be clarified. While eight principles may seem like a daunting number, they are interrelated and together form the basis of a cosmopolitan orientation.

The first principle is that the ultimate units of moral concern are individual human beings, not states or other particular forms of human association. Humankind belongs to a single 'moral realm' in which each person is regarded as equally worthy of respect and consideration (Beitz, 1994; Pogge, 1994b). To think of people as having equal moral value is to make a general claim about the basic units of the world comprising persons as free and equal beings (see Kuper, 2000). This notion can be denoted as the principle of individualist moral egalitarianism or, simply, egalitarian individualism. To uphold this principle is not to deny the significance of cultural diversity and difference – not at all – but it is to affirm that there are limits to the moral validity of particular communities – limits which recognize, and demand, that we must treat with equal respect the dignity of reason and moral choice in every human being (Nussbaum, 1997: 42–3). In the post-Holocaust world, these limits have been recognized in the UN Charter, in the human rights regime, and in many other legal instruments (see chapter 1; also see Held, 2004: Part III).

The second principle recognizes that, if principle one is to be universally recognized and accepted, then human agency cannot be understood as the mere expression of a given teleology, fortune or tradition; rather, human agency must be conceived as the ability to act otherwise – the ability not just to accept but to shape human community in the context of the choices of others. Active agency connotes the capacity of human beings to reason self-consciously, to be self-reflective and to be self-determining.[2] It bestows both opportunities and duties – opportunities to act (or not, as the case may be), and duties to ensure that independent action does not curtail and restrict the life chances and opportunities of others (unless, of course, sanctioned by negotiation or consent; see below). Active agency is a capacity both to make and pursue claims and to have such claims made and pursued in relation to oneself. Each person has an equal interest in active agency or self-determination.

The first and second principles cannot be grasped fully unless supplemented by the third principle: the principle of personal responsibility and accountability. At its most basic, this principle can be understood to mean that it is inevitable that people will choose different cultural, social and economic projects and that such differences need to be recognized. People develop their skills and talents differently, and enjoy different forms of ability and specialized competency. That they fare differently, and that many of these differences arise from a voluntary choice on their part, should be welcomed and accepted (see Barry, 1998a: 147–9). These prima facie legitimate differences of choice and outcome have to be distinguished from unacceptable structures of difference which reflect conditions that prevent, or partially prevent, the pursuit by some of their vital needs. Actors have to be aware of, and accountable for, the consequences of actions, direct or indirect, intended or unintended, which may radically restrict or delimit the choices of others. Individuals have both personal responsibility-rights as well as personal responsibility-obligations.[3]

The fourth principle, the principle of consent, recognizes that a commitment to equal worth and equal moral value, along with active agency and personal responsibility, requires a non-coercive political process in and through which people can negotiate and pursue their public interconnections, interdependencies and life chances. Interlocking lives, projects and communities require forms of public reasoning, deliberation and decision-making that take account of each person's equal standing in such processes. The principle of consent constitutes the basis of non-coercive collective agreement and governance.

The fourth and fifth principles must be interpreted together; the fifth principle acknowledges that while a legitimate public decision is one that results from consent, this needs to be linked with voting at the decisive stage of collective decision-making and with the procedures and mechanisms of majority rule. The consent of all is too strong a requirement of collective decision-making and the basis on which minorities can block or forestall public responses to key issues (see Held, 2002b: 26–7). Principle five recognizes the importance of inclusiveness in the process of granting consent, while interpreting this to mean that an inclusive process of participation, deliberation and debate can coalesce with a decision-making procedure that allows outcomes which accrue the greatest support (Dahl, 1989).[4]

The sixth principle, which I earlier referred to as the principle of inclusiveness and subsidiarity, seeks to clarify the fundamental criterion for drawing proper boundaries around units of collective decision-making, and on what grounds. At its simplest, it states that those significantly affected by public decisions, issues or processes, should, *ceteris paribus*, have an equal opportunity, directly or indirectly through elected representatives, to influence and shape them. By 'significantly affected' I mean that people are enmeshed in decisions and forces that impact on their capacity to fulfil their vital needs (Held, 2004; also see chapter 5). According to this principle, collective decision-making is best located when it is closest to and involves those whose life expectancy and life chances are determined by significant social processes and forces. On the other hand, this principle also recognizes that if the decisions at issue are translocal, transnational or transregional, then political associations need not only be locally or nationally based but must also have a wider scope and framework of operation.

The seventh principle is a leading principle of social justice: the principle of the avoidance of serious harm and the amelioration of urgent need. This is a principle for allocating priority to the most vital cases of need and, where possible, trumping other, less urgent, public priorities until such a time as all human beings, de facto and de jure, are covered by the first six principles; that is to say, until they enjoy the status of equal moral value, active agency and have the means to participate in their respective political communities and in the overlapping communities of fate which shape their needs and welfare. A social provision which falls short of the potential for active agency can be referred to as a situation of manifest harm in that the participatory potential of individuals and groups will not have been achieved; that is to say, people would not have adequate access to effectively resourced capacities which they might make use of in their particular circumstances (Sen, 1999). But even this significant shortfall in the realization of human potential should be distinguished from situations of the most pressing levels of vulnerability, defined by the most urgent need. The harm that follows from a failure to meet such needs can be denoted as 'serious harm', marked, as it often is, by immediate, life-and-death consequences. Accordingly, if the requirements specified by the principle of the avoidance of serious harm are to be met, public policy ought to be focused, in the first instance, on the prevention of such conditions; that is, on the eradication of severe harm inflicted on people 'against their will' and 'without their consent' (Barry, 1998b: 231, 207).

The eighth and final principle is the principle of sustainability, which specifies that all economic and social development must be consistent with the stewardship of the world's core resources – by which I mean resources which are irreplaceable and non-substitutable (Goodin, 1992: 62–5, 72). Such a principle discriminates against social and economic change which disrupts global ecological balances and unnecessarily damages the choices of future generations. Sustainable development is best understood as a guiding principle, as opposed to a precise formula, since we do not know, for example, how future technological innovation will impact on resource provision and utilization. Yet, without reference to such a principle, public policy would be made without taking account of the finite quality of many of the world's resources and the equally valid claims of future generations to well-being. Because the contemporary economic and military age is the first to be able to take decisions not just for itself but for all future epochs, its choices must be particularly careful not to pre-empt the equal worth and active agency of future generations.

The eight principles can best be thought of as falling into three clusters. The first cluster (principles 1–3) sets down the fundamental organizational features of the cosmopolitan moral universe. Its crux is that each person is subject of equal moral concern; that each person is capable of acting autonomously with respect to the range of choices before them; and that, in deciding how to act or which institutions to create, the claims of each person affected should be taken equally into account. Personal responsibility means, in this context, that actors and agents have to be aware of, and accountable for, the consequences of their actions, direct or indirect, intended or unintended, which may substantially restrict and delimit the opportunities of others. The second cluster (principles 4–6) forms the basis of translating individually initiated activity, or privately determined activities, more broadly, into collectively agreed or collectively sanctioned frameworks of action or regulatory regimes. Public power at all levels can be conceived as legitimate to the degree to which principles 4, 5 and 6 are upheld. The final principles (7 and 8) lay down a framework for prioritizing urgent need and resource conservation. By distinguishing vital from non-vital needs, the seventh principle creates an unambiguous starting point and guiding orientation for public decisions. While this 'prioritizing commitment' does not, of course, create a decision procedure to resolve all clashes of priority in politics, it clearly creates a moral framework for focusing public policy on those who are most vulnerable. By contrast, the eighth principle seeks to set down a prudential orientation to help ensure that public policy is consistent with global ecological balances and that it does not destroy irreplaceable and non-substitutable resources.

Thick or thin cosmopolitanism?

It could be objected at this point that, given the plurality of interpretive standpoints in the contemporary world (social, cultural, religious and so on), it is unwise to construct a political philosophy which depends upon overarching principles. For it is doubtful, the objection could continue, that a bridge can be built between 'the many particular wills' and 'the general will' (see McCarthy, 1991: 181–99). In a world marked by a diversity of value orientations, on what grounds, if any, can we suppose that all groups or parties could be argumentatively convinced about fundamental ethical and political principles?

It is important to stress that cosmopolitan philosophy does not deny the reality and ethical relevance of living in a world of diverse values and identities – how could it? It does not assume that unanimity is attainable on all practical-political questions. The elaboration of cosmopolitan principles is not an exercise in seeking a general and universal understanding on a wide spectrum of issues concerning the broad conditions of life or diverse ethical matters (for example, abortion, animal rights or the role of voluntary euthanasia). This is not how a modern cosmopolitan project should be understood. Rather, at stake is a more restrictive exercise aimed at reflecting on the moral status of persons, the conditions of agency, and collective decision-making. It is important to emphasize that this exercise is constructed on the assumption that ground rules for communication, dialogue and dispute settlement are not only desirable but essential, precisely because all people are of equal moral value and their views on a wide range of moral-political questions will conflict. The principles of cosmopolitanism are the conditions for taking cultural diversity seriously and for building a democratic culture to mediate clashes of the cultural good. They are, in short, about the prerequisites of just difference and democratic dialogue. The aim of modern cosmopolitanism is the conceptualization and generation of the necessary background conditions for a 'common' or 'basic' structure of individual action and social activity (see Rawls, 1985: 254ff.).

Contemporary cosmopolitans, it should be acknowledged, are divided about the demands that cosmopolitanism lays upon the individual and, accordingly, upon the appropriate framing of the necessary background conditions for a 'common' structure of individual action and social activity. Among them there is agreement that in deciding how to act, or which rules or regulations ought to be established, the claims of each person affected should be weighed equally – 'no matter where they live, which society they belong to, or how they are connected to us' (Miller, 1998: 165). The principle of egalitarian individualism is regarded as axiomatic. But the moral weight granted to this principle depends heavily upon the precise modes of interpretation of other principles.

Two broad positions exist in the literature. There are those for whom membership of humanity at large means that special relationships (including particular moral responsibilities) to family, kin, nation or religious grouping can never be justified because the people involved have some intrinsic quality which suffices to compel special moral attention, or because they are allegedly worth more than other people, or because such affiliations provide sufficient reason for pursuing particular commitments or actions. This does not mean that such relationships cannot be justified – they can, but only insofar as nurturing or honouring such ties is in the cosmopolitan interest; that is, is the best way to achieve the good for humanity overall (Nussbaum, 1996; Barry, 1998a). As Scheffler succinctly put it, 'special attention to particular people is legitimate only if it can be justified by reference to the interests of all human beings considered as equals' (1999: 259).

The second interpretation recognizes that while each person stands in 'an ethically significant relation' to all other people, this is only one important 'source of reasons and responsibilities among others' (ibid.: 260). Cosmopolitan principles are, in this context, quite compatible with the recognition of different 'spheres' or 'layers' of moral reasoning (Walzer, 1983).

In the light of this, it is useful to draw a distinction between 'strong' and 'weak' cosmopolitanism, or between thick and thin cosmopolitanism, as I refer to it. Miller has summarized the distinction well:

According to the strong [thick] version . . . [a]ll moral principles must be justified by showing that they give equal weight to the claims of everyone, which means that they must either be directly universal in their scope, or if they apply only to a select group of people they must be secondary principles whose ultimate foundation is universal. The weak [thin] version, by contrast, holds only that morality is cosmopolitan in part: there are some valid principles with a more restricted scope. According to . . . [thin] cosmopolitanism . . . we may owe certain kinds of treatment to all other human beings regardless of any relationship in which we stand to them, while there are other kinds of treatment that we owe only to those to whom we are related in certain ways, with neither sort of obligation being derivative of the other. (1998: 166–7)

Whether cosmopolitanism is an overriding frame of reference (trumping all other moral positions) or a distinctive subset of considerations (specifying that there are some substantive global rules, norms and principles of justice which ought to be balanced with, and take account of, those derived from individual societies or other human groupings) is not a question which will be focused on here at length (see Barry, 1998a; Miller, 1998). However, some comment is in order if the rationale and standing of the eight principles are to be satisfactorily illuminated.

I take cosmopolitanism ultimately to denote the ethical and political space occupied by the eight principles. Cosmopolitanism lays down the universal or regulative principles which delimit and govern the range of diversity and difference that ought to be found in public life. It discloses the proper basis or framework for the pursuit of argument, discussion and negotiation about particular spheres of value, spheres in which local, national and regional affiliations will inevitably be weighed. In some respects, this is a form of thick cosmopolitanism. However, it should not be concluded from this that the meaning of the eight principles can simply be specified once and for all. For while cosmopolitanism affirms principles which are universal in their scope, it recognizes, in addition, that the precise meaning of these is always fleshed out in situated discussions; in other words, that there is an inescapable hermeneutic complexity in moral and political affairs which will affect how the eight principles are actually interpreted, and the weight granted to special ties and other practical-political issues. I call this mix of regulative principles and interpretative activity neither thick nor thin cosmopolitanism, but, rather, a 'layered' cosmopolitan perspective (cf. Tully, 1995). This cosmopolitan point of view builds on principles that all could reasonably assent to, while recognizing the irreducible plurality of forms of life (Habermas, 1996). Thus, on the one hand, the position upholds certain basic egalitarian ideas – those which emphasize equal worth, equal respect, equal consideration and so on – and, on the other, it acknowledges that the elucidation of their meaning cannot be pursued independently of an ongoing dialogue in public life. Hence, there can be no adequate institutionalization of equal rights and duties without a corresponding institutionalization of national and transnational forms of public debate, democratic participation and accountability (McCarthy, 1999). The institutionalization of regulative cosmopolitan principles requires the entrenchment of democratic public realms.

A layered cosmopolitan perspective of this kind shares a particular affinity with thin cosmopolitanism insofar as it acknowledges a plurality of value sources and a diversity of moral conceptions of the good; it recognizes, accordingly, different spheres of ethical reasoning linked to everyday attempts to resolve matters concerning modes of living and social organization (Böhme, 2001). As such, it seeks to be ethically neutral with regard to many life questions. But ethical neutrality of this sort should not be confused with political neutrality and its core requirements (see Kuper, 2000: 649f.). The point has been succinctly stated by Tan: 'a commitment to ethical neutrality entails a particular type of political arrangement, one which, for one, allows for the pursuit of different private conceptions of the good' (1998: 283, quoted in Kuper, 2000: 649; see Barry, 1995: 263). Only polities that acknowledge the equal status of all persons, that seek neutrality or impartiality with respect to personal ends, hopes and aspirations, and that pursue the public justification of social, economic and political arrangements can ensure a basic or common structure of political action which allows individuals to pursue their projects – both individual and collective – as free and equal agents. Such a structure is inconsistent with, and, if applied systematically, would need to filter out, those ends and goods, whether public or private, which would erode or undermine the structure itself.[5] For value pluralism and social pluralism to flourish, political associations must be structured or organized in one general way; that is, according to the constituting, legitimizing and prioritizing principles specified above (cf. Pogge, 1994b: 117). Arguments can be had about the exact specification of these – that is, about how these notions are properly formulated – but the eight principles themselves constitute guiding notions or regulative ideals for a polity geared to autonomy, dialogue and tolerance.

Cosmopolitan justifications

While cosmopolitans must stand by these principles, they are not, of course, self-justifying. Or, to put the point another way, from whence come these principles? From the outset, it is important to distinguish two things that are too often run together: questions about the origins of principles, and questions about their validity or weight (see Weale, 1998). Both kinds of question are relevant. If the first illuminates the ethical circumstances or motivation for a preference for, or commitment to, a principle or set of principles, the second is the basis for testing their intersubjective validity. In this regard, the justificatory rationale of cosmopolitan principles is dependent on two fundamental metaprinciples or organizing notions of ethical discourse – one cultural and historical, the other philosophical. These are, respectively, the metaprinciple of autonomy and the metaprinciple of impartialist reasoning.

The metaprinciple of autonomy (henceforth, the MPA) is at the core of the democratic project. Its rationale and standing are 'political not metaphysical', to borrow a phrase from Rawls (1985). A basic concept or idea is political, in this sense, if it represents an articulation of an understanding latent in public political life and, in particular, if against the background of the struggle for a democratic culture in the West and elsewhere, it builds on the distinctive conception of the person as a citizen who is, in principle, 'free and equal' in a manner 'comprehensible' to everyone. In other words, the MPA can be understood as a notion embedded in the public political culture of democratic societies and emerging democracies.

The MPA is part of the 'deep structure' of ideas which have shaped the constitution of modern political life. It has roots in the ancient world, although many elements of its deep structure were not part of classical thinking, marked as the latter was by a very restricted view of who could count as a citizen and by a teleological conception of nature and the cosmos. It was not until the modern world that the MPA became more firmly entrenched (Held, 2006a). It became entrenched in the pursuit of citizenship, which has always been marked by 'an urge', as Marshall put it, to secure 'a fuller measure of autonomy' for each and every person; for autonomy is the 'stuff' of which modern citizenship is made (Marshall, 1973: 84). Or, to restate the point in the language used hitherto, it has been marked by an urge to realize the core elements of an egalitarian conception of the individual (with an emphasis upon people as free and equal, capable of active agency and accountable for their choices), of the democratic regulation of public life (including consent, deliberation, voting and inclusiveness) and of the necessity to ensure that, if people's equal interest in self-determination or self-governance is to be protected, attention must be focused on those who lack the capacity to participate in, and act within, key sites of power and political institutions (that is, that there must be a measure of social protection).

Another way to put these points is to say that the MPA is the guiding political thread of modern democratic societies and that the first seven cosmopolitan principles, suitably unfolded from a commitment to self-determination and autonomy, are the basis for specifying more fully the nature and form of a liberal and democratic order.[6] In short, these cosmopolitan principles are the principles of democratic public life, but without one crucial assumption – never fully justified in any case in liberal democratic thought, classic or contemporary – that these principles can only be enacted effectively within a single, circumscribed, territorially based political community (see Held, 1995). The cosmopolitan principles do not presume, as the sixth principle makes clear, that the link between self-determination, accountability, democracy and sovereignty can be understood simply in territorial terms. Hence, it is possible to have a modern democratic rendition of the aspiration of the Stoics to multiple forms of affiliation – local, national and global. The cosmopolitan principles are the core element of democratic public life, shed of the contingent link with the borders of nation-states. How these principles should be spliced with organizations, institutions and borders of political communities is a separate question, to which I will return.

It could be objected that the language of autonomy and self-determination has limited cross-culture validity because of its Western origins. But a distinction must be made between those political terms and discourses which obscure or underpin particular interests and power systems and those which seek to test explicitly the generalizability of claims and interests, and to render power, whether it be political, economic or cultural, accountable. What the language of autonomy and self-determination generates and, in particular, the language of the MPA, is what might be thought of as a commitment or pre-commitment to the idea that all persons should be equally free – that is to say, that they should enjoy equal liberty to pursue their own activities without arbitrary or unwarranted interference. If this notion is shared across cultures, it is not because they have acquiesced to modern Western political discourse; it is, rather, that they have come to see that there are certain languages which protect and nurture the notion of equal status and worth, and others which have sought to ignore or suppress it.

To test the generalizability of claims and interests involves 'reasoning from the point of view of others', as noted in chapter 1 (Benhabib, 1992: 9–10, 121–47). Attempts to focus on this 'social perspective' find their clearest contemporary elaboration in Rawl's original position, Habemas's ideal speech situation and Barry's formulation of impartialist reasoning (see Rawls, 1971; Habermas, 1973, 1996; Barry, 1989, 1995). These formulations have in common a concern to conceptualize an impartial moral standpoint from which to assess particular types of practical reasoning. This concern should not be thought of as over-demanding. All the impartiality thesis claims is that if one raises questions about fundamental moral standards, as one commentator aptly put it, 'the court of appeal that one addresses is a court in which no particular individual, group, or country has special standing' (Hill, 1987: 132, quoted in Barry, 1995: 226–7). Before the court, suggesting 'I like it', 'it suits me', 'it belongs to male prerogatives', 'it's a gay right', 'it is in the best interest of my country', does not settle the issue at hand, for principles must be defensible from a larger, human standpoint (ibid.). This social open-ended, moral perspective is a way for focusing our thoughts and testing the intersubjective validity of our conceptions of the good. I refer to it as the metaprinciple of impartialist reasoning (henceforth the MPIR).

The MPIR is a moral frame of reference for specifying rules and principles that can be universally shared; and, concomitantly, it rejects as unjust all those practices, rules and institutions anchored in principles not all could adopt (O'Neill, 1991). At issue is the establishment of principles and rules that nobody, motivated to establish an uncoerced and informed agreement, could reasonably discard (see Barry, 1989; cf. Scanlon, 1998). In order to meet the standard set by the MPIR a number of particular tests can be carried out, including an assessment of whether all perspectives have been taken into consideration; whether participants in decision-making are in a position to impose their will on others in such a way that would prove unacceptable to the latter, or to the originator of the action (or inaction), if the roles were reversed; and, finally, whether all parties would be equally willing to accept the outcomes proposed as fair and reasonable irrespective of the social positions they might occupy now or in the future (see Barry, 1989: 372, 362–3).

The MPIR can be thought as a heuristic device to test candidate principles of moral worth, democracy and social justice, and their forms of justification (Kelly, 1998: 1–8; Barry 1998b). Its tests are concerned with a process of reasonable rejectability, which can always be pursued in a dialogue open to fresh challenge and new questions and, hence, in an interpretive sense, can never be complete (Gadamer, 1975). Thus, the MPIR cannot produce a simple deductive proof of the ideal set of principles and conditions which can overcome the deficiencies of a political order; nor can it produce a deductive proof of the best or only moral principles that should guide institutional development. But to acknowledge this is not to say that theoretical conversation is devoid of value with respect either to principles or to the conditions of their entrenchment.

In the first instance, moral impartialism has a crucial critical and debunking role. This position is emphasized most clearly by O'Neill (1991). Impartialist reasoning, in this account, is a basis for disclosing non-generalizable principles, rules and interests, and for showing how justice is a matter of not basing actions, lives or institutions on principles that cannot be universally shared. The impartialist vantage point has efficacy qua critical stance.

The principles of coercion and deception are among the principles open to serious objection from this perspective. It is impossible for a principle of coercion to be universally shared, for those who are coerced are denied agency and so cannot share their coercer's principle of action. Likewise, it is impossible for a principle of deception to be universally upheld because those who are deceived cannot adopt their deceiver's underlying concerns or share the deceiver's principle of action. (If the deceiver's plan of action was known to all parties, the deception could not, of course, work.) Such arguments do not show 'that all coercion or deception is unjust: they show only that actions, institutions and lives which make coercion or deception fundamental are unjust' (ibid.: 298). Moreover, the same line of reasoning can disclose that human beings cannot construct a just order based on the neglect of need. For a principle of neglecting need will also fail the test of universal adoption. Human beings who sought to adopt such a principle would risk failing to meet their own finite, needy states, let alone those of others. But how, and to what extent, needs should be met remains unspecified in this account.

Impartialist reasoning, thus understood, is a critical device for highlighting non-generalizable principles and unjust institutions, but can it state a more positive position, which lays down the underlying principles of a just cosmopolitan order? I believe something more positive can be demonstrated in the pursuit of principles and rules that can be universally shared. In this regard, it is my contention that the eight cosmopolitan principles can all meet the test of impartiality, and form moral and political elements upon which all could act; for they are at the root of the equal consideration and treatment of all human beings, irrespective of where they were born or raised. The impartialist emphasis on taking account of the position of the other, of only treating political outcomes as fair and reasonable if there are good reasons for holding that they would be equally acceptable to all parties, and of only treating the position of some socio-economic groups as legitimate if they are acceptable to all people irrespective of where they come in the social hierarchy, is consistent with the eight principles and does not provide grounds on which they can be reasonably rejected. The principles of equal moral status, equal public engagement and the public justification of collective institutional arrangements are robust enough not to fall foul of these considerations.

Within this theoretical framework, it can be argued that individual or collective social arrangements generating serious harm cannot be justified by reference to a special social status, cultural identity, ethnic background or nationality – in fact, by reference to any particular grouping – if the latter sanctions closure or exclusion in relation to the core conditions of human autonomy, development and welfare (see Caney, 2001). To the extent that a domain of activity operates to structure and delimit life expectancy and life chances, deficits are disclosed in the structure of action of a political association. These deficits can, furthermore, be regarded as illegitimate to the extent that they could be rejected under the conditions of the MPIR. If people did not know their future social location and political standing, they would be unlikely to find the self-interested defence of specific exclusionary processes and mechanisms convincing. These justificatory structures cannot easily be generalized and are, thus, weak in the face of the test of impartiality. Unless exceptional arguments are available to the contrary, social mechanisms and processes generating serious harm for certain groups and categories of people fall to the requirement of impartiality (see Barry, 1995, 1998a).

Impartialist reasoning is a basis for thinking about the problems posed by asymmetries of power, unevenness of resource distribution and stark prejudices. It provides the means for questioning the rules, laws and policies that people might think right, justified or worthy of respect. It allows a distinction to be made between legitimacy as acquiescence to existing socioeconomic arrangements, and legitimacy as 'rightness' or 'correctness' – the worthiness of a political order to be recognized because it is the order people would accept as a result of impartialist reasoning. The latter can be conceived not as an optional element of a political and legal understanding, but as a requirement of any attempt to grasp the nature of the support and legitimacy enjoyed by particular social forces and relations; for without this form of reasoning, the distinction between legitimacy as 'acceptance' and legitimacy as 'rightness' could not be drawn.

It should be emphasized that the pursuit of impartial reasoning is a social activity – not a solitary theoretical exercise. For, as Arendt has written:

> The power of judgment rests on a potential agreement with others, and the thinking process which is active in judging something is not . . . a dialogue between me and myself, but finds itself always and primarily, even if I am quite alone in making up my mind, in an anticipated communication with others with whom I know I must finally come to some agreement. . . . And this enlarged way of thinking . . . cannot function in strict isolation or solitude; it needs the presence of others 'in whose place' it must think, whose perspective it must take into consideration, and without whom it never has the opportunity to operate at all. (1961: 220–1, as cited by Benhabib, 1992: 9–10)

The aim of a 'theoretical conversation' about impartiality is an anticipated agreement with all those whose diverse circumstances affect the realization of people's equal interest in self-determination and autonomy. Of course, as an 'anticipated agreement' it is a hypothetical ascription of an intersubjective or collective understanding. As such, the ultimate test of its validity must depend in contemporary life on the extension of the conversation to all those whom it seeks to encompass. Only under the latter circumstances can an analytically proposed interpretation become an actual understanding or agreement among others (Habermas, 1988). Critical reflection must conjoin with public debate and democratic politics.

Together, the MPA and MPIR provide the grounds of cosmopolitan thought. The MPA lays down the conceptual space in which impartialist reasoning can take place. For it generates a preoccupation with each person as a subject of equal moral concern; with each person's capacity to act autonomously with respect to the range of choices before them; and with each person's equal status with respect to the basic institutions of political communities; that is, with an entitlement to claim and be claimed upon (see Rawls, 1971: 544–5; Barry, 1989: 200). It provides motives, reasons and constraining considerations to help establish agreement on reasonable terms. The MPIR is the basis for pursuing this agreement. It is a device of argument that is designed to abstract from power relations in order to disclose the fundamental enabling conditions of active agency, rightful authority and social justice.[7] Of course, as a device of argument, it can be resisted by those who reject the language of autonomy and self-determination; but then we must be clear that this is precisely what they are doing.

From cosmopolitan principles to cosmopolitan law

Cosmopolitan law refers to a domain of law different in kind from the law of states and the law made between one state and another for the mutual enhancement of their geopolitical interests. Kant, the leading interpreter of the idea of such a law, interpreted it as the basis for articulating the equal moral status of persons in the 'universal community' (1970: 108). For him, cosmopolitan law is neither a fantastic nor a utopian way of conceiving law, but a 'necessary complement' to the codes of national and international law, and a means to transform them into a public law of humanity (see Held, 1995: ch. 10). While Kant limited the form and scope of cosmopolitan law to the conditions of universal hospitality – the right to present oneself and be heard within and across communities – I understand it more broadly as the appropriate mode of representing the equal moral standing of all human beings, their entitlement to equal liberty and to forms of governance founded on deliberation and consent. In other words, cosmopolitan law is the form of law which best articulates and entrenches the eight principles of cosmopolitan order. If these principles were to be systematically entrenched as the foundation of law on a global basis, the conditions of the cosmopolitan regulation of public life could be set down. This theme is taken up in the next chapter.

3

Cosmopolitan Law and Institutional Requirements

Thinking about the future of humankind on the basis of the early years of the twenty-first century does not give grounds for optimism. From 9/11 to the 2006 war in the Middle East, terrorism, conflict, territorial struggle and the clash of identities appear to define the moment. The wars in Afghanistan, Iraq, Israel/Lebanon, Israel/Gaza and elsewhere suggest that political violence is an irreducible feature of our age. Perversely, globalization seems to have dramatized the significance of differences between peoples; far from the globalization of communications easing understanding and the translation of ideas, it seems to have highlighted what it is that people do not have in common and find dislikeable about each other (cf. Bull, 1977: 127). Moreover, the contemporary drivers of political nationalism – self-determination, secure borders, geopolitical and geoeconomic advantage – place an emphasis on the pursuit of the national interest above concerns with what it is that humans might have in common.

Yet, it is easy to overstate the moment and exaggerate from one set of historical experiences. While each of the elements mentioned poses a challenge to a rule-based global order, it is a profound mistake to forget that the twentieth century established a series of cosmopolitan steps towards the delimitation of the nature and form of political community, sovereignty and 'reasons of state'. These steps were laid down after the First and Second World Wars, which brought humanity to the edge of the abyss – not once, but twice. At a time as difficult as the start of the twenty-first century, it is important to recall why these steps were taken and remind ourselves of their significance.

From the foundation of the UN system to the creation of the EU, from changes to the laws of war to the entrenchment of human rights, from the emergence of international environmental regimes to the establishment of the ICC, people have sought to reframe human activity and embed it in law, rights and responsibilities. As noted in the Introduction, many of these developments were initiated against the background of formidable threats to humankind – above all, Nazism, fascism and Stalinism. Those involved in them affirmed the importance of universal principles, human rights and the rule of law in the face of strong temptations simply to put up the shutters and defend the position of only some countries and nations. They rejected the view of national and moral particularists that belonging to a given community limits and determines the moral worth of individuals and the nature of their freedom, and they defended the irreducible moral status of each and every person. At the centre of such thinking is the cosmopolitan view that human well-being is not defined by geographical or cultural locations, that national or ethnic or gendered boundaries should not determine the limits of rights or responsibilities for the satisfaction of basic human needs, and that all human beings require equal moral respect and concern. The principles of equal respect, equal concern and the priority of the vital needs of all human beings are not principles for some remote utopia; for they are at the centre of significant post-Second World War legal and political developments.

What does 'cosmopolitanism' mean in this context? In the first instance, cosmopolitanism refers to those basic values which set down standards or boundaries which no agent, whether a representative of a global body, state or civil association, should be able to violate (see Held, 2002b). Focused on the claims of each person as an individual, these values encapsulate the idea that human beings are in a fundamental sense equal, and that they deserve equal political treatment; that is, treatment based upon the equal care and consideration of their agency, irrespective of the community in which they were born or brought up. After more than two centuries of nationalism, sustained nation-state formation and seemingly endless conflicts over territory and resources, such values could be thought of as being out of place. But such values are already enshrined in the law of war, human rights law and the statutes of the ICC, among many other international rules and legal arrangements (see chapter 1).

Second, cosmopolitanism can be taken to refer to those forms of political regulation and law-making which create powers, rights and constraints that go beyond the claims of nation-states and which have far-reaching consequences, in principle, for the nature and form of political power. These regulatory forms can be found in the domain between national and international law and regulation – the space between domestic law, which regulates the relations between a state and its citizens, and traditional international law, which applies primarily to states and interstate relations. This space is already filled by a host of legal regulation, from the legal instruments of the EU and the international human rights regime to the diverse agreements of the arms control system and environmental regimes. Within Europe, the European Convention for the Protection of Human Rights and Fundamental Freedoms, together with the EU, creates new institutions and layers of law and governance which have divided political authority; any assumption that sovereignty is an indivisible, illimitable, exclusive and perpetual form of public power – entrenched within an individual state – is now defunct (Held, 1995: 107–13). Within the wider international community, rules governing war, weapons systems, war crimes, human rights and the environment, among other areas, have transformed and delimited the order of states, embedding national polities in new forms and layers of accountability and governance. Accordingly, the boundaries between states, nations and societies can no longer claim the deep legal and moral significance they once did in the era of classic sovereignty.

Cosmopolitan Law and Institutional Requirements

Cosmopolitanism is not made up of political ideals for another age, but is embedded in rule systems and institutions which have already altered state sovereignty in distinct ways, and in societies of diverse faiths.

The idea of cosmopolitan law

The precise sense in which these developments constitute a form of 'cosmopolitanism' remains, however, to be clarified, especially given that the ideas of cosmopolitanism have a long and complex history. For my purposes in this chapter, cosmopolitanism can be taken as the moral and political outlook which builds upon the strengths of the post-1945 multilateral order, particularly its commitment to universal standards, human rights and democratic values, and which seeks to specify general principles upon which all could act. These are principles which can be widely shared and form the basis for the protection and nurturing of each person's equal interest in the determination of the forces and institutions which govern their lives.

Cosmopolitan values can be expressed formally, as noted earlier, in terms of a set of eight principles:

- equal worth and dignity;
- active agency;
- personal responsibility and accountability;
- consent;
- collective decision-making about public issues through voting procedures;

97

- inclusiveness and subsidiarity;
- avoidance of serious harm; and
- sustainability.

Since these principles have already been analysed earlier, I will not elucidate them further here (see chapter 2). But it is important to recall that their focus is on each person as a subject of equal moral concern, capable of acting autonomously with respect to the range of choices before them and able, through democratic organization and institutions, to take into account and weigh the claims of each person seriously affected by the decisions they take or do not take. Hence, cosmopolitan principles describe the conceptual core of democratic public life, stripped of one crucial (and unwarranted) assumption: the need for democratic principles to work only and exclusively in a self-contained, bounded political community.

Against this background, the nature and form of cosmopolitan law can begin to be addressed. In the first instance, the idea of cosmopolitan law invokes the notion of a domain of law different in kind from the law of states and the law made between one state and another for the mutual enhancement of their geopolitical interests. Kant understood the idea of such a law as the basis for articulating the equal moral status of persons in the 'universal community' (1970: 108). While he restricted the form and scope of cosmopolitan law to the conditions of universal hospitality – the right to present oneself and be heard within and across communities – it is interpreted here more broadly as the appropriate mode of representing the equal moral standing of all human beings, their entitlement to equal liberty and to forms of governance founded on deliberation and consent. In other words, cosmopolitan law should be thought of as the form of law which best entrenches the eight cosmopolitan principles and, hence, the appropriate basis of legitimate public power. Political power becomes legitimate power according to cosmopolitanism when, and only when, it is entrenched by, and constituted by, these cosmopolitan principles. If these were to be systematically entrenched as the foundation of law, the conditions for the possibility of the cosmopolitan regulation of public life could be set down.

Within the framework of cosmopolitan law, the idea of rightful authority, which has been so often connected to the state and particular geographical domains, has to be reconceived and recast. Sovereignty can be delinked from the idea of fixed borders and territories and thought of as, in principle, an attribute of basic cosmopolitan democratic law which can be drawn upon and enacted in diverse realms, from local associations and cities to states and wider global networks. Cosmopolitan law would thus require the subordination of regional, national and local 'sovereignties' to an overarching legal framework, but within this framework associations may be self-governing at diverse levels (Held, 1995: 234).

Clear contrasts with the classic and liberal regimes of sovereignty follow. Within the terms of classic sovereignty, the idea of the modern polity is associated directly with the idea of the state – the supreme power operating in a delimited geographic realm. The state has pre-eminent jurisdiction over a unified territorial area – a jurisdiction supervised and implemented by territorially anchored institutions. While the notion of the state within the frame of classic sovereignty is associated with an unchecked and overarching supreme power, in the liberal conception a legitimate political power is one marked by an impersonal, legally circumscribed structure of power, delimited nationally and (increasingly) internationally. The geopolitics and the geoeconomics of the liberal international sovereign order are fierce, but they are locked, at least in principle, into the universal human rights regime and the growing standards of democratic governance. Within the cosmopolitan framework, by contrast, the political authority of states is but one aspect of a complex, overlapping regime of political authority; legitimate political power in this framework embeds states in a complex network of authority relations, where networks are regularized or patterned interactions between independent but interconnected political agents, nodes of activity, or sites of political power (Modelski, 1972; Mann, 1986; Castells, 1996). Cosmopolitan sovereignty comprises networked realms of public authority shaped and delimited by cosmopolitan law. Cosmopolitan sovereignty is sovereignty stripped away from the idea of fixed borders and territories governed by states alone, and is instead thought of as a framework of political relations and regulatory activities, shaped and formed by an overarching cosmopolitan legal structure.

In this conception, the nation-state 'withers away'. But this is not to suggest that states and national democratic polities become redundant. Rather, states would no longer be regarded as the sole centres of legitimate power within their borders, as is already the case in diverse settings (see Held et al., 1999: Conclusion). States need to be articulated with, and relocated within, an overarching cosmopolitan framework. Within this framework, the laws and rules of the nation-state would become but one focus for legal development, political reflection and mobilization.

At the heart of a cosmopolitan conception of global order is the idea that citizenship can be based, not on an exclusive membership of a territorial community, but on general rules and principles which can be entrenched and drawn upon in different settings. The meaning of citizenship thus shifts from membership in a community which bestows, for those who qualify, particular rights and duties to an alternative principle of world order in which all persons have equivalent rights and duties in the cross-cutting spheres of decision-making which can affect their vital needs and interests. As Habermas has written, 'only a democratic citizenship that does not close itself off in a particularistic fashion can pave the way for a *world citizenship* . . . State citizenship and world citizenship form a continuum whose contours, at least, are already becoming visible' (1996: 514–15). There is only a historically contingent connection between the principles underpinning citizenship and the national community; as this connection weakens in a world of overlapping communities and fate, the principles of citizenship must be rearticulated and re-entrenched. Under these conditions, people would come, in principle, to enjoy multiple citizenships – political membership, that is, in the diverse political communities which significantly affect them. In a world of overlapping communities of fate, individuals would be citizens of their immediate political communities, and of the wider regional and global networks which impact upon their lives. This overlapping cosmopolitan polity would be one that in form and substance reflected and embraced the diverse forms of power and authority that operate within and across borders.

Moreover, in the light of these considerations, the connection between patriotism and nationalism becomes easier to call into question, and a case built to bind patriotism to the defence of core civic and political principles – not to the nation or country for their own sake (Heater, 2002). Only national identities open to diverse solidarities, and shaped by respect for general rules and principles, can accommodate themselves successfully to the challenges of the global age. Ultimately, diversity and difference, accountability and political capacity, can flourish only in a cosmopolitan legal community (see Brunkhorst, 2005). The global challenges we face are better met in a cosmopolitan legal framework.

The key reasons for this should be highlighted for clarity. First, cosmopolitan values have played a constitutive role in the development of important aspects of the international and global political realm, and these continue to be of great relevance in the framing of core civic and political principles. Second, the world of overlapping communities of fate, of interlocking and interdependent relations across borders and sectors of society, generated by globalization, binds the fortunes of people together across countries in dense networks and processes. Third, if the complex and demanding political issues that this gives rise to are to be resolved, not by markets or geopolitical might, but by mechanisms of deliberation, accountability and democracy, then a cosmopolitan legal order can be seen to set down a fair and inclusive political framework to address them, internationally and globally.

Institutional requirements

The institutional requirements of a cosmopolitan polity are many and various. In thinking about the relevance and efficacy of cosmopolitanism to international legal and political arrangements, it is helpful to break down these requirements into a number of different dimensions. All relate to the idea of cosmopolitanism but function analytically and substantively at different levels, ranging from the legal and the political to the economic and the socio-cultural. Four institutional dimensions of cosmopolitanism will be set out below and related to the key problems embedded in the international order (see chapter 1). Each of the different dimensions can contribute to an expansion of the resources necessary to move beyond these problems and, eventually, to the entrenchment of a cosmopolitan conception of sovereignty.

Legal cosmopolitanism

Legal cosmopolitanism explores the tension between legal claims made on behalf of the state system and those made on behalf of an alternative organizing principle of world order in which all persons have equivalent rights and duties (Pogge, 1994b: 90f.). It posits an ideal of a global legal order in which people can enjoy an equality of status with respect to the fundamental institutions of the legal system. At the centre of legal cosmopolitanism is *legalis homo*, someone free to act by law, free to ask for and expect the law's protection, free to sue and be sued in certain courts, but who does not directly make or determine the law (Pocock, 1995: 36ff.). The focus of *legalis homo* is equal legal standing and personal rights.

Legal cosmopolitanism is universalizing and potentially inclusive. It is not, as one commentator usefully put it, 'tied to a particular collective identity, or membership of a demos' (Cohen, 1999: 249). It can be deployed to create the basis for the equal treatment of all, the entrenchment of a universal set of rights and obligations, and the impartial delimitation of individual and collective action within the organizations and associations of state, economy and civil society (Held, 1995: ch. 12). As such, it is a resource to help resolve the challenges posed by asymmetries of power, the externalities produced by national policy, and the overlapping fortunes of countries.

The institutional requirements of legal cosmopolitanism include:

- the entrenchment of cosmopolitan democratic public law and a related charter of rights and obligations embracing political, social and economic power;

- an interconnected global legal system, embracing elements of criminal, human rights and environmental law; and
- submission to ICJ and ICC jurisdiction; the creation of a new international human rights court, and an international environmental court to address legal issues involving the global commons.

Political cosmopolitanism

Without complementary forms of law-making and enforcement, however, there is no reason to think that the agenda of *legalis homo* will satisfactorily mesh with that of the protection of equal membership in the public realm and the requirements of active citizenship. For this, legal cosmopolitanism needs to be related to political cosmopolitanism. Political cosmopolitanism involves the development of regional and global governance and the creation of political organizations and mechanisms which would provide a cosmopolitan framework of regulation and law-enforcement across the globe. Although cosmopolitan positions often differ on the precise nature and form of such a framework, they are generally committed to the view that political cosmopolitanism entails that institutions and organizations of regional and global governance are a necessary supplement and complement to those of the state.

From this perspective, the rights and duties of individuals can only be nurtured adequately if, in addition to their proper articulation in national constitutions, they are underwritten by regional and global regimes, laws and institutions. The promotion of the political good and of principles of egalitarian political participation and justice are rightly pursued at regional and global levels. Their conditions of possibility are inextricably linked to the establishment and development of transnational organizations and institutions of regional and global governance. The latter are a necessary basis of cooperative relations and just conduct.

Political cosmopolitanism, accordingly, takes as its starting point a world of overlapping communities of fate. In the classic and liberal regimes of sovereignty, nation-states largely dealt with issues which spilled over boundaries by pursuing 'reasons of state', backed, ultimately, by coercive means. But this power logic is singularly inappropriate to resolve the many complex issues, from economic regulation to resource depletion and environmental degradation, which engender an intermeshing of national fortunes. Recognizing the complex structures of an interconnected world, political cosmopolitanism views certain issues as appropriate for delimited (spatially demarcated) political spheres (the city, state or region), while it sees others – such as climate change, global infectious diseases and financial market regulation – as needing new, more extensive institutions to address them. Deliberative and decision-making centres beyond national territories are appropriately situated (see principle 6 – pp. 72–3) when the cosmopolitan principles of equal worth, impartial treatment and so on can only be properly redeemed in a transnational context; when those significantly affected by a public matter constitute a cross-border or transnational grouping; and when 'lower' levels of decision-making cannot manage and discharge satisfactorily transnational or international policy questions. Only a cosmopolitan political outlook can ultimately accommodate itself to the political challenges of a more global era, marked by policy spill-overs, overlapping communities of fate and growing global inequalities.

The institutional requirements of political cosmopolitanism include:

- multilayered governance, diffused authority;
- a network of democratic fora from the local to global;
- enhanced political regionalization; and
- the establishment of effective, accountable, international security forces for last resort use of coercive power in defence of cosmopolitan law.

Economic cosmopolitanism

Economic cosmopolitanism enters an important proviso about the prospects of political cosmopolitanism, for unless the disjuncture between economic and political power is addressed, resources will remain too skewed to ensure that formally proclaimed liberties and rights can be enjoyed in practice by many; in short, 'nautonomy' will prevail – the asymmetrical production and distribution of life chances which erode the possibilities of equal participative opportunities and place artificial limits on the creation of a common structure of political action (Held, 1995: ch. 8). At issue is what was earlier referred to as the tangential impact of the liberal international order on the regulation of economic power and market mechanisms, and on the flourishing socio-economic inequalities which exist side by side with the spread of liberal democracy (see chapter 1). A bridge has to be built between human rights law and international economic law, between a formal commitment to the impartial treatment of all and a geopolitics driven too often by special economic interests and between cosmopolitan principles and cosmopolitan practices.

This understanding provides a rationale for a politics of intervention in economic life – not to control and regulate markets per se, but to provide the basis for self-determination and active agency. Economic cosmopolitanism connotes the enhancement of people's economic capacities to pursue their own projects – individual and collective – within the constraints of community and interdependence between communities, i.e. within the constraints created by taking each human being's interest in declared liberties equally seriously. It thus specifies good reasons for being committed to reforming and regulating all those forms of economic power which compromise the possibility of equal worth and active agency. It aims to establish fair conditions for economic competition and cooperation as the background context of the particular choices of human agents (see Pogge, 1994a).

It follows from this that political intervention in the economy is warranted when it is driven by the objective of ensuring that the basic requirements of individual autonomy are met within and outside of economic organizations. Moreover, it is warranted when it is driven by the need to overcome those consequences of economic interaction, whether intended or unintended, which generate damaging externalities, such as health-threatening environmental pollution. The roots of such intervention lie in the indeterminacy of the market system itself (see Sen, 1985: 19). Market economies can only function in a manner commensurate with self-determination and equal freedom if this indeterminacy is addressed systematically and if the conditions of the possibility of self-governance are met.

In addition, a transfer system has to be established within and across communities to alleviate the most pressing cases of avoidable economic suffering and harm. If such measures involved the creation of new forms of regional and global taxation – for instance, a consumption tax on energy use, or a tax on carbon emissions, or a global tax on the extraction of resources within national territories, or a tax on the GNP of countries above a certain level of development, or a transaction tax on the volume of financial turnover in foreign exchange markets – independent (non-national) funds could be established to meet the most extreme cases of need. Sustained social investments in the conditions of autonomy (sanitation, health, housing, education and so on) could then follow. Moreover, the raising of such funds could also be the basis for a critical step in the realization of political cosmopolitanism: the creation of an independent flow of economic resources to fund regional and global governance, a vital move in reducing the latter's dependence on leading politicians and the most powerful countries.

Cosmopolitan Law and Institutional Requirements

The institutional requirements of economic cosmopolitanism include:

- reframing market mechanisms and leading sites of economic power;
- expanding the representative base of the international financial institutions to include developing countries and emerging markets;
- global taxation mechanisms; and
- the transfer of resources to the most economically vulnerable in order to protect and enhance their agency.

Cultural cosmopolitanism

Cultural cosmopolitanism is the capacity to mediate between national traditions, communities of fate and alternative styles of life. It encompasses the possibility of dialogue with the traditions and discourses of others with the aim of expanding the horizons of one's own framework of meaning and prejudice. Political agents who can 'reason from the point of view of others' are likely to be better equipped to resolve, and resolve fairly, the new and challenging transboundary issues and processes that create overlapping communities of fate. The development of this kind of cultural cosmopolitanism depends on the recognition by a growing number of people of the increasing interconnectedness of political communities in diverse domains, including the economic, cultural and environmental, and the development of an understanding of overlapping 'collective fortunes' which require collective solutions – locally, nationally, regionally and globally.

The formation of cultural cosmopolitanism has been given an enormous impetus by the sheer scale, intensity, speed and volume of global cultural communication, which today has reached unsurpassed levels (see Held et al., 1999: ch. 7). Global communication systems are transforming relations between physical locales and social circumstances, altering the 'situational geography' of political and social life (Meyrowitz, 1985). In these circumstances, the traditional link between 'physical setting' and 'social situation' is broken. Geographical boundaries can be overcome, as individual and groups experience events and developments far afield. Moreover, new understandings, commonalties and frames of meaning can be elaborated without direct contact between people. As such, they can serve to detach – or disembed – identities from particular times, places and traditions, and can have a 'pluralizing impact' on identity formation, producing a variety of options which are 'less fixed or unified' (Hall, 1992). While everyone has a local life, the ways people make sense of the world are now increasingly interpenetrated by developments and processes from diverse settings. Hybrid cultures and transnational media organizations have made significant inroads into national cultures and national identities (see Held and Moore, 2008: Parts I and II). The cultural context of national traditions is transformed as a result.

Cultural cosmopolitanism emphasizes 'the fluidity of individual identity, people's remarkable capacity to forge new identities using materials from diverse cultural sources, and to flourish while so doing' (Scheffler, 1999: 257). It celebrates, as Rushdie put it, 'hybridity, impurity, intermingling, the transformation that comes of new and unexpected combinations of human beings, cultures, ideas, politics, movies, songs' (quoted in Waldron, 1992: 751). But it is the ability to stand outside a singular cultural location (the location of birth, land, upbringing, conversion), and to mediate traditions, that lies at its core. However, there are no guarantees about the extent to which such an outlook will prevail; for it has to survive and jostle for recognition alongside often deeply held national, ethnic and religious traditions (see Held and McGrew, 2000: 13–18, Part III). It is a cultural and cognitive orientation, not an inevitability of history.

The institutional requirements of cultural cosmopolitanism include:

- recognition of increasing interconnectedness of political communities in diverse domains, including the social, economic and environmental;
- development of an understanding of overlapping 'collective fortunes' which require collective solutions – locally, nationally, regionally and globally; and
- the celebration of difference, diversity and hybridity, while learning how to 'reason from the point of view of others' and mediate traditions.

In sum

The core of the cosmopolitan political project involves reconceiving legitimate political authority in a manner which disconnects it from its traditional anchor in fixed territories and, instead, articulates it as an attribute of basic cosmopolitan democratic arrangements or basic cosmopolitan law which can, in principle, be entrenched and drawn upon in diverse associations. Significantly, this process of disconnection has already begun, as political authority and forms of governance are diffused 'below', 'above' and 'alongside' the nation-state (see Held, 2004).

Recent history embraces many different forms of globalization. There is the rise of neoliberal deregulation, so much emphasized from the mid-1970s. But there is also the growth of major global and regional institutions, from the UN to the EU. The latter are remarkable political innovations in the context of state history. The UN remains a creature of the interstate system; however, it has, despite all its limitations, developed an innovative system of global governance which delivers significant international public goods – from air-traffic control and the management of telecommunications to the control of contagious diseases, humanitarian relief for refugees and some protection of the environmental commons. The EU, in remarkably little time, has taken Europe from the disarray of the post-Second World War era to a world in which sovereignty is pooled across a growing number of areas of common concern. Again, despite its many limitations, the EU represents a highly innovative form of governance which creates a framework of collaboration for addressing transborder issues.

In addition, it is important to reflect upon the growing scope and content of international law (see chapters 1 and 4). Twentieth-century forms of international law have taken the first steps towards a framework of universal law, law which circumscribes and delimits the political power of individual states. In principle, states are no longer able to treat their citizens as they think fit. Moreover, the twentieth century saw the beginnings of significant efforts to reframe markets – to use legislation to alter the background conditions and operations of firms in the marketplace. While efforts in this direction failed with respect to the NAFTA agreement, the 'Social Chapter' of the Maastricht Agreement, for instance, embodies principles and rules which are compatible with the idea of restructuring aspects of markets. While the provisions of this agreement fall far short of what is ultimately necessary if judged by the standards of a cosmopolitan conception of law and regulation, they set down new forms of regulation which can be built upon.

Furthermore, there are, of course, new regional and global transnational actors contesting the terms of globalization – not just corporations but new social movements as well. These are the 'new' voices of an emergent 'transnational civil society', heard, for instance, at the Rio Conference on the Environment, the Cairo Conference on Population Control, the Beijing Conference on Women and at the Copenhagen Conference on Climate Change. In short, there are forces at work seeking to create new forms of public life and new ways of debating regional and global issues.

These changes are all in early stages of development, and there are no guarantees that the balance of political interests will allow them to develop. Nor are there any guarantees that those who push for change will accept the necessity of deliberation with all key stakeholders, or recognize the time it takes to create and develop institutions. But the changes under way point in the direction of establishing new modes of holding transnational power systems to account – that is, they help open up the possibility of a cosmopolitan order. Together, they form an anchor on which a more accountable form of globalization can be established.

Political openings

Surprisingly, perhaps, it is an opportune moment to rethink the nature and form of contemporary global governance and the dominant policies of the last decade or so. The policy packages that have largely set the global agenda – in economics and security – are failing. The Washington Consensus and Washington security doctrines – or market fundamentalism and unilateralism – have dug their own graves. The most successful developing countries in the world (China, India, Vietnam, Uganda, among them) are successful because they have not followed the Washington Consensus agenda, and the conflicts that have most successfully been diffused (the Balkans, Sierra Leone, Liberia, among others) are ones that have benefited from concentrated multilateral support and a human security agenda. Here are clues as to how to proceed in the future. We need to follow these clues and learn from the mistakes of the past if the rule of law, accountability and the effectiveness of the multilateral order are to be advanced.

115

In addition, the political tectonic plates appear to be shifting. With the faltering of unilateralism in US foreign policy, uncertainty over the role of the EU in global affairs, the crisis of global trade talks, the growing confidence of leading emerging countries in world economic fora (China, India, Brazil), and the unsettled relations between elements of Islam and the West, business as usual seems unlikely at the global level in the decades ahead. It is highly improbable that the multilateral order can survive for very much longer in its current form. A new political space is being opened up.

4

Violence, Law and Justice in a Global Age

On Sunday, 23 September 2001, the novelist, Barbara Kingsolver (2001) wrote in the *Los Angeles Times*:

> It's the worst thing that's happened, but only this week. Two years ago, an earthquake in Turkey killed 17,000 people in a day, babies and mothers and business-men . . . . The November before that, a hurricane hit Honduras and Nicaragua and killed even more . . . . Which end of the world shall we talk about? Sixty years ago, Japanese airplanes bombed Navy boys who were sleeping on ships in gentle Pacific waters. Three and a half years later, American planes bombed a plaza in Japan where men and women were going to work, where schoolchildren were playing, and more humans died at once than anyone thought possible. Seventy thousand in a minute. Imagine . . .
>
> There are no worst days, it seems. Ten years ago, early on a January morning, bombs rained down from the

sky and caused great buildings in the city of Baghdad to fall down – hotels, hospitals, palaces, buildings with mothers and soldiers inside – and here in the place I want to love best, I had to watch people cheering about it. In Baghdad, survivors shook their fists at the sky and said the word 'evil'. When many lives are lost all at once, people gather together and say words like 'heinous' and 'honor' and 'revenge' . . . . They raise up their compatriots' lives to a sacred place – we do this, all of us who are human – thinking our own citizens to be more worthy of grief and less willingly risked than lives on other soil.

This is an unsettling and challenging passage. When I first read it, I felt angered and unsympathetic to its call to think systematically about 9/11 in the context of other disasters, acts of aggression and wars. A few days later I found it helpful to connect its sentiments to my own cosmopolitan approach.

Immanual Kant wrote more than 200 years ago that we are 'unavoidably side by side'. A violent challenge to law and justice in one place has consequences for many other places and can be experienced everywhere (1970: 107–8). While he dwelt on these matters and their implications at length, he could not have known how profound and immediate his concerns would become.

Since Kant, our mutual interconnectedness and vulnerability have grown rapidly. We no longer live, if we ever did, in a world of discrete national communities. Instead, we live in a world of overlapping communities of fate, where the trajectories of countries are heavily enmeshed with each other. In our world, it is not only the violent exception that links people together across borders; the very nature of everyday problems and processes joins people in multiple ways. From the movement of ideas and cultural artefacts to the fundamental issues raised by genetic engineering, from the conditions of financial stability to environmental degradation, the fate and fortunes of each of us are thoroughly intertwined.

The story of our increasingly global order – 'globalization' – is not a singular one. Globalization is not a one-dimensional phenomenon. For example, there has been an expansion of global markets which has altered the political terrain, increasing exit options for capital of all kinds, putting pressure on polities everywhere (see Held et al., 1999: chs. 3–5; and Held and McGrew, 2000: ch. 25). But the story of globalization is not just economic: it is also one of growing aspirations for international law and justice. From changes to the laws of war to the entrenchment of human rights, from the emergence of international environmental regimes to the foundation of the International Criminal Court, there is also another narrative being told – a narrative which seeks to reframe human activity and entrench it in law, rights and responsibilities. In the first section of this chapter, I would like to reflect on this second narrative and highlight some of its strengths and limitations. Once this background is sketched, elements of the legal and political context of 9/11 can be better grasped.

Reframing human activity: International law, rights and responsibilities

The process of the gradual delimitation of political power, and the increasing significance of international law and justice, can be illustrated by reflecting on a strand in international legal thinking which has overturned the exclusive position of the state in international law, and buttressed the role of the individual in relation to, and with responsibility for, systematic violence against others.

In the first instance, by recognizing the legal status of conscientious objection, many states – particularly Western states (I shall return to the significance of this later) – have acknowledged there are clear occasions when an individual has a moral obligation beyond that of his or her obligation as a citizen of a state (see Vincent, 1992: 269–92). The refusal to serve in national armies triggers a claim to a 'higher moral court' of rights and duties. Such claims are exemplified as well in the changing legal position of those who are willing to go to war. The recognition in international law of the offences of war crimes, genocide and crimes against humanity make clear that acquiescence to the commands of national leaders will not be considered sufficient grounds for absolving individual guilt in these cases. A turning point in this regard was the judgment of the international tribunal at Nuremberg (and the parallel tribunal in Tokyo). The tribunal laid down, for the first time in history, that when *international rules* that protect basic humanitarian values are in conflict with *state laws*, every individual must transgress the state laws (except where there is no room for 'moral choice', i.e. when a gun is being held to someone's head) (Cassese, 1988: 132). Modern international law has generally endorsed the position taken by the Tribunal, and has affirmed its rejection of the defence of obedience to superior orders in matters of responsibility for crimes against peace and humanity. As one commentator has noted: 'since the Nuremberg Trials, it has been acknowledged that war criminals cannot relieve themselves of criminal responsibility by citing official position or superior orders. Even obedience to explicit national legislation provides no protection against international law' (Dinstein, 1993: 968).

A most notable recent extension of the application of the Nuremberg principles has been the establishment of the war crimes tribunals for the former Yugoslavia (established by the UN Security Council in 1993) and for Rwanda (set up in 1994) (cf. Chinkin, 1998; *Economist*, 1998). The Yugoslav tribunal issued indictments against people from all three ethnic groups in Bosnia, and investigated crimes in Kosovo, although it encountered serious difficulty in obtaining custody of many of the key accused. Although neither the tribunal for Rwanda nor the Yugoslav tribunal had the ability to detain and try more than a small fraction of those engaged in atrocities, both took important steps towards implementing the law governing war crimes and, thereby, helped reduce the credibility gap between the promises of such law, on the one hand, and the weakness of its application, on the other.

Most recently, the proposals put forward for the establishment of a permanent ICC were designed to further close this gap in the longer term (cf. Crawford, 1995; Dugard, 1997; Weller, 1997). Several major hurdles remain to its successful operation, including the continuing opposition from the United States (which fears its soldiers will be the target of politically motivated prosecutions) and dependency upon individual state consent for its effectiveness (Chinkin, 1998: 118–19). However, the Court is formally established and marks another significant step away from the classic regime of state sovereignty – sovereignty, that is, as effective power – and towards the firm entrenchment of the liberal regime of international sovereignty – sovereignty shaped and delimited by new broader frameworks of governance and law.

The ground now being staked out in international legal agreements suggests something of particular importance: that the containment of armed aggression and abuses of power can only be achieved through both the control of warfare and the prevention of the abuse of human rights. For it is only too apparent that many forms of violence perpetrated against individuals, and many forms of abuse of power, do not take place during declared acts of war. In fact, it can be argued that the distinctions between war and peace, and between aggression and repression, are eroded by changing patterns of violence (Kaldor, 1998a, 1998b). The kinds of violence witnessed in Bosnia and Kosovo highlight the role of paramilitaries and organized crime, and the use of parts of national armies which may no longer be under the direct control of a state. What these kinds of violence signal is that there is a very fine line between explicit formal crimes committed during acts of national war, and major attacks on the welfare and physical integrity of citizens in situations that may not involve a declaration of war by states. While many of the new forms of warfare do not fall directly under the classic rules of war, they are massive violations of international human rights. Accordingly, the rules of war and human rights law can be seen as two complementary forms of international rules which aim to circumscribe the proper form, scope and use of coercive power (see Kaldor, 1998a: chs. 6 and 7). For all the limitations of its enforcement, these are significant changes which, when taken together, amount to the rejection of the doctrine of legitimate power as effective control, and its replacement by international rules which entrench basic humanitarian values as the criteria for legitimate government.

How do the terrorist attacks on the World Trade Center and the Pentagon fit into this pattern of legal change? A wide variety of legal instruments, dating back to 1963 (the Convention on Offences and Certain Other Acts Committed on Board Aircraft), enable the international community to take action against terrorism, and bring those responsible to justice. Any person responsible for aiding and abetting the 9/11 attacks could face prosecution in virtually any country that obtains custody of them. In particular, the widely ratified Hague Convention for the Suppression of Unlawful Seizure of Aircraft (1970) makes the hijacking of aircraft an international criminal offence. The offence is regarded as extraditable under any extradition treaty in force between contracting states, and applies to accomplices as well as to the hijackers. In addition, the use of hijacked aircraft as lethal weapons can be interpreted as a crime against humanity under international law (although there is some legal argument about this). Frederic Kirgis has noted that the statute of the ICC 'defines a crime against humanity as any of several listed acts "when committed as part of a widespread or systematic attack directed against any civilian population . . ."'. The acts include murder and 'other inhumane acts of a similar character intentionally causing great suffering, or serious injury to body or to mental or physical health' (Kirgis, 2001).

Changes in the law of war, human rights law and in other legal domains have placed individuals, governments and non-governmental organizations under new systems of legal regulation – regulation which, in principle, recasts the legal significance of state boundaries. The regime of liberal international sovereignty entrenches powers and constraints, and rights and duties in international law which – albeit ultimately formulated by states – go beyond the traditional conception of the proper scope and boundaries of states, and can come into conflict, and sometimes contradiction, with national laws. Within this framework, states may forfeit claims to sovereignty, and individuals their right to sovereign protection, if they violate the standards and values embedded in the liberal international order; and such violations no longer become a matter of morality alone. Rather, they become a breach of a legal code, a breach that may call forth the means to challenge, prosecute and rectify it (see Habermas, 1999). To this end, a bridge is created between morality and law where, at best, only stepping-stones existed before in the era of classic sovereignty. These are transformative changes which alter the form and content of politics, nationally, regionally and globally. They signify the enlarging normative reach, extending scope and growing institutionalization of international legal rules and practices – the beginnings of a 'universal constitutional order' in which the state is no longer the only layer of legal competence to which people have transferred public powers (Crawford and Marks, 1998: 72; Weller, 1997: 45).

In short, boundaries between states are of decreasing legal and moral significance. States are no longer regarded as discrete political worlds. International standards breach boundaries in numerous ways. Within Europe, new institutions and layers of law and governance have reframed political authority; any assumption that sovereignty is an indivisible, exclusive and perpetual form of public power – entrenched within an individual state – is now erroneous (Held, 1995: 107–13). Within the wider international order, new rules and regimes have transformed and delimited the order of states, embedding national polities in new forms and layers of accountability and governance (from particular regimes such as the Nuclear Non-Proliferation Treaty to wider frameworks of regulation laid down by the UN Charter and a host of specialized agencies) (see Held et al., 1999: chs. 1 and 2). Accordingly, the boundaries between states, nations and societies can no longer claim the deep legal and moral significance they once had; they can be judged, along with the communities they embody, by general, if not universal, standards. That is to say, they can be scrutinized and appraised in relation to standards which, in principle, apply to each person, each individual, who is held to be equally worthy of concern and respect. Concomitantly, shared membership in a political community, or spatial proximity, is not regarded as a sufficient source of moral privilege (Beitz, 1998, cf. 1979; Pogge, 1989, 1994a, 1994b; Barry, 1999; also see below).

The political and legal transformations of the past 50 years or so have gone some way towards circumscribing and delimiting political power on a regional and global basis. Several major difficulties remain, nonetheless, at the core of the liberal international regime of sovereignty which create tensions, if not faultlines, at its centre (see Held, 2002b). I shall dwell on just one aspect of these here.

Serious deficiencies can, of course, be documented in the implementation and enforcement of democratic and human rights, and of international law more generally. Despite the development and consolidation of the regime of liberal international sovereignty, massive inequalities of power and economic resources continue to grow. There is an accelerating gap between rich and poor states as well as between peoples in the global economy (UNDP, 1999; Held and Kaya, 2007). The human rights agenda often has a hollow ring. The development of regional trade and investment blocs, particularly the Triad (NAFTA, the EU and Japan), has concentrated economic transactions within and between these areas (Thompson, 2000). The Triad accounts for two-thirds to three-quarters of world economic activity, with shifting patterns of resources across each region. However, one further element of inequality is particularly apparent: a significant proportion of the world's population remains marginal to these networks (Pogge, 1999: 27; also see UNDP, 1997, 1999; Held and McGrew, 2000).

Does this growing gulf in the life circumstances and life chances of the world's population highlight intrinsic limits to the liberal international order or should this disparity be traced to other phenomena – the particularities of nation-states or of regions with their own distinctive cultural, religious and political problems? The latter phenomena are contributors to the disparity between the universal claims of the human rights regime and its often tragically limited impact (see Pogge, 1999; Leftwich, 2000). But one of the key causes of the gulf lies, in my judgement, elsewhere – in the tangential impact of the liberal international order on the regulation of economic power and market mechanisms. The focus of the liberal international order is on the curtailment of the abuse of political power, not economic power. It has few, if any, systematic means to address sources of power other than the political (see chapter 1; also see Held, 1995: Part III). Its conceptual resources and leading ideas do not suggest or push towards the pursuit of self-determination and autonomy in the economic domain; they do not seek the entrenchment of democratic rights and obligations outside the sphere of the political. Hence, it is hardly a surprise that liberal democracy and flourishing economic inequalities exist side by side.

Thus, the complex and differentiated narratives of globalization point in stark and often contradictory directions. On the one side, there is the dominant tendency of economic globalization over the past three decades towards a pattern set by the deregulatory, neo-liberal model; an increase in the exit options of corporate and finance capital relative to labour and the state; an increase in the volatility of market responses, which has exacerbated a growing sense of political uncertainty and risk; and the marked polarization of global relative economic inequalities (as well as serious doubt as to whether there has been a 'trickle down' effect to the world's poorest at all). (See chapter 6 for an exploration of the impact of the global financial crisis on these trends.) On the other side, there is the significant entrenchment of cosmopolitan values concerning the equal dignity and worth of all human beings, the reconnection of international law and morality, the establishment of regional and global systems of governance, and growing recognition that the public good – whether conceived as financial stability, environmental protection, or global egalitarianism – requires coordinated multilateral action if it is to be achieved in the long term.

9/11, war and justice

If 9/11 was not a defining moment in human history, it certainly was for today's generations. The terrorist violence was an atrocity of extraordinary proportions. It was a crime against America and against humanity; a massive breach of many of the core codes of international law; and an attack on the fundamental principles of freedom, democracy, justice and humanity itself, i.e. those principles which affirm the sanctity of life, the importance of self-determination and of equal rights and liberty.

These principles are not just Western principles. Elements of them had their origins in the early modern period in the West, but their validity extends much further than this. For these principles are the basis of a fair, humane and decent society, of whatever religion or cultural tradition. To paraphrase the legal theorist Bruce Ackerman, there is no nation without a woman who yearns for equal rights, no society without a man who denies the need for deference and no developing country without a person who does not wish for the minimum means of subsistence so that they may go about their everyday lives (1994; also see Sen, 1992, 1999). The principles of freedom, democracy and justice are the basis for articulating and entrenching the equal liberty of all human beings, wherever they were born or brought up. They are the basis of underwriting the liberty of others, not of obliterating it. Their concern is with the irreducible moral status of each and every person – the acknowledgement of which links directly to the possibility of self-determination and the capacity to make independent choices (see Nussbaum, 1997).

The intensity of the range of responses to the atrocities of 9/11 is fully understandable. There cannot be many people in the world who did not experience shock, revulsion, anger and a desire for vengeance, as the Kingsolver passage acknowledges. This emotional range is perfectly natural within the context of the immediate events. But it cannot be the basis for a more considered and wise response.

The founding principles of our society dictate that we do not overgeneralize our response from one moment and one set of events; that we do not jump to conclusions based on concerns that emerge in one particular country at one moment; and that we do not rewrite and rework international law and governance arrangements from one place – in other words, that we do not think and act hastily, taking the law into our own hands. Clearly, the fight against terror must be put on a new footing. Terrorists must be brought to heel and those who protect and nurture them must be brought to account. Zero tolerance is fully justified in these circumstances. Terrorism does negate our most elementary and cherished principles and values. But any defensible, justifiable and sustainable response to 9/11 must be consistent with our founding principles and the aspirations of international society for security, law and the impartial administration of justice – aspirations painfully articulated after the Holocaust and the Second World War – and embedded, albeit imperfectly, in regional and global law and the institutions of global governance. If the means deployed to fight terrorism contradict these principles and achievements, then the emotion of the moment might be satisfied, but our mutual vulnerability will be deepened.

War and bombing were and are one option. President Bush described the attacks of 9/11, and the US-led coalition response, as a 'new kind of war'; and, indeed, the attacks of 9/11 can be viewed as a more dramatic version of patterns of violence witnessed during the previous decade, in the wars in the Balkans, the Middle East and Africa. These wars were quite different from, for example, the Second World War. They are wars which are difficult to end and difficult to contain, where, typically, there have been no clear victories and many defeats for those who champion the sanctity of human life, human rights and human welfare. There is much that can be learned from these experiences that is relevant to the post-9/11 world.

The contours of these 'new wars' are distinctive in many respects because the range of social and political groups involved no longer fit the pattern of a classical interstate war; the type of violence deployed by the terrorist aggressors is no longer carried out by the agents of a state (although states, or parts of states, may have a supporting role); violence is dispersed, fragmented and directed against citizens; and political aims are combined with the deliberate commission of atrocities which are a massive violation of human rights (see Kaldor, 1998a). Such a war is not typically triggered by a state interest, but by religious identity, zeal and fanaticism. The aim is not to acquire or control territory, as was the case in 'old wars', but to gain political power through generating fear and hatred. War itself becomes a form of political mobilization in which the pursuit of violence promotes extremist causes.

In Western security policy, there is a dangerous gulf between the dominant thinking about security based on 'old wars' – like the Second World War and the Cold War – and the reality in the field. The so-called 'Revolution in Military Affairs', the development of 'smart' weaponry to fight wars at long distance, and the proposals for the National Missile Defence programme were all predicated on outdated assumptions about the nature of war – the idea that it is possible to protect territory from attacks by outsiders. The language of President Bush, with its emphasis on the defence of America and of dividing the world between those 'who are with us or against us', tended to reproduce the illusion, drawn from the experience of the Second World War, that this war is simply between 'good' states – led by the United States – and 'bad' states. Such an approach is regrettable and, potentially, very dangerous.

Today, a clear-cut military victory is very difficult to achieve because the advantages of supposed superior technology have been eroded in many contexts. As the Russians discovered in Afghanistan, the Americans in Vietnam and the Israelis in the current period, conquering people and territory by military means has become an increasingly problematic form of warfare. These military campaigns have all been lost or suffered serious and continuous setbacks as a result of the stubborn refusal of movements for independence or autonomy to be suppressed; the refusal to meet the deployment of the conventional means of interstate warfare with similar forces which play by the same set of rules; and by the constantly shifting use of irregular or guerrilla forces which sporadically but steadily inflict major casualties on states (whose domestic populations become increasingly anxious and weary). And the costs of using high-tech weapon systems, carpet bombing and other very destructive means of interstate warfare are very high, to say the least.

The risk of concentrating military action against states like Afghanistan is that of ratcheting-up fear and hatred, of actually creating a 'new war' between the

132

West and Islam, a war which is not only between states but within every community in the West as well as in the Middle East and elsewhere. No doubt, the terrorists always hoped for air strikes, which would rally more supporters to their cause. No doubt, they hoped for a global division between those states that side with America and those that do not. The fanatical Islamic networks that were responsible for the attacks have groups and cells in many places including Britain and the United States. The effect of the US-led war might very well be, now and in the future, to expand the networks of fanatics, who may gain access to even more horrendous weapons, to increase racist and xenophobic feelings of all kinds, and to increase repressive powers everywhere, justified in the name of fighting terrorism.

An alternative approach existed – and might even be salvageable in some respects, although the longer the bombing goes on, and the longer the forces of the US and its allies have to remain in place to secure foreign lands, the less optimistic one can be. An alternative approach is one which counters the strategy of 'fear and hate'. What is needed, as Mary Kaldor and I have argued (2001), is a movement for global, not American, justice and legitimacy, aimed at establishing and extending the rule of law in the place of war, and at fostering understanding between communities in the place of terror. Such a movement must press upon governments and international institutions the importance of three things.

First, there must be a commitment to the rule of law not the prosecution of war. Civilians of all faiths and nationalities need protection, wherever they live, and terrorists must be captured and brought before an international criminal court, which could be either permanent or modelled on the Nuremberg or Yugoslav war crimes tribunals. The terrorists must be treated as criminals, and not glamorized as military adversaries. This does not preclude internationally sanctioned military action under the auspices of the United Nations both to arrest suspects and to dismantle terrorist networks – not at all. But such action should always be understood as a robust form of policing, above all as a way of protecting civilians and bringing criminals to trial. Moreover, this type of action must scrupulously preserve the laws both of war and of human rights. Imran Khan (2001) put a similar point forcefully:

> The only way to deal with global terrorism is through justice. We need international institutions such as a fully empowered and credible world criminal court to define terrorism and dispense justice with impartiality . . . . The world is heading towards disaster if the sole superpower behaves as judge, jury and executioner when dealing with global terrorism.

The intense pattern of extra-judicial, outlaw killings (organized, targeted murders) on both sides of the Israeli-Palestine conflict compounds anxieties about the breakdown of the rule of law, nationally and internationally. This way only leads one way; that is, towards Hobbes's state of nature: the 'war of every one against every one' – life as 'solitary, poor, nasty, brutish, and short'.

134

Second, a massive effort has to be undertaken to create a new form of global political legitimacy, one which must confront the reasons why the West is so often seen as self-interested, partial and insensitive. This must involve condemnation of all human rights violations wherever they occur, renewed peace efforts in the Middle East, talks between Israel and Palestine, and rethinking policy towards Iraq, Iran, Afghanistan and elsewhere. This cannot be equated with an occasional or one-off effort to create a new momentum for peace and the protection of human rights. It has to be part of a continuous emphasis in foreign policy, year-in, year-out. Many parts of the world will need convincing that the West's interest in security and human rights for all regions and peoples is not just a product of short-term geopolitical or geoeconomic interests.

And, finally, there must be a head-on acknowledgement that the ethical and justice issues posed by the global polarization of wealth, income and power, and with them the huge asymmetries of life chances, cannot be left to markets to resolve. Those who are poorest and most vulnerable, locked into geopolitical situations which have neglected their economic and political claims for generations, will always provide fertile ground for terrorist recruiters. The project of economic globalization has to be connected to manifest principles of social justice; the latter need to reframe global market activity.

To date, the US-led coalition, in pursuing, first and foremost, a military response to 9/11, has chosen *not* to prioritize the development of international law and UN institutional arrangements (point 1); and *not* to emphasize the urgency of building institutional bridges between the priorities of social justice and processes of economic globalization (point 3), although one or two coalition politicians have made speeches acknowledging the importance of this question. Peace in the Middle East has been singled out as a priority by some coalition leaders, but there is little sign as yet that this is part of a broader rethinking of foreign policy in the Middle East, and of the role of the West in international affairs more generally (point 2). These are political choices and, like all such choices, they carry a heavy burden of possibility and lost opportunity.

Of course, terrorist crimes of the kind we have just witnessed on 9/11 may often be the work of the simply deranged and the fanatical, and so there can be no guarantee that a more just world will be a more peaceful one in all respects. But, if we turn our back on this challenge, there is no hope of ameliorating the social basis of disadvantage often experienced in the poorest and most dislocated countries. Gross injustices, linked to a sense of hopelessness born of generations of neglect, feed anger and hostility. Popular support against terrorism depends upon convincing people that there is a legal and pacific way of addressing their grievances. Without this sense of confidence in public institutions and processes, the defeat of terrorism becomes a hugely difficult task, if it can be achieved at all.

Kant was right; the violent abrogation of law and justice in one place ricochets across the world. We cannot accept the burden of putting justice right in one dimension of life – security – without at the same time seeking to put it right everywhere. A socioeconomic order in which whole regions and peoples suffer serious harm and disadvantage independently of their will or consent will not command widespread support and legitimacy. If the political, social and economic dimensions of justice are separated in the long term – as is the tendency in the global order today – the prospects of a peaceful and civil society will be bleak indeed.

Islam, the Kantian heritage and double standards

The responsibility for the pursuit of justice does not just fall on the West. It is not simply the USA and Europe that must look critically at themselves in the aftermath of 9/11; there is a chronic need for self-examination in parts of Islamic world as well. The Muslim writer, Ziauddin Sardar, wrote (2001):

> To Muslims everywhere I issue this fatwa: any Muslim involved in the planning, financing, training, recruiting, support or harbouring of those who commit acts of indiscriminate violence against persons . . . is guilty of terror and no part of the *ummah*. It is the duty of every Muslim to spare no effort in hunting down, apprehending and bringing such criminals to justice. If you see something reprehensible, said the Prophet Muhammad, then change it with your hand; if you are not capable of that then use your tongue (speak out against it); and if you are not capable of that then detest it in your heart. The silent Muslim majority must now become vocal.

Iman Hamza, a noted Islamic teacher, has spoken of the 'deep denial' many Muslims seem to be in. He is concerned that 'Islam has been hijacked by a discourse of anger and a rhetoric of rage' (quoted in Young, 2001). The attacks of 9/11 appear to have been perpetrated in the name of Islam, albeit a particular version of Islam. It is this version of Islam which must be repudiated by the wider Islamic community, which needs to reaffirm the compatibility of Islam with the universal, cosmopolitan principles that put life, and the free development of all human beings, at their centre.

Hugo Young (2001) made the same point rather bluntly in the *Guardian*:

> The September terrorists who left messages and testaments described their actions as being in the name of Allah. They made this their explicit appeal and defence. Bin Laden himself . . . clothes their murders and their suicides in religious glory. A version of Islam – not typical, a minority fragment, but undeniably Islamic – endorses the foaming hatred for America that uniquely emanates, with supplementary texts, from a variety of mullahs.

Accordingly, it is not just enough for the West to look critically at itself in the shadow of 9/11. Muslim countries need to confront their own ideological extremists and reject without qualification any doctrine or action which encourages or condones the slaughter of innocent human beings. In addition, they need to reflect on their own failings to ensure minimum standards of living, and a decent, free and democratic life for all their citizens. As Bhikhu Parekh, former Chair of the Commission on the Future of Multiethnic Britain, put it, Muslims must 'stop blaming the West for all their ills' and must grapple with the temptation to locate all the main sources of their problems elsewhere (2001).

9/11 can be linked to a new, integrated political crisis developing in West Asia. The crisis has been well analysed by Fred Halliday (2001):

> [I]n several countries, there has been a weakening, if not collapse, of the state – in the 1970s and 1980s in Lebanon, more recently in Afghanistan and Yemen . . . . It is in these countries, where significant areas are free of government control, or where the government seeks to humour autonomous armed groups, like al-Qaeda, that a culture of violence and religious demagogy has thrived . . . . This is compounded by the way in which the historically distinct conflicts of Afghanistan, Iraq and Palestine have, in recent years, come to be more and more connected. Militants in each – secular nationalist (Saddam) as well as Islamist (Osama bin Laden) – see the cause of resistance to the West and its regional allies as one.

Hence, Osama bin Laden's first target was the government of Saudi Arabia, to which he later added the governments of Egypt and Jordan (and the Shi'ite Republic of Iran). Only later did he formally connect (via a declared fatwa in 1998) his war against these governments to the US, which he came to see as the key source of, and support for, the corruption of Islamic sovereignty in the Middle East (Armstrong, 2001).

The fundamental fissure in the Muslim world is between those who want to uphold universal standards, including the standards of democracy and human rights, and want to reform their societies, dislodging the deep connection between religion, culture and politics, and those who are threatened by this and wish to retain and/ or restore power to those who represent 'fundamentalist' ideals. The political, economic and cultural challenges posed by the globalization of (for want of a better shorthand) 'modernity' now face the counterforce of the globalization of radical Islam. This poses many big questions, but one in particular should be stressed; that is, how far and to what extent Islam – and not just the West – has the capacity to confront its own ideologies, double standards, and limitations. Clearly, the escape from dogma and unvindicated authority – the removal of constraints on the public use of reason – has a long way to go, East and West. The Kantian heritage should be accepted across Islam as well.

It's a mistake to think that this is simply an outsider's challenge to Islam. Islam, like the other great world religions, has incorporated a diverse body of thought and practice. In addition, it has contributed and accommodated itself to ideas of religious tolerance, secular political power and human rights. It is particularly in the contemporary period that radical Islamic movements have turned their back on these important historical developments and sought to deny Islam's contribution to both the Enlightenment and the formulation of universal ethical codes. There are many good reasons for doubting the often expressed Western belief that thoughts about justice and democracy have only flourished in the West (Sen, 1996: 118). Islam is not a unitary or explanatory category (see Halliday, 1996). Hence, the call for cosmopolitan values and principles speak to a vital strain within Islam which affirms the importance of rights and justice.

Concluding reflections

It is useful to return to the passage with which I started this chapter. It makes uncomfortable reading because it invites reflection on 9/11 in the context of other tragedies and conflict situations, and asks the reader to step outside of the maelstrom of 9/11 and consider those events in a wider historical and evaluative framework. Uncomfortable as this request is, we have to accept it if we are to find a satisfactory way of making sense of 9/11. To begin with, as the passage suggests, it is important to affirm the irreducible moral status of each and every person and, concomitantly, reject the view of moral particularists that belonging to a given community limits and determines the moral worth of individuals and the nature of their freedom. At the centre of this kind of thinking is the cosmopolitan view that human well-being is not defined by geographical and cultural locations, that national or ethnic or gendered boundaries should not determine the limits of rights or responsibilities for the satisfaction of basic human needs, and that all human beings require equal moral respect and concern. Cosmopolitanism builds on the basic principles of equal dignity, equal respect and the priority of vital need in its preoccupation with what is required for the autonomy and development of all human beings.

141

Cosmopolitan principles are not principles for some remote utopia; for they are at the centre of significant post-Second World War legal and political developments, from the 1948 UN Declaration of Human Rights to the 1998 adoption of the Statute of the ICC. The framers of these initiatives affirmed the importance of universal principles, human rights and the rule of law when there were strong temptations simply to put up the shutters and defend the position of some nations and countries only. The response to 9/11 could have followed in the footsteps of these achievements and strengthened our multilateral institutions and legal arrangements; instead, it took us further away from these fragile gains towards a world of further antagonisms and divisions – a distinctively uncivil society. At the time of writing the signs are not good, but we have not yet run out of choices – history is still with us and can be made.

5

Reframing Global Governance: Apocalypse Soon or Reform!

The paradox of our times

The paradox of our times can be stated simply: the collective issues we must grapple with are increasingly global and, yet, the means for addressing these are national and local, weak and incomplete. Three pressing global issues highlight the urgency of finding a way forward.

First, little, if any, progress has been made in creating a sustainable framework for the management of climate change. The concentration of carbon dioxide in the global atmosphere is now almost 35 per cent higher than in pre-industrial times (Byers, 2005: 4). The former British chief scientist, Sir David King, has warned that 'climate change is the most serious problem we are facing today, more serious than the threat of terrorism' (2004). Irrespective of whether one finds this characterization completely convincing, climate change has the capacity to wreak havoc on the world's diverse species,

143

biosystems and socioeconomic fabric. Violent storms will become more frequent, water access a battleground, rising sea levels will displace millions, the mass movement of desperate people will become more common, and deaths from serious diseases in the world's poorest countries will rise rapidly (largely because bacteria will spread more quickly, causing greater contamination of food and water). The overwhelming body of scientific opinion now maintains that climate change constitutes a serious threat not in the long term, but in the here and now. The failure of the international community to generate a sound framework for managing climate change is one of the most serious indications of the problems facing the multilateral order.

Second, little progress has been made towards achieving the Millennium Development Goals – the agreed human development targets of the international community, or, one could say, its moral consciousness. The Millennium Goals set down minimum standards to be achieved in relation to poverty reduction, health, educational provision, the combating of HIV/AIDS, malaria and other diseases, environmental sustainability and so on. Progress towards these targets has been lamentably slow, and there is evidence that they will be missed by a very wide margin. In fact, there is evidence that there may have been no point in setting these targets at all, so far are we from attaining them in many parts of the world. Underlying this human crisis is, of course, the material vulnerability of half of the world's population: 45 per cent of humankind live below the World Bank's $2/day poverty line, and 18 per cent (or some 1,089 million people) live below the $1/day poverty line. As

Thomas Pogge has appropriately put it, 'people so incredibly poor are extremely vulnerable to even minor shifts in natural and social conditions . . . . Each year, some 18 million of them die prematurely from poverty-related causes. This is one third of all human deaths – 50,000 every day, including 29,000 children under age five' (Pogge, 2007: 207; cf. UNDP, 2005). And, yet, the gap between rich and poor countries continues to rise, and there is evidence that the bottom 5 per cent of the world have become poorer still (Milanovic, 2002: 88; Pogge, 2007).

Third, the threat of nuclear catastrophe may seem to have diminished, but it is only in abeyance, as Martin Rees has argued (2003: 8, 27, 32–3, 43–4). Huge nuclear stockpiles remain; nuclear proliferation among states is continuing (for example, in Iran); nuclear weapons and materials, due to poor accounting records, may have been purloined (after the demise of the Soviet Union); new generations of tactical nuclear weapons are being built; and 'dirty bomb' technology (the coating of plutonium on the surface of a conventional bomb) makes nuclear terrorism a serious threat. Other dangers include terrorist attacks on nuclear power stations, many of which may be in countries with little protective capacity. Adding to these considerations the disquieting risks stemming from microbiology and genetics (engineered viruses), Rees concludes that 'the odds are no better that fifty-fifty that our present civilization on Earth will survive to the end of the present century without a serious setback' (2003: 8). Certainly, huge questions are raised about accountability, regulation and enforcement.

These global challenges are indicative of three core sets of problems we face – those concerned with:

- sharing our planet (climate change, biodiversity and ecosystem losses, water deficits);
- sustaining our humanity (poverty, conflict prevention, global infectious diseases); and
- developing our rulebook (nuclear proliferation, toxic waste disposal, intellectual property rights, genetic research rules, and trade, finance and tax rules). (See Rischard, 2002: 66.)

In our increasingly interconnected world, these global problems cannot be solved by any one nation-state acting alone. They call for collective and collaborative action – something that the nations of the world have not been good at, and which they need to be better at if these pressing issues are to be adequately tackled. Yet, the evidence is wanting that we are getting better at building appropriate governance capacity.

Why be concerned with global challenges?

Why do these global issues matter? The answer to this may seem intuitively obvious, but four separate reasons are worth stressing: solidarity, social justice, democracy and policy effectiveness. It is important to clarify each of these because they provide a map of the dimensions we need to keep in mind for thinking about the nature and adequacy of governance at the global level. By solidarity, I mean not just empathetic recognition of another's plight, but the willingness to stand side-by-side with others in the creation of solutions to pressing collective problems. Without solidarity between rich and poor, developed and developing countries, the Millennium Development Goals will not be met and, as Kofi Annan simply put it, 'millions of people will die, prematurely and unnecessarily' (2005: 139). These deaths are all the more poignant because solutions are within our grasp. Insofar as challenges like climate change and nuclear proliferation are concerned, we need to add to the definition of solidarity a focus on our own sustainability, never mind that of citizens of the future. Contemporary global challenges require recognition of, and active participation in, the forces that shape our overlapping communities of fate.

A second reason to focus on global challenges is social justice. Standards of social justice are, of course, controversial. To make the argument I want to make here as accessible as possible, I will, following Pogge, take social justice to mean the fulfilment of human rights in an institutional order to the extent that it is reasonably possible (Pogge, 2007; also see chapter 2). Of course, most argue that social justice requires more, and so it can be claimed with some confidence that an institutional order that fails to meet these standards cannot be just. Accordingly, it can be reasoned that, insofar as our existing socioeconomic arrangements fail to meet the Millennium Goals, and the broader challenges of climate change and the risks of nuclear proliferation, they are unjust, or, simply, beyond justice.

The third reason is democracy. Democracy presupposes a non-coercive political process in and through which people can pursue and negotiate the terms of their interconnectedness, interdependence and difference. In democratic thinking, 'consent' constitutes the basis of collective agreement and governance. For people to be free and equal there must be mechanisms in place through which consent can be registered in the determination of the government of public life (see chapter 2). Yet, when millions die unnecessarily, and billions are threatened unnecessarily, it can clearly be held that serious harm can be inflicted on people 'without their consent' and 'against their will' (Barry, 1998b: 201, 231). The recognition of this reveals fundamental deficits in our governance arrangements which go to the heart of both justice and democracy.

Finally, the failure to act sooner rather than later on pressing global issues generally escalates the costs of dealing with them. In fact, the costs of inaction are high and often vastly higher than the costs of action. For instance, it has been estimated that the costs of inaction in dealing with communicable diseases in Africa are about 100 times greater than the costs of corrective action (see Conceição, 2003). Similar calculations have also been undertaken in areas of international financial stability, the multilateral trade regime and peace and security, all of which show that the costs of deficient global public goods provision are extremely large and outweigh, by significant margins, the costs of corrective policies (ibid.). And yet we too often stand paralysed in the face of urgent collective challenges or actively engage in the reproduction of political and social arrangements that fail to meet the minimum standards that solidarity, justice and democracy require.

Deep drivers and governance challenges

The post-1945 multilateral order is threatened by the intersection and combination of humanitarian, economic and environmental crises. There are, moreover, forces pushing them from bad to worse; I call these the emergent system of structural global vulnerability, the Washington policy packages and the constellation of contemporary geopolitics. The first factor – structural global vulnerability – is a feature of our contemporary global age, and in all likelihood is here to stay. The other two factors are the outcomes of clear political choices, and they can be modified. Their force is willed, even though it has often presented itself in the form of inevitability. Or, to put the point another way, the current form of globalization is open to transformation, even if the Doomsday clock (the logo on the Bulletin of Atomic Scientists) is rather too close to midnight.

The world we are in is highly interconnected. The interconnectedness of countries – or the process of 'globalization' as it is often called – can readily be measured by mapping the ways in which trade, finance, communication, pollutants, violence and many other factors flow across borders and lock the well-being of countries into common patterns (see Held et al., 1999). The deep drivers of this process will be operative for the foreseeable future, irrespective of the exact political form that globalization takes. Among these drivers are:

- the changing infrastructure of global communications linked to the IT revolution;

149

- the development of global markets in goods and services, connected to the new worldwide distribution of information;
- the pressure of migration and the movement of peoples, linked to shifts in patterns of economic demand, in demography and in environmental degradation;
- the end of the Cold War and the diffusion of democratic and consumer values across many of the world's regions, alongside some marked reactions to this; and
- the emergence of a new type and form of global civil society, with the crystallization of elements of a global public opinion.

Despite the fractures and conflicts of our age, societies are becoming more interconnected and interdependent. As a result, developments at the local level – whether economic, political or social – can acquire almost instantaneous global consequences and vice versa (Giddens, 1990: ch. 2; Held, 2004: chs. 4–6). Link to this the advances in science across many fields, often now instantly diffused through global communication networks, and the global arena becomes both an extraordinary potential space for human development as well as for disruption and destruction by individuals, groups or states (all of whom can, in principle, learn the lessons of nuclear energy, genetics, bacteriology and computer networking) (Rees, 2003: 62, 65).

The second set of driving forces, referred to in the Introduction, can be summed up in two phrases: the Washington Consensus and the Washington security agenda. I take a detailed look at these in *Global*

Covenant (Held, 2004) and *Debating Globalization* (Held et al., 2005). Any assessment of them must be grounded in the issues each seeks to address. But they are now also connected drivers of the specific form that globalization takes (cf. chapter 6 for an analysis of how far the global financial crisis has triggered a shift in global economic governance). Together, they promulgate the view that a positive role for government is to be fundamentally distrusted in core areas of socioeconomic life – from market regulation to post-conflict planning – and that the sustained application of internationally adjudicated policy and regulation threatens freedom, impedes development and restrains the good. Of course, neither exhaustively explains the current structures of globalization, but they form a core part of its political circumstances.

For the past two to three decades, the agenda of economic liberalization and global market integration (the Washington Consensus) has been the mantra of many leading economic powers and international financial institutions. The standard view of economic development has maintained that the path to economic and social well-being is economic liberalization and international market integration. As Martin Wolf put it, 'all else is commentary' (2004: 144). But is this true? There are strong grounds for doubting that the standard liberal economic approach delivers on promised goods and that global market integration is the indispensable condition of development. Moreover, their forceful implementation by the World Bank, IMF and leading economic powers has often led to counter-productive results.

Countries that have benefited most from globalization are those that have not played by the rules of the standard liberal market approach, including China, India and Vietnam (Rodrik, 2005). In addition, those that have – for example, the Latin American and Caribbean countries – have done worse, judged by the standards of East Asia and their own past. In other words, the link between growth, economic openness and liberalization is weaker than the standard liberal argument suggests. The widespread shift among developing countries to greater openness has coincided with a slowdown in the rate of world economic growth compared to earlier in the post-1945 period, from 2.7 per cent in 1960–78 to 1.5 per cent from 1979–2000 (Milanovic, 2005).

The link between economic liberalization, growth and poverty reduction is also not as close as the liberal argument would predict. Accounts of this type generally assume a catch-up or convergence story whereby poorer countries, opening their markets and liberalizing, are expected to grow faster and richer so that income differentials narrow over time. However, the evidence to support this is controversial, at best. In the first instance, outside the phenomenal development of China and, to some extent, (urban) India, the reported number of people living below the World Bank poverty line of $1 a day has actually risen in the two decades since 1981 (see Wade, 2006). In addition, there is a near perfect correlation between an income group's relative standing at the beginning of the 1990s and its real cumulative income gains in the years that followed (see Pogge, 2006). The evidence shows that gains at the bottom of the global income hierarchy were minimal or even negative, as the first, that is to say, bottom percentile, lost 7.3 per cent and the second gained only 1 per cent. Moreover, the World Bank's measure of absolute poverty, based on $1 a day, is to a large extent arbitrary; if you take the figure of $2 a day, you can actually show the reverse trend (see Held and Kaya, 2007).

Examining and evaluating trends in income inequality between countries, it is clear that much depends again on how China's economic success and subsequent reduction in poverty is treated. If China is excluded from consideration, inequality between countries can be shown to have increased since 1980. This is an important date because it is often claimed to be the moment when income inequality between countries reached its peak. Of course, there is much to be said for including China in the account, but then it has to be borne in mind that China's success has depended significantly on a host of factors, not all of which fit neatly into the liberal argument. For example, China has staggered and regulated its entry into the global market; tariffs have been cut, but only after economic take-off, particularly in the last couple of decades or so; capital movements have remained tightly regulated; and FDI is locked into partnerships often with significant political controls.

None of this is to argue that trade and international capital flows do not provide important potential gains to many countries. The question is: under what conditions are trade and capital flows (and what kinds of trade and capital flows) introduced to maximize benefit? Thinking of globalization as either an inextricably positive

153

force or the opposite is likely to miss the core conditions for successful development and political change. The choice is not between globalization in its liberal free market form or no globalization. Rather, what is at issue is the proper form globalization should take.

This critical issue cannot be resolved within the terms of the Washington Consensus because its thrust is to enhance economic liberalization and to adapt public policy and the public domain to market-leading institutions and processes. It thus bears a heavy burden of responsibility for the common political resistance or unwillingness to address significant areas of market failure, including the problem of externalities (for example, the environmental degradation caused by current forms of economic growth); the inadequate development of non-market social factors, which alone can provide an effective balance between 'competition' and 'cooperation'; the underemployment or unemployment of productive resources in the context of the demonstrable existence of urgent and unmet need; and the emergence of global financial flows which can rapidly destabilize national economies. Moreover, to the extent that pushing back the boundaries of state action or weakening governing capacities means increasing the scope of market forces, and cutting back on services which have offered protection to the vulnerable, the difficulties faced by the poorest and the least powerful – North, South, East and West – are exacerbated.

The Washington Consensus has, in sum, weakened the ability to govern – locally, nationally and globally – and it has eroded the capacity to provide urgent public goods. Economic freedom is championed at the expense of social justice and environmental sustainability, with long-term damage to both. And it has confused economic freedom and economic effectiveness. Moreover, the systematic political weaknesses of the Washington Consensus have been compounded by the Washington security doctrines promulgated by the Bush administrations.

The rush to war in Afghanistan in 2001 and Iraq in 2003 gave priority to a narrow security agenda which was at the heart of the Bush administration's security doctrine. This doctrine contradicts many of the core tenets of international politics and international agreements since 1945 (Ikenberry, 2002). It sets out a policy which is essentially hegemonic, which seeks order through dominance, which pursues the pre-emptive use of force, which relies on a conception of leadership based on a coalition of the willing and which aims to make the world safe for freedom and democracy – by globalizing American rules and conceptions of justice. The doctrine was enacted as the War on Terror. The language of interstate warfare was preserved intact and projected onto a new enemy. As a result, the terrorists of 9/11 were dignified as soldiers and war prosecuted against them. But this strategy was a distortion and simplification of reality and a predictable failure. In pursuing dominance through force, the War on Terror killed more innocent civilians in Iraq than the terrorists achieved on 9/11, humiliated and tortured many Iraqis, created numerous innocent victims and acted as a spur to terrorist recruitment (see Soros, 2006). It showed little, if any, understanding of the dignity, pride and fears of others, and of the way the fate and fortune of

155

all peoples are increasingly tied together in our global age. And it unleashed an orgy of sectarian killing among the Sunni and Shia in Iraq, and the displacement of more than 300,000 people. Instead of seeking to extend the rule of law, ensuring that no party – terrorist or state – acts as judge, jury and executioner, seeking dialogue with the Muslim world, strengthening the multilateral order, and developing the means to deal with the criminals of 9/11, the US and its allies (notably the UK) pursued 'old war' techniques that have made nearly everyone less secure (see chapter 4).

The new doctrine has many serious implications (Hoffmann, 2003, 2006). Among these are a return to an old realist understanding of international relations as a sphere in which states rightly pursue their national interests unencumbered by attempts to establish internationally recognized limits (self-defence, collective security) on their ambitions. Moreover, 'freedom of anticipation' (or pre-emption) is a Hobbesian doctrine, one that creates both incentives and legitimacy for military action. Of course, international institutions have flaws. But the latter should not be used as an excuse for the further weakening of the rule-governed system that regulates the legitimate use of force in international society. For if freedom to dispense with the law is exercised by one country, soon others will choose to follow in its footsteps.

It would be wrong to link current threats to the multilateral order just to these policy packages, and specifically to policy shifts introduced by the Bush administrations. First, elements of the Washington Consensus clearly predate Bush. Second, the end of the

Cold War and the huge geopolitical shifts that have come in its wake may also form a key geopolitical factor. John Ikenberry has formulated the argument thus: '[T]he rise of America's unipolar power position during the 1990s has complicated the old postwar logic of cooperation among allied democratic states. America's power advantages make it easier for it to say no to other countries or to go it alone' (2005: 32). Connected to the decline in incentives for US multilateral cooperation are the divisions within Europe, which make it less effective in promulgating an alternative model of global governance. The current state of the leading organizations and institutions of the multilateral order needs unfolding.

Global governance: Contemporary surface trends

In a recent survey of the current state of key global and regional governance arrangements – the UN, EU and NATO prominent among them – Ikenberry has suggested that they have all weakened. He puts the point thus: '[T]oday the machinery of the post-war era is in disrepair. No leader, international body or group of states speaks with authority or vision on global challenges' (ibid.: 30). The value of the UN system has been called into question, the legitimacy of the Security Council has been challenged, as have the working practices of many multilateral bodies.

While the UN still plays a vital and effective role in peacekeeping, natural disaster mitigation and the protection of refugees, among many other tasks, the war in

Iraq dramatized the weakness of the UN system as a vehicle for global security cooperation and collective decision-making on the use of force. The management of the UN system has also been under suspicion, with the oil-for-food programme in Iraq becoming a scandal and UN-helmeted troops in Africa being implicated in sexual violence and the abuse of children. In September 2005, the UN members came together to try to establish new rules and institute bold reforms. But member states were unable to agree on a new grand vision and the summit failed in many key respects. (I return to these issues later.) As a result, the deeply embedded difficulties of the UN system remain unresolved – the marginalization or susceptibility of the UN to the agendas of the most powerful states, the weaknesses of many of its enforcement operations (or lack of them altogether), the underfunding of its organization, the inadequacies of the policing of many environmental regimes (regional and global) and so on.

The future direction of the EU is also highly uncertain. There is a deep sense of unease in Brussels about what the next few years will bring. Anxious about the increasing success of 'low-cost' economies, notably China, India and Brazil, and about whether the European social model can survive in its current form, voters are increasingly expressing scepticism both about the European integration and expansion. The French 'no' to the proposed European constitution partly reflected this, as did the Dutch 'no', although the latter was also fuelled by a perception that the Dutch 'host culture' was under threat from historical waves of immigration. The capacity of Europe to project its 'soft power' alternative to US 'hard power' looks frail, as does its capacity to play a more active global leadership role. In the absence of the negative unity provided by the Cold War, old foreign policy rivalries and differences among the big states are reasserting themselves (ibid.). Add to this the limited impact of the Lisbon process, the mixed results, at best, of the Growth and Stability Pact, and it is clear that the European model, for all its extraordinary innovation and progress, is suffering something of an identity crisis (cf. Held, 2006a: ch. 11).

While the economic multilaterals are still functioning (although the WTO faces a critical test over whether the Doha Round can be brought to a successful conclusion), many of the multilaterals that coordinate the activities of the US, EU and other leading states all look weaker now: NATO, the G8 and treaty-based arms control, among others. Since 9/11, the future of NATO has become clouded. The global redeployment of US forces, and divisions in Europe about the conditions for the use of NATO troops, have rendered the role of NATO increasingly unclear. The G8 has always been more of a 'talking shop' than a vehicle for collective action, but today its meetings appear to have minimal, if any, lasting impact. Arms agreements like the non-proliferation treaty are similarly in crisis. The US under President George Bush ignored its NPT obligations, announcing that it would create a new generation of tactical 'bunker-busting' missiles, and so introducing new levels of uncertainty about nuclear risks. In addition, the US ignored protocol III on the use of incendiary weapons of the 1980 Convention on Certain Conventional Weapons (and, arguably, the 1993 Chemical Weapons

Convention) by deploying white phosphorus in Falluja, an area of concentrated civilian population.[1] How far President Obama intends and is able to reverse these trends remains to be seen.

The post-war multilateral order is in trouble. With the resurgence of nationalism and unilateralism in US foreign policy, EU disarray and the growing confidence of China, India and Brazil in world economic fora, the political tectonic plates appear to be shifting. Clear, effective and accountable global decision-making is needed across a range of global challenges; and, yet, the collective capacity for addressing these matters is in serious doubt.

Problems and dilemmas of global problem-solving

The field of contemporary geopolitics is merely the chaff, significant though it is. Prior to it, beneath it, underlying it and restricting it are the limits of the post-war settlement itself and of the institutional nexus of the multilateral order. Four deep-rooted problems need highlighting.

In the first instance, there is no clear division of labour among the myriad of international governmental agencies; functions often overlap, mandates frequently conflict and aims and objectives too often get blurred. There are a number of competing and overlapping organizations and institutions, all of which have some stake in shaping different sectors of global public policy. This is true, for example, in the area of health and social policy, where the World Bank, the IMF and the World Health Organisation (WHO) often have different or competing priorities (Deacon, 2003); or, more specifically, in the area of AIDS/HIV treatment, where the WHO, the Global Fund, UN AIDS, the G1 and many other interests vie to shape reproductive healthcare and sexual practices.

Reflecting on the difficulties of interagency cooperation during his time as Director-General of the WTO, Mike Moore wrote: '[G]reater coherence amongst the numerous agencies that receive billions of taxpayers' dollars would be a good start . . . this lack of coherence damages their collective credibility, frustrates their donors and owners and gives rise to public cynicism . . . the array of institutions is bewildering . . . our interdependent world has yet to find the mechanism to integrate its common needs' (2003: 220–3).

A second set of difficulties relates to the inertia found in the system of international agencies, or the inability of these agencies to mount collective problem-solving solutions faced with disagreement over means, objectives, costs and so on. This often leads to the situation where, as mentioned previously, the cost of inaction is greater than the cost of taking action. Bill Gates recently referred to the developed world's efforts in tackling malaria as 'a disgrace'. Malaria causes an estimated 500 million bouts of illness a year, kills an African child every 30 seconds and costs an estimated $12 billion a year in lost income; and, yet, investment in insecticide-treated bed nets and other forms of protective treatment would be a fraction of this (Meikle, 2005: 22). The failure to act decisively in the face of urgent global problems not only compounds the costs of dealing with these issues in the long run, but it can also reinforce a widespread perception that these agencies are not just ineffective but unaccountable and unjust.

A third set of problems emerges as a result of issues which span the distinction between the domestic and the foreign. A growing number of issues can be characterized as 'intermestic'; that is, issues which cross the *inter*national and do*mestic* (Rosenau, 2002). These are often insufficiently understood, comprehended or acted upon. For there is a fundamental lack of ownership of global problems at the global level. It is far from clear which global public issues – such as climate change or the loss of biodiversity – are the responsibility of which international agencies, and which issues ought to be addressed by which particular agencies. The institutional fragmentation and competition lead not just to the problem of overlapping jurisdictions among agencies, but also to the problem of issues falling between agencies. This latter problem is also manifest between the global level and national governments.

The fourth set of difficulties relates to an accountability deficit, itself linked to two interrelated problems: the power imbalances among states as well as those between state and non-state actors in the shaping and making of global public policy. Multilateral bodies need to be fully representative of the states involved in them, and they are rarely so. In addition, there must be arrangements in place to engage in dialogue and consultation between state and non-state actors, and these conditions are only partially met in multilateral decision-making bodies. Investigating this problem,

162

Inge Kaul and her associates at UNDP have made the telling point that 'the imbalances among states as well as those between state and non-state actors are not always easy to detect, because in many cases the problem is not merely a quantitative issue – whether all parties have a seat at the negotiating table'. The main problem is often qualitative, 'how well various stakeholders are represented' (2003: 30). Having a seat at the negotiating table in a major IGO or at a major conference does not ensure effective representation. For even if there is parity of formal representation, it is often the case that developed countries have large delegations equipped with extensive negotiating and technical expertise, while poorer developing countries often depend on one-person delegations, or have even to rely on the sharing of a delegate. The difficulties that occur range from the significant under-representation of developing countries in agencies such as the IMF – where 24 industrial countries hold 10–11 seats on the executive board, while 42 African countries hold only 2 – to problems that result from an inability to develop adequate negotiating and technical expertise, even with one-person one-country decision-making procedures (see Chasek and Rajamani, 2003; Mendoza, 2003). In sum, many people are stakeholders in the global political problems that affect them, but remain excluded from the political institutions and strategies needed to address these problems.

Underlying these institutional difficulties is the breakdown of symmetry and congruence between decision-makers and decision-takers (Held, 1995: Part III). The point has been well articulated recently by Kaul and her associates in their work on global public goods. They speak about the forgotten *equivalence* principle (see Kaul et al., 2003: 27–8). This principle suggests that the span of a good's benefits and costs should be matched with the span of the jurisdiction in which decisions are taken about that good. At its simplest, the principle suggests that those who are significantly affected by a global good or bad should have a say in its provision or regulation. Yet, all too often there is a breakdown of 'equivalence' between decision-makers and decision-takers, between decision-makers and stakeholders, and between the inputs and outputs of the decision-making process. To take some topical examples: a decision to permit the 'harvesting' of rain forests (which contributes to carbon dioxide build-up in the atmosphere) may contribute to ecological damage far beyond the borders which formally limit the responsibility of a given set of decision-makers; a decision to build nuclear plants near the frontiers of a neighbouring country is a decision likely to be taken without consulting those in the nearby country (or countries), despite the possible risks for them.

As a result, we face the challenge of:

- *Matching circles of stakeholders and decision-makers*: to create opportunities for all to have a say about global public goods that affect their lives.
- *Systematizing the financing of global public goods*: to get incentives right and to secure adequate private and public resources for these goods.
- *Spanning borders, sectors, and groups of actors*: to foster institutional interaction and create space for

policy entrepreneurship and strategic issue management. (Ibid.: 5–6)

Failures or inadequacies in global political processes often result from the mismatch between the decision-making circles created in international arenas, and the range of spill-overs associated with specific public goods or public bads. 'The challenge is to align the circles of those to be consulted (or to take part in the decision-making) with the spill over range of the good under negotiation' (ibid.: 28).

Strengthening global governance

To restore symmetry and congruence between decision-makers and decision-takers and to entrench the principle of equivalence require a strengthening of global governance and a resolve to address those institutional challenges just discussed, as well as those underlying faultlines running through global governance provision set out earlier. In the first instance, this agenda can be thought of as comprising three interrelated dimensions: promoting coordinated state action to tackle common problems, reinforcing those international institutions that can function effectively, and developing multilateral rules and procedures that lock all powers, small and major, into a multilateral framework (see Hirst and Thompson, 2002: 252–3). But to do what exactly? It cannot be to pursue more of what we have had: the misleading and destructive policy packages of the

Washington Consensus and the Washington security agenda. Indeed, both need to be replaced by a policy framework that:

- encourages and sustains the enormous enhancement of productivity and wealth that the global market and contemporary technology make possible;
- addresses the extremes of poverty and ensures that the benefits are fairly shared;
- creates avenues of 'voice', deliberation and democratic decision-making in regional and global public domains;
- puts environmental sustainability at the centre of global governance;
- provides international security which engages with the causes as well as the crimes of terrorism, war and failed states.

I call the approach that sets itself this task 'social democratic globalization' and a 'human security agenda' – core elements of a cosmopolitan politics.

The Washington Consensus needs to be replaced by a wider vision of institutions and policy approaches. Liberal market philosophy offers too narrow a view, and clues to an alternative vision can be found in an old rival – social democracy (see Ruggie, 2003; Held, 2004). Traditionally, social democrats have sought to deploy the democratic institutions of individual countries on behalf of a particular project; they have accepted that markets are central to generating economic well-being, but recognized that in the absence of appropriate regulation they suffer serious flaws – especially the generation of unwanted risks for their citizens, and an unequal distribution of those risks.

Social democracy at the level of the nation-state means supporting free markets while insisting on a framework of shared values and common institutional practices. At the global level, it means pursuing an economic agenda which calibrates the freeing of markets with poverty reduction programmes and the protection of the vulnerable. Moreover, this agenda must be pursued while ensuring, on the one hand, that different countries have the freedom they need to experiment with their own investment strategies and resources and, on the other, that domestic policy choices uphold basic universal standards. How can self-determination, markets and core universal standards coexist?

To begin with, a bridge has to be built, as noted in chapter 1, between international economic law and human rights law, between commercial law and environmental law, and between state sovereignty and transnational law (see Chinkin, 1998). What is required is not only the firm enactment of existing human rights and environmental agreements and the clear articulation of these with the ethical codes of particular industries (where they exist or can be developed), but also the introduction of new terms of reference into the ground rules or basic laws of the free market system. Attempts have been made, for instance, in the Social Chapter of the Maastricht Agreement or in the efforts to introduce labour and environmental requirements into the NAFTA regime, to attain this objective.

At stake, ultimately, are three interrelated transformations. The first would involve engaging companies in the promotion of core UN universal principles (as the UN's Global Compact does at present). To the extent that this would lead to the entrenchment of human rights and environmental standards in corporate practices, it would be a significant step forward. But if this is to be something other than a voluntary initiative, vulnerable to being side-stepped or ignored, then it needs to be elaborated in due course into a set of codified and mandatory rules. The second set of transformations would, thus, involve the entrenchment of revised codes, rules and procedures – concerning health, child labour, trade union activity, environmental protection, stakeholder consultation and corporate governance, among other matters – in the articles of association and terms of reference of economic organizations and trading agencies. The key groups and associations of the economic domain would have to adopt, within their very *modus operandi*, a structure of rules, procedures and practices compatible with universal social requirements, if the latter are to prevail. This would require a new international treaty, laying down elements of universal jurisdiction and clear avenues of enforcement.

There are many possible objections to such a scheme. However, most of these are misplaced (Held, 2002a: 72ff.). The framework of human rights and environmental values is sound, preoccupied as it is with the equal liberty and development possibilities of all human beings. But it cannot be implemented without a third set of transformations, focused on the most pressing cases of economic suffering and harm. Without this commitment, the advocacy of such standards can descend into *high-mindedness*, which fails to pursue the socioeconomic changes that are a necessary part of such a commitment.

Accordingly, this means that development policies must be directed to promote the 'development space' necessary for national trade and industrial incentives, to build robust public sectors nurturing political and legal reform, to develop transparent, accountable political institutions, to ensure long-term investment in health-care, human capital and physical infrastructure, to challenge the asymmetries of access to the global marketplace, and to ensure the proper sequencing of global market integration, particularly of capital markets. Moreover, it means eliminating unsustainable debt, seeking ways to reverse the outflow of capital assets from the poorest countries to the north, and creating new finance facilities for development purposes. Furthermore, if the latter measures were combined with a (Tobin) tax on financial transactions, and/or a carbon tax on fossil fuels, and/or a different order of priorities concerning the relationship between military expenditure and the alleviation of severe need (the former running to nearly $1.5 trillion per annum globally, while the latter is only some $70 billion per annum globally), then the developmental agenda of Western and Northern nation-states could begin to be reconciled with the prospects of those nations struggling for survival and development.

The shift in the agenda of globalization I am arguing for – in short, a move from liberal to social democratic globalization – would have pay-offs for today's most pressing security concerns. At the centre of this argument is the need to connect the security and human rights agendas and to bring them into a coherent international framework. This is the second aspect of global policy: replacing the Washington security agenda. If developed countries want swift movement to the establishment of global legal codes that will enhance security and ensure action against the threats of terrorism, then they need to be part of a wider process of reform that addresses the insecurity of life experienced in developing societies. Across the developing or majority world, issues of justice with respect to government and terrorism are not regarded as a priority on their own, and are unlikely to be perceived as legitimate concerns unless they are connected with fundamental humanitarian issues rooted in social and economic well-being, such as basic education, clean water and public hygiene. At issue is what I call a new 'global covenant' or, as the High-level Panel on UN reform recently put it, a new 'grand bargain' (Held, 2004; UN High-level Panel, 2005).

Specifically, what is needed is to link the security and human rights agenda in international law; reform the UN Security Council to improve the legitimacy of armed intervention, with credible threshold tests; amend the now outmoded 1945 geopolitical settlement that shapes decision-making in the Security Council, extending representation to all regions on a fair and equal footing; expand the remit of the Security Council or create a parallel social and economic Security Council to examine and, when necessary, intervene in the full gamut of human crises – physical, social, biological, environmental – that can threaten human agency; and found a world environmental organization to promote the implementation of existing environmental agreements

170

and treaties, and whose main mission would be to ensure that the world trading and financial systems are compatible with the sustainable use of the world's resources. This would be a grand bargain indeed!

Of course, it has to be conceded that the moment to pursue this agenda has been missed, marked by the limits of the UN Summit in September 2005 and the 'no' vote on the European constitution. But some progress at the Summit was made on human rights (with an agreement, in principle, to create a Human Rights Council), on UN management (with a commitment to strengthen mechanisms of internal accountability), on peace-building (with the establishment of a Peace Building Commission), and on the acceptance of the 'responsibility to protect' those facing grave harm irrespective of borders (see Feinstein, 2005). And there is some measure of agreement about what needs doing in the area of UN institutional reform, which can be evinced by comparing the UN High-level Panel (2005) with the Newt Gingrich and George Mitchell report to Congress (2004).

But even if the moment has been missed, it has not been lost. The Washington Consensus and Washington security doctrine are failing – market fundamentalism and unilateralism have disclosed their weaknesses and self-defeating tendencies (Held, 2004, 2005). The most successful cases of development, seen in China, India, Vietnam and Uganda, among other countries, do not owe their success to the Washington Consensus (see Rodrik, 2005), while the conflicts that have been most effectively diffused (in the Balkans, Sierra Leone and Liberia, for example) were the ones that received concentrated multilateral support informed by a human security agenda (see Human Security Centre, 2005). These cases reveal clear evidence and clues of alternative (and better) approaches to security and development than the erstwhile dominant doctrines. The table at the end of this chapter summarizes some of the key policy shifts involved.

Global governance and the democratic question

The reflections developed so far are about taking steps towards solidarity, democracy, social justice and policy effectiveness after the failures of current policy have come home to roost. Yet, the problems of global governance today require a much longer time horizon to address them fully. The problems of democracy and social justice will only be institutionally resolved if we grasp the structural limits of the present global political arrangements, limits which can be summed up as 'realism is dead' or, to put it more moderately, *raison d'état* must know its place (cf. the Introduction).

Traditionally, the tension between the sphere of decision-makers and the sphere of decision-takers has been resolved by the idea of political community – the bounded, territorially delimited community in which decision-makers and decision-takers create processes and institutions to resolve the problem of accountability. During the period in which nation-states were being forged, the idea of a close mesh between geography, political power and democracy could be assumed. It seemed compelling that political power, sovereignty, democracy and citizenship were simply and appropriately bounded by a delimited territorial space (Held, 1995). But this is no longer the case. Globalization, global governance and global challenges raise issues concerning the proper scope of democracy, and of a democracy's jurisdiction, given that the relation between decision-makers and decision-takers is not necessarily symmetrical or congruent with respect to territory.

The principle of all-inclusiveness is often regarded in democratic theory as the conceptual means to help clarify the fundamental criterion for drawing proper boundaries around those who should be involved in particular decision-making domains, those who should be accountable to a particular group of people, and why. At its simplest, it states that those significantly affected by public decisions, issues, or processes should have an equal opportunity, directly or indirectly through elected delegates or representatives, to influence and shape them. Those significantly affected by public decisions ought to have a say in their making. But the question today is: how is the notion of 'significantly affected' to be understood when the relation between decision-makers and decision-takers is more spatially complex – when, that is, decisions affect people outside a circumscribed democratic entity, as is the case, for example, with agricultural subsidies, the rules governing stem cell research, and carbon emissions. In an age of global interconnectedness, who should key decision-makers be accountable to? The set of people they affect? The answer is not so simple. As Bob Keohane has noted, 'being affected cannot be sufficient to create a valid claim. If it were, virtually nothing could ever be done, since there would be so many requirements for consultation and even veto points' (2003: 141). This is a hard issue to think through. The matter becomes a little easier to address if the 'all-affected' concept is connected directly to the idea of impact on people's needs or interests.

If we think of the impact of powerful forces on people's lives, then impact can be divided into three categories: strong, moderate and weak. By 'strong' I mean that vital needs or interests are affected (from health to housing) with fundamental consequences for people's life expectancy. By 'moderate' I mean that needs are affected in such a way that people's ability to participate in their community (in economic, cultural and political activities) is in question. At stake here is the quality of life chances. By 'weak' I mean an affect which impacts upon particular lifestyles or the range of available consumption choices (from clothes to music). These categories are not watertight, but they provide some useful guidance:

- if people's urgent needs are unmet, their lives will be in danger – in this context, people are at risk of serious harm;
- if people's secondary needs are unmet, they will not be able to participate fully in their communities and their potential for involvement in public and private life will remain unfulfilled; their choices will be restricted or depleted – in this context, people are at risk of harm to their life opportunities;

- if people's lifestyle needs are unmet, their ability to develop their lives and express themselves through diverse media will be thwarted – in this context, unmet need can lead to anxiety and frustration.

In the light of these considerations, the principle of all-inclusiveness needs restating. I take it to mean that those whose life expectancy and life chances are significantly affected by social forces and processes ought to have a stake in the determination of the conditions and regulation of these, either directly or indirectly through political representatives. Democracy is best located when it is closest to and involves those whose life expectancy and life chances are determined by powerful entities, bringing the circles of stakeholders and decision-makers closer together. The argument for extending this consideration to decisions and processes which affect lifestyle needs is less compelling, since these are fundamentally questions of value and identity for communities to resolve for themselves. For example, whether McDonald's should be allowed access across China, or US media products given free range in Canada, are questions largely for those countries to resolve, although clearly serious cross-border issues concerning, for example, the clash of values and consumption choices can develop, posing questions about regional or global trade rules and regulations.

The principle of all-inclusiveness points to the necessity of both the decentralization *and* the centralization of political power. If decision-making is decentralized as much as possible, it maximizes each person's opportunity to influence the social conditions that shape his or her life. But if the decisions at issue are translocal, transnational or transregional, then political institutions need not only be locally based but must also have a wider scope and framework of operation. In this context, the creation of diverse sites and levels of democratic fora may be unavoidable. It may be unavoidable, paradoxically, for the very same reasons as decentralization is desirable: it creates the possibility of including people who are significantly affected by a political issue in the public (in this case, transcommunity public) sphere.

To restore symmetry and congruence between decision-makers and decision-takers, and to entrench the principle of all-inclusiveness, requires a redevelopment of global governance and a resolve to address those challenges generated by cross-border processes and forces. This project must take as its starting point, in other words, a world of overlapping communities of fate. Recognizing the complex processes of an interconnected world, it ought to view certain issues – such as industrial and commercial strategy, housing and education – as appropriate for spatially delimited political spheres (the city, region or state), while seeing others – such as the environment, pandemics and global financial regulation – as requiring new, more extensive institutions to address them. Deliberative and decision-making centres beyond national territories are appropriately situated when the principle of all-inclusiveness can only be properly upheld in a transnational context, when those whose life expectancy and life chances are significantly affected by a public matter constitute a transnational grouping and when 'lower' levels of decision-making cannot manage satisfactorily transnational or global policy questions. Of course, the boundaries demarcating different levels of governance will always be contested, as they are, for instance, in many local, subnational regional and national polities. Disputes about the appropriate jurisdiction for handling particular public issues will be complex and intensive; but better complex and intensive in a clear public framework than left simply to powerful geopolitical interests (dominant states) or market-based organizations to resolve them alone. In short, the possibility of a long-term institutional reform must be linked to an expanding framework of states and agencies bound by the rule of law, democratic principles and human rights. How should this be understood from an institutional point of view?

Multilevel citizenship, multilayered democracy

In the long term, the realignment of global governance with solidarity, democracy and social justice must involve the development of both independent political authority and administrative capacity at regional and global levels. It does not call for the diminution per se of state power and capacity across the globe (see chapter 3). Rather, it seeks to entrench and develop political institutions at regional and global levels as a necessary supplement to those at the level of the state. This conception of politics is based on the recognition of the continuing significance of nation-states, while arguing for layers of governance to address broader and more global questions. The aim is to forge an accountable and responsive politics at local and national levels alongside the establishment of representative and deliberative assemblies in the wider global order; that is, a political order of transparent and democratic cities and nations as well as of regions and global networks within an overarching framework of social justice.

The long-term institutional requirements include:

- multilayered governance and diffused authority;
- a network of democratic fora from the local to the global;
- strengthening the human rights conventions and creating regional and global human rights courts;
- enhancing the transparency, accountability and effectiveness of leading IGOs, and building new ones where there is demonstrable need for greater public coordination and administrative capacity;
- improving the transparency, accountability and 'voice' of non-state actors;
- use of diverse forms of mechanisms to access public preferences, test their coherence and inform public will formation;
- establishment of an effective, accountable, regional and global police/military force for the last resort use of coercive power in defence of international humanitarian or cosmopolitan law.

Over the years, I (alongside Daniele Archibugi) have called this agenda, and the institutions to which it gives rise, 'cosmopolitan democracy' (see Archibugi and Held,

1995; Held, 1995, 2004, 2006a; Archibugi, 2009). Since I have elaborated it elsewhere (and set out its institutional dimensions in this volume in chapter 3), I will restrict myself here to the change it entails in the meaning of citizenship.

At the heart of a cosmopolitan conception of citizenship is the idea that citizenship can be based not on exclusive membership of a territorial community, but on general rules and principles which can be entrenched and drawn upon in diverse settings (see chapter 2). This conception relies on the availability and clarity of the principles of democracy and human rights. These principles create a framework for all persons to enjoy, in principle, equal moral status, equal freedom and equal participative opportunities. The meaning of citizenship thus shifts from membership in a community which bestows, for those who qualify, particular rights and duties to an alternative principle of world order in which all persons have equivalent rights and duties in the cross-cutting spheres of decision-making which affect their vital needs and interests. It posits the idea of a global political order in which people can enjoy an equality of status with respect to the fundamental processes and institutions which govern their life expectancy and life chances.

Within this context, the puzzling meaning of a cosmopolitan or global citizenship becomes a little clearer. Built on the fundamental rights and duties of all human beings, cosmopolitan citizenship underwrites the autonomy of each and every human being, and recognizes their capacity for self-governance at all levels of human affairs. Although this notion needs further clarification and unpacking, its leading features are within our grasp. Today, if people are to be free and equal in the determination of the conditions which shape their lives, there must be an array of fora, from the city to global associations, in which they can hold decision-makers to account. If many contemporary forms of power are to become accountable and if many of the complex issues that affect us all – locally, nationally, regionally and globally – are to be democratically regulated, people will have to have access to, and membership in, diverse political communities. As Jürgen Habermas has written, 'only a democratic citizenship that does not close itself off in a particularistic fashion can pave the way for a *world citizenship* . . . . State citizenship and world citizenship form a continuum whose contours, at least, are already becoming visible' (1996: 514–15). There is only a historically contingent connection between the principles underpinning citizenship and the national community; as this connection weakens in a world of overlapping communities of fate, the principles of citizenship must be rearticulated and re-entrenched. Core civic and political principles can be embedded at different levels in a 'global legal community' (see Brunkhorst, 2005). It is to these principles that citizens owe their political capacities and allegiance – not to the nation or country for its own sake.

There was once a time when the idea that the old states of Europe might share a set of economic, monetary and political institutions seemed improbable, to say the least. It also appeared improbable that the Cold War would be brought to an end by a peaceful revolution.

The notion that Nelson Mandela would be released
from jail alive and that apartheid would be undone
without substantial violence was not anticipated by
many. That China and India would be among the fastest
growing economies in the world once seemed unlikely.
Let us hope that the task of reframing global governance
– through cosmopolitan principles, law and policies – is
similarly possible, even though now it seems remote!

Table 5.1: Sifting the Global Policy Agenda

The Original Washington Consensus	*The Social Democratic Agenda*
	NATIONAL
• fiscal discipline	• sound macroeconomic policy
• reorientation of public expenditure	• nurturing of political/legal reform
• tax reform	• state-led economic and investment strategy in sectors of strategic significance, enjoying sufficient development space to experiment with different policies
• financial liberalization	
• unified and competitive exchange rates	
• trade liberalization	
• openness to foreign direct investment (FDI)	
• privatization	• sequencing of global market integration
• deregulation	• priority investment in human and social capital
• secure property rights	• public capital expenditure on infrastructure
	• poverty reduction and social safety nets
	• strengthening civil society

Table 5.1 *(Continued)*

Washington Consensus (augmented)	*The Social Democratic Agenda*
The original list plus:	GLOBAL
• legal/political reform	• salvaging Doha
• regulatory institutions	• cancellation of unsustainable debt
• anti-corruption	• reform of trade-related intellectual property rights (TRIPS)
• labour market flexibility	
• WTO agreements	• creation of fair regime for transnational migration
• financial codes and standards	• expand negotiating capacities of developing countries at international financial institutions (IFIs)
• 'prudent' capital-account opening	
• non-intermediate exchange rate regimes	• increase developing countries' participation in the running of IFIs
• social safety nets	• establish new financial flows and facilities for investment in human capital and internal country integration
• poverty reduction	
	• reform of UN system to enhance accountability and effectiveness of poverty reduction, welfare and environmental programmes

Table 5.1 (*Continued*)

The Washington Security Doctrine	*The Human Security Doctrine*
• hegemonic	• multilateralism and common rules
• order through dominance	• order through law and social justice
• 'flexible multilateralism' or unilateralism when necessary	• enhance multilateral, collective security
• pre-emptive and preventive use of force	• last resort use of internationally sanctioned force to uphold international humanitarian law
• security focus: geopolitical and, secondarily, geoeconomic	• security focus: relinking security and human rights agendas; protecting all those facing threats to life, whether political, social, economic, or environmental
• collective organization where pragmatic (UN, NATO), otherwise reliance on US military and political power	• strengthen global governance: reform UN Security Council; create Economic and Social Security Council; democratize UN
• leadership: the US and its allies	• leadership: develop a worldwide dialogue to define new global covenant
• aims: making world safe for freedom and democracy; globalizing American rules and justice	• aims: making world safe for humanity; global justice and impartial rules

6

Parallel Worlds: The Governance of Global Risks in Finance, Security and the Environment

The world has recently witnessed the largest and most widespread financial crisis in nearly 80 years.[1] What is the significance of this event? Most commonly, the calamity is seen through the prism of policy failure, albeit on a massive scale – a failure of corporate governance, a failure of financial risk models, or of monetary policy. Even more widespread is the view that the financial crisis has signified the failure of a particular ideology, neoliberalism, with its emphasis on efficient markets and deregulation. While there are elements of truth to each of these observations, comparatively less attention has been paid to the global governance dimensions of the recent financial crisis. Yet it is from the deficiencies of global financial governance that some of the most important lessons can be drawn. In this chapter, it is argued that the global financial crisis and its fallout speak to broader problems of contemporary world order. Rather than a calamity specific to the domain of

184

financial affairs, the recent global financial crisis is only a symptom of more general problems of global governance. These deficiencies are present not just in the system of global financial governance, but also in the domains of security and global environmental governance.

The chapter proceeds as follows. The first section begins by outlining some of the basic characteristics of contemporary global governance, briefly describing some central problems therein. The sections that follow show that the three policy domains of finance, security and the environment have remarkable similarities both in the way in which they underscore human interconnectedness and in the ways in which the governance of these domains remains quite inadequate to manage contemporary global risks. Finally, the closing section highlights that recent attempts to address deficiencies in global financial governance, imperfect as they are, demonstrate that focused, politicized attention to the global nature of risks can yield progressive reform.

Global governance and the paradox of our times

It is now increasingly acknowledged that complex global processes, from the financial to the ecological, connect the fates of communities to each other across the world. Global interconnectedness means that emerging risks or policy failures generated in one part of the world can travel quickly across the world to affect those that had no hand in their generation. Yet the problem-solving capacity of the existing system of global institutions is in many areas not effective, accountable or responsive enough to resolve current global dilemmas. The paradox of our times, discussed in previous chapters, refers to the fact that the collective issues with which we must grapple are of growing extensity and intensity, and yet the means for addressing these are nationally rooted, inadequate and incomplete (Held, 2006b). Global public goods seem to be chronically undersupplied, and global bads build up and continue to threaten livelihoods. While there are a variety of reasons for the persistence of these problems, at the root the problem is an institutional one, a problem of *governance*. Problem-solving capacities at the global and regional levels are weak because of a number of structural difficulties which compound the problems of generating and implementing urgent policies. These difficulties are rooted in the post-war settlement and the subsequent development of the multilateral order itself (see Held, 2004).

Such problems of governance have a variety of manifestations, which can be succinctly grouped into two categories. The first can be called 'the capacity problem'. While the globalization of persistent risks means that a growing number of issues span both the domestic and the international domains, the character and scope of institutions are insufficient to deal with the systemic nature of these risks. Institutional fragmentation and competition between states can lead to such policy issues being addressed in an ad hoc, dissonant manner. Even when the global dimension of a problem is acknowledged, there is often no clear division of labour among the myriad of international institutions that seek to address them: their functions often overlap, their mandates conflict and their objectives often become blurred. In this regard, existing multilateral institutions are seldom afforded the institutional resources to tackle what are effectively global-level policy issues (see chapter 5). The second problem can be called 'the responsibility problem'. Put succinctly, the existing system of global governance suffers from severe deficits of accountability and inclusion. Less economically powerful states, hence their entire populations, are either marginalized or excluded from decision-making altogether. The severity of this problem is exacerbated, and its persistence sustained, by the fact that the relative costs associated with global risks can be larger for those who play little or no role in the generation of the problems in the first place.

These deficiencies in global governance can be seen within three policy domains which each constitute a part of what can be referred to as the 'global commons' – the collectively shared domains that tie diverse populations, interests and concerns together into a global community of fate. Each of the three policy domains has at its core a central element which has near-universal value for human welfare in the contemporary period. In the case of finance, it is the international organization of a particular social construction central to economic development: the management of credit. In the case of the environment, it is the complex resource systems of the natural world, natural systems which challenge modern notions of sovereignty. In the case of security, it is the access to basic means of physical well-being, most commonly understood as the protection from arbitrary violence. Despite the importance of each of these core elements to the well-being of every human being on the planet, the governance of each of these policy domains remains plagued by deficiencies. The global governance of finance, the environment and security all remain, to different degrees, subject to both the capacity problem and the responsibility problem.

The global governance of finance

The recent financial crisis demonstrates an important feature of our contemporary world. The interconnectedness afforded by globalization, for all its benefits, also disperses global risks on a large scale. The globalization of financial markets has integrated the global economy in unprecedented ways, and yet the rules and institutions that monitor and regulate financial market activity have not kept pace. There are many factors at play in the recent global financial crisis – the near universal incapacity to ameliorate systemic risk, excessive confidence in the efficient market hypothesis, the powerful private authority of private sector actors to increase the riskiness of their institutions, to name but a few. These contributing forces are highly complex, and are beyond the scope of this chapter. It is unquestionable that key national public institutions in the Anglo-American world failed in important ways. Yet another important feature of the recent financial crisis is the failure at the global level of the existing multilateral institutions which exist to monitor, contain and manage global financial risks and their contagion. Existing institutions that govern the way in which financial markets are managed around the world were weak and largely unprepared for the events of autumn 2008. The global financial crisis has made it clear that the problem-solving capacity of the global system is in many areas not effective, accountable or rapid enough to resolve current global policy challenges.

The capacity problem runs deep in global financial governance. The existing system of global financial governance has been, for most intents and purposes, weak and highly fragmented. One institution exists for the management of stock exchanges (the International Organization of Securities Commissioners), one for accounting (the International Accounting Standards Board), one for money-laundering (the Financial Action Task Force), one for insurance (the International Association of Insurance Supervisors) and one for banking regulation (the Basel Committee on Banking Supervision). Some institutions, such as the Bank for International Settlements and the Financial Stability Forum, have developed as overarching institutions which seek to monitor and conduct research on global financial risks and disseminate ideas. Yet, their ability to guide the existing constellations of institutions has been weak at best. The historical evolution of global financial governance can go a long way to explain the level of institutional fragmentation which has existed. While the protection of other areas of the global commons, such as the environment and interstate security, has been organized under UN auspices, institutions of global financial governance have had much more ad hoc arrangements, arising from informal policy communities reacting to particular collective problems. More well-known institutions, such as the IMF, had their beginnings firmly entrenched in the UN system, but other institutions just as vital to the governance of international finance have not. For example, the Basel Committee on Banking Supervision was established in 1974 in direct reaction to the contagion effects of cross-border bank failures. Similarly, the Financial Stability Forum was established in 1999 after widespread concerns over the contagion of financial instability following the East Asian financial crises. Each of these institutions have housed their secretariats in the Bank for International Settlements, an institution established in 1930 with the initial remit to manage German war reparations. In subsequent decades it expanded to focus on international financial cooperation among central bankers, and to conduct research and disseminate monetary policy ideas. Other institutions, such as the International Accounting Standards Board, are not even governed by public institutions at all, but reflect private sector self-regulatory initiatives.

Existing institutions have, of course, communicated with each other in important ways, and together these institutions have in some respects made significant advances, being involved, for example, in the limitation of financial regulatory competition among states, the provision of emergency liquidity, the occasional coordination of monetary policies and the combating of money laundering. Yet the capacity of this system to both detect and take action on the development of global financial risks has been poor. While the build-up of these risks can be traced back to features of the Anglo-American economies, it is notable that the existing institutions of global financial governance did not restrain them, but rather amplified the regulatory framework of these countries and made them models for all – the global standard.[2] Even if one puts aside the biases of existing governance institutions, none of them, it can be noted, has possessed much power to actually take action on important regulatory issues, and instead have executed what has been called 'soft law' through the production of global standards and codes (see Singer, 2007).

Compounding this institutional fragmentation has been the fact that most institutions at the centre of global financial governance have adopted an exclusionary model in relation to how they are run and how policy decisions are made, reflecting the responsibility problem in global governance more generally. Despite the wide membership of the IMF, its voting rules skew decision-making power towards the United States (Rapkin and Strand, 2006; Broz and Brewster Hawes, 2006). This has wider implications than is often assumed, especially given the fact that private interests within the United States have been shown to influence IMF policies through the lobbying of Congress (Broz, 2008). Other governance institutions, however, have operated on a different decision-making rule, but still exclude the vast majority of the world's population from any representative hand in formal decision-making. For example, the Basel Committee on Banking Supervision, the institution effectively setting the regulatory banking standards for the entire world, has maintained a highly exclusive approach to its membership for years. It has failed to expand its membership to include formal representation of developing countries, and right up to 2008 its membership reflected the status of international financial power in the 1970s, rather than the 2000s. During this period nothing changed in the Committee's membership, while countries like Japan, France and Germany experienced a relative decline in the position of their largest banks, and countries like China and Brazil a relative increase (Griffith-Jones and Young, 2009). This meant that up to and including the worst moments of the recent financial crisis, many countries (without any formal representation in the Basel Committee) had a much more prominent role in banking than many of those within the Committee. Other institutions, such as the Bank for International Settlements, have had a less embarrassing record of participation in governance; since 2006 central bankers from Mexico and China have been included in its board of directors. Nonetheless, the general picture of the responsibility problem has persisted, and this despite UN declarations, such as the Monterrey Consensus, that global financial governance institutions should review their membership to include adequate participation from developing countries (see Kregel, 2006; Germain, 2004).

The responsibility problem in global financial governance is particularly striking when one considers the global dispersion of costs associated with the recent financial crisis. Not only has world output declined, but global economic interconnectedness has meant that the costs of governance failures are widely dispersed (World

Bank, 2009a: 25).[3] While some of the poorest countries are unaffected by direct shocks of the financial turmoil itself, with contracting world trade, deteriorating terms of trade, and sharp rises in the cost of external financing, overall growth in emerging economies was expected to decline sharply from 6.1 per cent in 2008 to 1.5 per cent by the end of 2009. Some of the poorest regions of the world have experienced severe shocks – sub-Saharan Africa, for example, will have experienced a drop in output from 5.5 to 1.7 per cent in 2009 (ibid.). The need for emergency international financial assistance, mostly by less-developed countries, has exploded. While before September 2008 only 6 countries had stand-by arrangements and flexible credit lines with the IMF, totalling less than $1.7 billion, by September 2009 this had risen to 21 countries, drawing a total of over $165.7 billion (only one of these countries, Iceland, was a rich developed country). Such dispersion of negative economic shocks affects extremely vulnerable segments of the world population. While those in the rich developed world are bombarded daily with news of the deepness of the economic slowdown, less prominent in the headlines are the effects of the crisis on the most vulnerable populations of the world. The World Bank estimated that as many as 90 million people would be trapped in extreme poverty in 2009 as the result of the global financial crisis, and the number of chronically hungry people is expected to climb to more than a billion (World Bank, 2009b).

The global economic slowdown as the result of the crisis will have extremely damaging effects on developing countries. Even if the negative economic shocks associated with the crisis were somehow evenly placed for every single country, the adjustment burdens are never equivalent in relative terms, with significant adjustment burdens facing those with no hand in the making of the problem in the first place.[4] As Supachai Panitchpakdi, Secretary General of UNCTAD has pointed out, while few developing countries have been directly exposed to securitized mortgages or failed US financial institutions, the vast majority of them have been significantly affected indirectly through the reduced availability of credit, stock market panics and the slowdown in the real economy. Such sudden shocks to developing economies have substantial effects given the precariousness of the social conditions faced by many people there. The World Bank estimates that, as a result of sharply lower growth rates, between 200,000 and 400,000 more infants may die each year, school enrolments will suffer (especially for girls), and the prospect of reaching the Millennium Development Goals, already a serious cause for concern, now appears even more distant than before (World Bank, 2009a: 11). The ILO expects record rates of unemployment in Asia, and a recent report has warned that the global financial crisis could push an increasing number of children, particularly girls, into child labour (ILO, 2009a, 2009b).

The characteristics of the system of global financial governance reflect both the capacity problem, that existing institutions created to address global risks are not fit for the tasks at hand, and the responsibility problem, that the generation of risks and their costs are not commensurate with the scope of their governance. Recently, there have been some changes. After widespread politicization of financial regulation around the world, there have been new – partially successful – demands for some of these deficiencies to be addressed. Before reviewing these changes, however, it is critical to point out that the problems of global financial governance are not discrete to this policy area. Rather, as argued below, they reflect governance problems persistent in other areas as well, such as the global governance of human security and global environmental governance.

The global governance of security

If the global financial governance system integrates a common infrastructure for the management of credit, the international security system provides an arrangement for the management of conflict and violence. This domain of our shared existence, like the others discussed here, does have an existing set of institutions and rules which govern it. These institutions have evolved over time, but most of their structure and content reflects the security dilemmas of a world which is fast disappearing. From the end of the Second World War until 1991, the nature of national security was shaped decisively by the contest between the US and the Soviet Union. The dominance of the US and the USSR as world powers, and the operation of alliances like NATO and the Warsaw Pact, constrained decision-making for many states in the post-war years. In the post-Cold War world of the 1990s and 2000s, the constraints upon state security policy have not been eradicated but reconfigured. Instead of bipolarity, the global system now exhibits more of the characteristics of a multipolar distribution of political-economic power. Within this more complex structure, while the strategic and foreign policy options confronting an individual state are still shaped by its location in the global power hierarchy, there is a great deal more indeterminacy and volatility in the system.

Most armed forces of the world are still developed on a model of nation-states at war with one another, and based on the organizational principle of geopolitical state interests. Global military spending, fuelled by such preconceptions, has been on a sustained upward trend. Total global military expenditure in 2008 is estimated to have totalled $1.464 trillion, representing an increase of 4 per cent in real terms compared to 2007, and of 45 per cent over the 10-year period 1999–2008 (SIPRI, 2009).[5] The effects of the global financial crisis – in particular, growing government budget deficits and the economic stimulus packages that are aimed at countering the crisis – seem to have had little effect to date on military spending, with most countries, including the US and China, remaining committed to further increases in the years ahead. However, of the 16 major armed conflicts that were active in 15 locations around the world in 2008, not one was a major interstate conflict (ibid.: 69).

Institutional fragmentation persists within the security domain. Militaries remain organized on a national, rather than a regional or multilateral basis, with vast duplication, overlap and waste of resources. In countries like the UK, France and the US, spending levels are now far in excess of any plausible *defensive* needs, and are no longer justified on such grounds. With the exception perhaps of the US and China, no country is capable of acting independently in major conflicts or of intervening against regimes that threaten global peace and security. As noted in the Introduction, there is something quite baroque about existing defence positions and tactics (Kaldor, 1982). Against this background, the way we conduct and organize military spending looks increasingly anachronistic. It bears pointing out that total global spending on multilateral operations, such as peacekeeping, was just $8.2 billion, or 0.56 per cent of total global military expenditures (SIPRI, 2010).

Despite the evident failures of the Bush Doctrine, the capacity problem in global security runs deeper than disregard for effective multilateralism. The very instruments of international security provision are perversely oriented for a world that we no longer live in. Our military capacity and technologies are all geared to fighting wars in terms of combating physical forces in discrete and bounded space and time. At the present time, this model cannot deliver in many areas where security is most needed – and as such there is a need to create military capacity which is based on cooperation and collaboration of armed forces. This poses not only important questions about the collaboration of, and sharing of, personnel, technology and intelligence; it also poses questions about how to link international security to human security more broadly – through commitments to sustainable development and social justice. The emphasis has to be not just on fighting wars, but on securing the safety of human beings more generally (see Kaldor, 1998a). In other words, substantial institutional capacity exists, but it is the wrong kind of capacity. Learning has been slow, but now some of the world's most senior military figures have taken up the challenge and are changing the way warfare is being conceived (*Independent*, 2009; Petraeus, 2010).

The global governance of the environment

Until the middle of the last century, most known forms of negative environmental impact were largely localized. Since then, the impact and scale of environmental change has dramatically intensified, with issues such as declining biodiversity, deforestation and a plethora of water resource problems becoming effectively globalized (see Stevis, 2005; Brimblecombe, 2005). While the problems associated with climate change have received considerable attention and have correctly been framed as quintessentially 'global' public policy problems, the failure to generate a sound and effective framework for managing global climate change remains one of the most serious indications of the deficiencies of the current system of global governance (see chapter 5). There have been important advances in this area; both states, through multilateral cooperative efforts, and civil society networks have played a prominent role in pushing this issue onto the global agenda.[6] Nonetheless, like other pressing global public policy challenges, the threats posed by global climate change are vastly greater than even those relatively coordinated efforts currently existing at the global level. In parallel with the policy domains of finance and security, the climate change problem suffers from institutional arrangements which are not fit for purpose.

The capacity problem in global environmental governance is striking. While a number of individual international environmental agreements exist, and may even possess admirable characteristics, they are often both weakly enforced and poorly coordinated amongst each other. Furthermore, they are supported by a plethora of different international organizations fulfilling various functions. The current global environmental governance regime features a diverse set of players whose roles are largely uncoordinated among each other: the UN Environment Program, the Global Environment Facility, the Environment Management Group, the OECD Environment Directorate, the Commission for Sustainable Development, ECOSOC and the Environmental Chamber of the International Court of Justice, to name the most prominent (see Mabey, 2007; Keohane and Raustiala, 2008). The current constellation of more than 200 international environmental agreements suffers from a problem of what might be called 'anarchic inefficiency'. Firm institutionalized commitment to solve pressing issues has been only slowly, and unevenly, forthcoming. There have been some important advances in the governance of climate change, with the Kyoto Protocol being a significant first step, followed by increasing recognition and multilateral commitment at the UN level at the Bali and Poznań conferences. However, there is a very long way to go to establish a new global deal for climate change, and it is already clear that the international negotiations in

Copenhagen in 2009 failed decisively in this respect, and did not succeed in creating a framework to cut carbon emissions fast enough to lay the foundations for a new low carbon world economy (see chapter 7).

Global climate change has recently been called the greatest market failure the world has ever seen (see King, 2004; Stern and Tubiana, 2008). If this failure is to be addressed, it will require considerable administrative capacity in order to encourage and institutionalize industrial and energy reform and ensure an ongoing multilateral engagement with the problem. The goal of achieving this capacity, and the means to get there, will be undermined if countries at all stages of development are not directly involved in the shaping of solutions. In this regard, there is a strong parallel with global financial governance: accountability and inclusion represent serious challenges to addressing the problem. Poorer developing countries very often lack the resources, capacity and technology to come into compliance because of the relative costs that they would face (Linnér and Jacob, 2003). The Clean Development Mechanism, and the eventual emergence of a global market in carbon credits may help to resolve these relative costs, but they will do little to address more underlying problems (see Giddens, 2009). Other sources of global funds for adaptation are insufficient at current levels. The various funds established by the UN Framework Convention on Climate Change and the Global Environment Facility have started to fund small-scale adaptation projects, but the level of funding is still woefully inadequate (see Jones et al., 2009: 30). At issue is not only the inequality of resources; the problem also reflects the inequality of access to decision-making in international institutions, which often puts developing countries on the defensive when new sustainability initiatives are proposed.[7] In order to be effective, any new global deal must be equitable in a very particular sense; it would have to require commitments from individual states to be graduated according to their respective stages of economic development.[8]

While the potential dangers of climate change are increasingly widely known to the public, less well known is the way in which the costs of adaptation to climate change are more or less arbitrarily distributed in relation to the source of the problem. In this respect, the responsibility problem looms large. The poorest and most vulnerable populations of the world are expected to be most negatively affected by climate change. A plethora of developing countries in Africa and Latin America and South Asia are expected to experience considerable reductions in cereal yields, and more populations will become susceptible to diarrhoea, cholera, dengue fever and malnutrition (see Nyong, 2009: 47–54; Stern, 2006: 79–86). And even while some negative effects from climate change, such as extreme weather events, heat stress, growing water scarcity and the reshaping of coastal geographies, might be mitigated in the future, the ability to do so will clearly be a function of access to resources – leaving the poorest populations in the world subject to what Archbishop Desmond Tutu has recently dubbed the prospect of 'adaptation apartheid' (UNDP, 2008: 73–207). The asymmetry of costs resulting from climate change stands in great contrast to the massive global asymmetries in carbon footprints. As the

201

UNDP has recently pointed out, a single standard air-conditioning unit in Florida emits more carbon dioxide than an average person in Cambodia or Afghanistan does in a lifetime; the population of New York State has a higher carbon footprint than the 766 million people living in the 50 least developed countries of the world (see ibid.: 43–4). And while countries like China and India are increasing their per capita carbon footprint at a dangerous rate (especially given their large populations and projected levels of industrialization), the historical picture is sobering – with the mass of responsibility lying with already industrialized states such as the United States and Britain (see ibid.: 41).[9] Once again, the parallels with global financial governance are striking.

Conclusion: Crisis, politicization and reform

The global financial crisis reflects general deficiencies in the system of global governance, deficiencies that are also reflected in the policy domains of security and the environment. In this way, the recent financial crisis underscores the profundity of the dilemmas we face in managing some of the most extensive global risks which persistently confront us, and will continue to threaten livelihoods in the future. The institutions governing the global risks present in finance, security and the environment all suffer from what can be called the 'capacity problem'. In the case of global financial governance, institutional fragmentation and lack of enforcement capability has been particularly striking. In the case of global security, existing institutions are at odds with a world in which patterns of conflict no longer merely reflect the old structures of interstate relations. In the case of global environmental governance, the capacity problem is also evident, with institutional fragmentation thus far undermining a much-needed capacity for collective problem-solving.

Each of these domains also suffers from a responsibility problem, since the generation of risks, and the costs borne by their realization, are not commensurate with their governance. This has been particularly pernicious in the case of global financial governance, where the dominant approach to participation in decision-making has been highly regressive, to say the least. While the responsibility problem in security is more well known, in global environmental governance it exists in symbiotic relation to the failure to engage in multilateral agreement.

While the failures in global financial governance can be linked with failures in other domains as well, parallels also exist in the progressive transformation of governance. It is often forgotten that many of the strengths of the multilateral governance arrangements in the domain of security have been the result of previous crises, such as wars and humanitarian disasters.[10] This has been no less true in the domain of international finance, where the genesis of nearly every governance institution can be linked to a crisis (see Germain, 2001).[11] In the domain of global environmental governance, at least in the case of climate change, it has taken a series of crises as well. While countless scientists, environmental activists and NGOs have campaigned for many years, warning of global-level risks in this domain, it

has taken the possibility of the full-blown global cata-
clysm of future climate change to put the issue on the
international agenda in a serious way. Given that the
worst and most acute ecological crises are likely still to
be ahead of us, efforts after Copenhagen will prove a
litmus test for the capacity of the international community to reform the drivers of global risk proactively,
rather than retroactively after disaster, as has been the
case all too often.

The reaction to the financial crisis has also shown that
focused, critical public attention and a renewed commitment to multilateralism in the face of demonstrable
failure can lead to the reform of global governance
institutions. In particular, the São Paulo and Washington
G20 summits in November 2008 saw an unprecedent-
edly successful attempt by developing countries to
extend their participation in key institutions of global
financial governance. Countries such as Brazil, China
and India argued for inclusion in the Financial Stability
Forum – a substantial reform that soon cascaded to
expand participation to the entire G20 plus Spain and
the European Commission (see Helleiner and Pagliari,
2009). The Financial Stability Forum has now been
renamed the Financial Stability Board (FSB), and the
new institution has also expanded its institutional
capacities through a full-time Secretary-General, a steer-
ing committee and three standing committees (see FSB,
2009). In addition to serving as a centralized hub of
global financial governance coordination, the FSB will
also undertake reviews of the existing international
standard-setting bodies, to ensure higher levels of
accountability. Furthermore, the G20 has commissioned

the FSB to develop 'supervisory colleges' to track major international financial institutions, and to work with the IMF to assess the systemic risks associated with large financial institutions and potentially risky financial instruments as they emerge. These changes in institutional capacity reflect a proactive function previously very weak in the system of global financial governance.

How far the FSB will go to mitigate the new and evolving global financial risks of the future remains to be seen, but these changes are an important, albeit partial, step towards resolution of both the capacity and responsibility problems which have traditionally plagued global financial governance.

Strong reactions to the global financial crisis have enhanced governance capacities in existing institutions. The IMF, which was seen by many as an increasingly redundant international institution, has been given a new lease on life as a result of the crisis (see Helleiner and Momani, 2008). At the G20 meeting in April 2009, leaders agreed to support a tripling of resources to the IMF, as well as a general increase in Special Drawing Rights, with substantial increases allocated directly to developing countries. Recognizing the disastrous effect of the global financial crisis on the financing of basic infrastructure in the developing world, the World Bank also launched a new programme to ensure infrastructure recovery by filling the funding gap caused by the crisis, providing at least $15 billion per year over the following three years (see World Bank, 2009b). Serious problems still exist with the governance of the IMF and World Bank, but in this regard the increasingly well-organized demands of the G24 group of developing countries to increase their representation, participation and negotiation capacity gives ground for hope for future change (G24, 2009).

Significant participatory reform has also taken place. The G20's call for participatory reform of international standard-setting bodies has resulted in extensive reform of global financial governance institutions with direct regulatory functions. For example, the Basel Committee on Banking Supervision has been expanded, first in March 2009 to include Australia, Brazil, China, India, South Korea, Mexico and Russia, and then a second time in June 2009 to include the entire G20, along with Hong Kong and Singapore. The International Organization of Securities Commissions has also experienced similar participatory reforms on its Technical Committee. Within both institutions, broader questions of governance remain, such as the transparency of decision-making and the fuller participation of stakeholders (Bhattacharya, 2009). Despite these ongoing challenges, it is remarkable how such a closed policy network can be opened up in the face of major events.

Further reform of the institutions of global financial governance could be guided by the notion that fuller and more accountable participation can help to underwrite effectiveness. Participation could be guided by a concept of the global commons, not only as a shared set of resources, but a shared community of fate – the very basis of contemporary globalization. At its normative core it could enshrine the principle of equivalence; that is, the principle that the span of a good's benefits and costs should be matched with the span of the jurisdiction in which decisions are taken about that good (see chapter 5). At its root, such a principle suggests that those who are significantly affected by a global public good or bad should have some say in its provision or regulation. Such a principle of equivalence could be circumscribed by a concept of the right to protection from grievous harm. In this way, all-inclusiveness would require deliberation and engagement with respect to policies that seriously affect life expectations and chances. The equivalence principle helps to underwrite effectiveness in that, in the protection of a global public good, such as financial stability and soundness, there are inherent problems when that global public good is protected and managed by a minority of stakeholders, since any minority group will necessarily suffer only a portion of the full consequences of their actions when it is ineffective.

It remains to be seen how and if the significant reforms begun in global financial governance can be reproduced in resolving the security and environmental challenges ahead. Certainly, the creation of effective institutions to address climate change and the movement to a low carbon economy, on the one hand, and effective military capacity to resolve new patterns of conflict, on the other, is a long way off. Nonetheless, a new space for global politics has emerged as a result of both the failures of old institutional structures and the new political opportunities created by a widely shared sense of the urgency of finding new ways ahead.

7

Democracy, Climate Change and Global Governance

This chapter examines the role of democracy in meeting the urgent challenge of climate change.[1] The challenge is multifaceted and multilayered, involving many actors and agencies, and demanding effective policy at the level of both the nation-state and global governance. Moreover, it is difficult to address because it requires long-term policy commitments and solutions that depend on complex scientific and technical developments. It is also difficult to solve because it involves great costs and effort, and because of the complicated distributive implications involved at every turn.

In order to unpack the issues at stake, the chapter is structured in five parts. The first section examines the relationship between democracy and climate change at the level of the nation-state, briefly reviewing existing literature and examining evidence for and against the claim that democracies are unable to address the problem. The second section focuses on the same issues in relation to global governance, concentrating on the enormous collective action problem that climate change poses to an international community of distinct nation-states, and the problem of multiple actors, organizational overlap and representation and accountability in international environmental institutions. The third section examines the policy debates about climate change, asking about the range of options available to nation-states and, in particular, liberal democracies. The fourth section focuses on the political elements of a democratic global deal on climate change, and the final section draws together the various arguments presented around the theme of democracy and the policy menu ahead.

Democracy I: *The democratic nation-state and climate change*

At the most basic level, it can be argued that modern liberal democracies suffer from a number of structural characteristics that prevent them from tackling global collective action problems, in general, and climate change, in particular. These are:

1 *Short-termism*. The electoral cycle tends to focus policy debate on short-term political gains and satisfying the median voter. The short duration of electoral cycles ensures that politicians are concerned with their own re-election, which may compromise hard policy decisions that require a great deal of political capital. It is extremely difficult for governments to impose large-scale changes on an electorate, whose votes they depend

on, in order to tackle a problem whose impact will only be felt by future generations.

2 *Self-referring decision-making.* Democratic theory and politics builds on a notion of accountability linked to home-based constituencies. It assumes a symmetry and congruence between decision-makers and decision-takers within the boundaries of the nation-state. Any breakdown of equivalence between these parties, i.e. between decision-makers and stakeholders, or between the inputs and outputs of the decision-making process, tends not to be heavily weighed. Democratic 'princes' and 'princesses' owe their support to that most virtuous source of power: their people. The externalities or spill-over border effects of decisions they take are not their primary concern.

3 *Interest group concentration.* In democracies, greater interest group pluralism reduces the provision of public goods because politicians are forced to adopt policies that cater to the narrow interests of small groups (Olson, 1982). The democratic process rewards small, well-organized interest groups and results in their proliferation. Also, strong competition among such groups leads to gridlock in public decision-making, delaying both the implementation and effectiveness of public goods provision (Midlarsky, 1998).

4 *Weak multilateralism.* Governments accountable to democratic publics often seek to avoid compliance with binding multilateral decisions if this weakens their relationship to their electorate. There is a notable exception:

it occurs when strong democratic governments can control the multilateral game.

Concerns such as these have generated scepticism about the compatibility of democratic forms of governance with the need for the drastic and urgent changes in policy required to combat climate change. The implication is that they are unable to meet the scale of the challenge posed by climate change, and that more coercive forms of government may be necessary. Such thinking finds its historical precedent in the work of the 'eco-authoritarians' of the 1970s, who argued that it might be difficult in democracies to constrain economic activity and population growth that results in pressures on the environment. They suggested that some aspects of democratic rule would have to be sacrificed to achieve sustainable future outcomes, since authoritarian regimes are not required to pay as much attention to citizens' rights in order to establish effective policy in key areas (Hardin, 1968; Heilbroner, 1974; Ophuls, 1977).

This type of argument has, however, been undermined by a body of theory arguing that there are a number of reasons why democracies are more likely than authoritarian regimes to protect environmental quality (Holden, 2002). Democracies have better access to information, with fewer restrictions on media and sources of information, and greater transparency in decision-making procedures. They encourage the advance of science, which is responsible for our awareness about climate change and other forms of environmental threat in the first place (Giddens, 2009: 74). Scientists and other experts are free to engage in research, exchange new evidence and travel to and obtain information from other countries. These factors make it more likely that environmental issues will be identified and placed on the political agenda, and tackled according to appropriate measures of risk. Moreover, concerned citizens can influence political outcomes not only through the ballot box, but also through pressure groups, social movements and the free media – channels that are closed in autocracies. The presence of civil society also serves to inform the public, act as a watchdog on public agencies and directly lobby government (Payne, 1995). There are many examples of cases where environmental interest groups have been able to overwhelm business interests pursuing environmentally damaging practices, and of cases where they have changed the public agenda (Bernauer and Caduff, 2004; Falkner, 2007).

At the same time, authoritarian regimes have fewer incentives to adopt or stick to sustainable policies. Environmental concerns are often trumped by economic development plans and external security, as was the case with the Soviet regime (Porritt, 1984). Leaders are unaccountable to the public, and have fewer grounds to enact long-term policy (Congleton, 1992). And in authoritarian regimes, those in power control a substantial fraction of society's resources, encouraging pay-offs to a relatively small elite, resulting in less public goods provision (Bueno de Mesquita et al., 2003).

It does not seem unreasonable, then, to expect a strong correlation between democracy and environmental quality. Indeed, among the 40 highest carbon emitters internationally (cumulatively responsible for 91 per cent of total world emissions), the countries that have the best records are all democracies (see table 7.1).[2]

However, upon closer examination, the record is less compelling, and detailed empirical evidence is inconclusive. Environmental quality is not just measured by a broad-based commitment to addressing emissions of carbon and other greenhouse gases (GHGs). While some studies have shown that authoritarian regimes have worse records than democracies on environmental protection (Desai 1998; Jancar-Webster, 1993), others find no evidence to suggest that this is the case (Grafton and Knowles, 2004). Indeed, across a range of measures and geographical areas numerous studies prove that outcomes are varied (see Midlarsky, 1998).[3]

On balance, while evidence on the link between political institutions and environmental sustainability does seem to suggest that democracies are preferable to authoritarian regimes, we might expect the effect to be far greater than it actually is. Why is this the case? Part of the reason might be attributed to the different types of transmission mechanisms that translate policy commitment into policy outcomes. Bättig and Bernauer (2009), for example, find that, while the effect of democracy on political commitment to climate change is positive, the effect on policy outcomes, measured in terms of emissions and trends, is ambiguous. They observe that the causal chain from environmental risks to public perceptions of such risks, to public demand for risk mitigation and to policy output is shorter than the one leading from risk via policy output to policy outcome. Because of that, outcomes are influenced by a range of other factors, such as the properties of the resource in

Table 7.1: World Carbon Emissions, by Country (measured in millions of metric tonnes of CO_2)

Rank	Country	2000	2006	per capita (tonnes), 2006	percentage change since 2000
1	China	2966.52	6017.69	4.58	103
2	United States	5860.38	5902.75	19.78	1
3	Russia	1582.37	1704.36	12.00	8
4	India	1012.34	1293.17	1.16	28
5	Japan	1203.71	1246.76	9.78	4
6	Germany	856.92	857.60	10.40	0
7	Canada	565.22	614.33	18.81	9
8	United Kingdom	561.23	585.71	9.66	4
9	South Korea	445.81	514.53	10.53	15
10	Iran	320.69	471.48	7.25	47
11	Italy	448.43	468.19	8.05	4
12	South Africa	391.67	443.58	10.04	13
13	Mexico	383.44	435.60	4.05	14

14	Saudi Arabia	290.54	424.08	15.70	46
15	France	402.27	417.75	6.60	4
16	Australia	359.80	417.06	20.58	16
17	Brazil	344.91	377.24	2.01	9
18	Spain	326.92	372.62	9.22	14
19	Ukraine	326.83	328.72	7.05	1
20	Poland	295.00	303.42	7.87	3
21	Taiwan	252.15	300.38	13.19	19
22	Indonesia	273.93	280.36	1.21	2
23	Netherlands	251.73	260.45	15.79	3
24	Thailand	161.86	245.04	3.79	51
25	Turkey	202.38	235.70	3.35	16
26	Kazakhstan	143.45	213.50	14.02	49
27	Malaysia	112.14	163.53	6.70	46
28	Argentina	138.42	162.19	4.06	17
29	Venezuela	134.46	151.97	5.93	13
30	Egypt	119.32	151.62	1.92	27

Table 7.1 (*Continued*)

Rank	Country	2000	2006	per capita (tonnes), 2006	percentage change since 2000
31	United Arab Emirates	115.72	149.52	35.05	29
32	Belgium	148.57	147.58	14.22	−1
33	Singapore	107.64	141.10	31.41	31
34	Pakistan	109.11	125.59	0.78	15
35	Uzbekistan	106.35	120.84	4.43	14
36	Czech Republic	113.45	116.30	11.36	3
37	Greece	101.27	107.07	10.02	6
38	Nigeria	80.75	101.07	0.77	25
39	Iraq	73.58	98.95	3.69	34
40	Romania	93.33	98.64	4.42	6

Source: EIA (2006)

question, mitigation costs and the efficiency of implementing agencies. Politicians might easily declare a set of public policy commitments to climate change mitigation, but the outcome of such efforts is affected by factors that are often outside their control. The result is that policymakers respond quite well to public demands for more environmental protection, but tend to discount implementation problems, hoping that voters will not be able to identify these within a short enough time period to use their votes as a punishment for any failure to deliver.

An additional concern is that political commitment to tackling climate change is critical, yet may require political leaders to adhere to a particular course of action that is potentially unpopular, and hence contrary to structural democratic pressures. The actual implementation of policies that reduce global warming may infringe on the democratic preferences of citizens. In such a context, political leaders can be caught between a desire for recognition and esteem in the international community – recognition that comes from peer admiration for leadership – and the need to ensure accountability to domestic electorates (Keohane and Raustiala, 2008). However, good democratic leadership is not confined to policymaking alone – it also involves educating constituents about pressing issues that may not be obvious to them. In this sense, the fact that democratic publics do not always have fully formed preferences is an advantage as well as a risk. Citizens can significantly shift their preferences, faced with new information and evidence about pressing issues. The democratic citizen that is capable of being 'fact-regarding, future-regarding and other-regarding', is not simply a myth (Offe and Preuss, 1991: 156–7, cited in Held, 2006a: 232).

Such an approach to democratic 'will formation' can be found within the tradition of what is known as deliberative democracy, broadly defined as 'any one of a family of views according to which the public deliberation of free and equal citizens is the core of legitimate political decision-making and self-governance' (Bohman, 1998: 401). Deliberative democrats advocate that democracy moves away from any notion of fixed and given preferences, to be replaced with a view that democracy should become a learning process in, and through which, people come to terms with the range of issues they need to understand in order to hold defensible positions. They argue that no set of values or particular perspectives can lay claim to being correct and valid by themselves, but, rather, are valid only insofar as they are capable of public justification (Offe and Preuss, 1991: 168). Individual points of view need to be tested in and through social encounters which take into account the point of view of others. Ultimately, the key objective is the transformation of private preferences via a process of deliberation into positions that can withstand public scrutiny and test. Empirical findings show that citizens can and do alter their preferences when they engage with new information, fresh evidence and debate (Held, 2006a: 247–55). This can lead to new and innovative ideas about public policy and about how democracy might function and work.

Deliberative democracy can, in principle, increase the quality, legitimacy and, therefore, the sustainability of environmental policy decisions. This is partly due to the uncertainty associated with environmental issues, which demands a wide range of experience, expertise and consultation. The complexity of climate change problems also requires integrated solutions that have been vetted by multiple actors and that cut across the narrow confines of expert knowledge and the responsibilities of established institutions and organizations. And the concerns of environmental justice require the political process to be as inclusive as possible, giving voice to the under-represented, including future generations. Effective and just action on climate change depends upon the continuing involvement of citizens in the making and delivery of policy; conventional representative democracy alone is a poor way to achieve this. To remodel environmental politics around deliberative democracy is thus to create an opening for a change in the way democracies address environmental management, in general, and climate change, in particular.

In shifting from policy commitments to real and binding action, democracies have all too often been unable to override the problems of short-termism, collective action and other factors that cut against emission reduction efforts. This is not to say that democracies are incapable of tackling climate change (certainly the alternative, in the form of authoritarian regimes, seems to be far worse). Rather, certain aspects of them typically fall short. The question now is whether democratic systems can be evolved to handle the problem better, and how this may be achieved.

Democracy II: Global governance and climate change

Complex global processes, from the ecological to the financial, connect the fate of communities to each other across the world, yet the problem-solving capacity of the global system is in many areas not effective, accountable or fast enough to resolve current global challenges. What I have earlier called the paradox of our times, in chapter 5, refers to the fact that the collective issues we must grapple with are of growing cross-border extensity and intensity, but the means for addressing these are state-based, weak and incomplete. While there are a variety of reasons for the existence of these problems, at the most basic level the persistence of the paradox remains a problem of governance. The abilities of states to address critical issues at the regional and global level are handicapped by a number of structural difficulties, domestic and international, which compound the problems of generating and implementing urgent policies with respect to global goods and bads (see chapter 5, pp. 160–5).

Today, there is a newfound recognition that global problems cannot be solved by any one nation-state acting alone, nor by states just fighting their corner in regional blocs. What is required is collective and collaborative action – something that the states of the world have not been good at, and which they need to reconsider and advance if the most pressing issues are to be adequately tackled. The number of actors and variety of organizations involved in both agenda setting and policymaking at the level of global environmental governance has increased substantially over the past decade. In addition to private, public and civil society actors, new types of actors have emerged, such as transnational activist networks (Keck and Sikkink, 1998), private rule-making organizations (Prakash and Potoski, 2006), government agencies, and public-private partnerships (Börzel and Risse, 2005). Moreover, established organizations have adopted new roles and responsibilities. For example, IGOs have acquired a higher degree of autonomy from the governments that have established them, and many NGOs now engage in agenda setting, policy formulation and the establishment of rules and regulations (Betsill and Corell, 2001). However, the increased engagement of diverse actors does not necessarily guarantee either effectiveness or equal access of diverse voices. In fact, it often leads to double representation of the West and North through both powerful states and NGOs (Kahler, 2005; Biermann and Pattberg, 2008).

At the institutional level, while many international environmental agreements exist, and possess some admirable characteristics, they are often both poorly coordinated and weakly enforced. Furthermore, they are supported by a plethora of different international organizations fulfilling various functions, and a diverse set of players whose roles are largely uncoordinated among each other. The most prominent include:[4]

1 *The UN system*, including the *United Nations Framework Convention on Climate Change (UNFCCC), the Environmental Management Group (EMG)* and the *Centre for Sustainable Development (CSD)*. While

international action on climate change relies overwhelmingly on the evidence presented by the UNFCCC (including the Kyoto Protocol), the UN system overall has so far been ineffective in reducing GHG emissions, and is hampered by major divisions between the North and South. The internal UN system is also still arguably uncoordinated on climate change, although there are plans to change this (UN System Chief Executives Board for Coordination, 2008). The EMG, chaired by United Nations Environmental Program (UNEP), is a key vehicle for this cooperation, but it remains too early to judge its progress. The CSD has engaged with NGOs in a constructive manner, and has an important agenda-setting role, but is also relatively ineffective.

2 *Global Environment Facility (GEF)*. The GEF has a climate change remit, including serving as the main financial mechanism for the UNFCCC. However, it has suffered legitimacy problems: developing countries have opposed GEF control of the Kyoto Adaptation Fund, perceiving a voting bias in favour of richer countries and the control of the World Bank. The current governance structure of the Adaptation Fund is regarded as an interim solution until this can be resolved. Elsewhere, the GEF has delivered important grants for climate change mitigation and adaptation, but has a tendency to support smaller technical or pilot projects that are not mainstreamed in countries or economic sectors.

3 *The OECD Environmental Directorate*. While this division of the OECD is technically proficient (having conducted agenda-setting work, for example,

on environmental indicators and economic modelling of carbon markets), it is globally unrepresentative. It also regards climate change as amenable to technical, pro-growth economic solutions, contrary to the views held by many of the key actors in the debate.

4 *The WTO Committee on Trade and Environment.* Collaboration between the UNEP and the WTO was proposed in 2006, yet the Committee has not even been able to agree to a limited environmental package within the Doha Round. There is little appetite to recognize climate change damage as grounds for unilateral member state exceptions (GATT/WTO Article XX) to world trade rules. Collaboration is, therefore, largely symbolic – the WTO is seeking more environmental legitimacy, while the UNEP wants access to WTO deliberations.

5 *Environmental Chamber of the International Court of Justice (ICJ).* The ICJ has thus far played an insignificant role, with no cases since its formation in 1993. It has been hampered by limited rules of standing and divided opinion over the need for a separate International Court for the Environment (Stephens, 2009).

Problems with representation at the level of global governance are high on the list of obstacles to addressing climate change (see Mason, 2008). Multilateral bodies need to be inclusive; unless both developed and less developed states come on board, the net reduction of GHG emissions becomes a much harder task, if it can be achieved at all. Ensuring effective representation is not a question of just providing a seat at the negotiating

223

table in a major IGO or at a major conference. For even if there is parity of formal representation (a condition typically lacking), it is generally the case that developed countries have large delegations equipped with extensive negotiating and technical expertise, while poorer developing countries frequently depend on one person delegations, or have to rely on the sharing of a delegate, and lack the negotiating strength to participate fully in discussions (Chasek and Rajamani, 2003). This is indicative not only of the problem of unequal access to decision-making, but of inequality of all types of resource. Many developing countries do not readily command the public funds, capacity or technology to come into compliance with agreed regulations designed to reduce emissions. As a result, any future agreement cannot simply build on the traditional burden-sharing approach to dealing with a problem inherent in the global commons; given the scale of transformation that is required for a sustainable future, wealthy industrialized states will have to bear a significant part of the cost of the transformation in developing countries.

The policy debate: Squaring the circle?

The greatest differences in the debate about the politics of climate change tend be revealed in issues of how to square the circle of participation, effectiveness and compliance. Or, to put the point more broadly, is it possible to combine coherently democracy, markets and universal standards? (See chapter 1.) The answer is far from straightforward. If international rules become stricter, we can expect reluctant states to become even more reluctant to be bound by them, while if participation increases, agreement may only become possible via lax rules (Keohane and Raustiala, 2008).

A critical component of a global deal will be the way in which market incentives are structured. In terms of targeting GHG emissions, two principal market-based instruments exist: cap and trade and taxation. Supporters of the former include Stern (2009), who points out a number of disadvantages with taxes: that they do not allow certainty over how big future GHG reductions will be, since estimates are imprecise and there is a long lag time between policy output and actual outcomes; that they are hard to coordinate internationally; and that developing countries are unlikely to agree to such arrangements, which impose economic burdens on industries without offering the offsetting gain of being able to sell emissions permits. Moreover, electorates in general are mistrustful of governments' use of tax resources, potentially opposing them in the belief they provide an excuse for 'stealth taxation'. A better approach is to set targets and then seek out the cheapest method (via the price mechanism) of reaching those.

The cap and trade system

According to its supporters, cap and trade makes the most sense of the options available because it allows for greater certainty about eventual emissions levels and produces better incentives for producers.[5] At this point, it also appears to be the approach most likely to be adopted at the global level, with a European Union Emission Trading System (EU ETS) already in place, and a successful precedent in the form of markets for sulphur in the United States. However, global markets in carbon and other GHGs are likely to be far larger and more complex than any previous emissions trading schemes, with a commensurate increase in levels of risk, opportunity for leakage and distributional consequences. Negotiating a comprehensive global accord and meshing national systems so that they operate coherently will be a highly fraught and difficult process, if it can be achieved at all.

Indeed, while cap and trade seems to be an ideal solution on the surface, it is in fact an odd way to do business. Politicians like it because it is market-based, does not require the imposition of unpopular taxes and can be worked out with special interest groups in backroom negotiations. Indeed, with regular auctions to sell off emitting rights, and the lack of a long-term or stable price, cap and trade is a lobbyist and trader's dream (Helm, 2008). Yet, putting the dangers of rent seeking aside, it is not even clear that cap and trade will lead to required emissions reductions. As Sachs observes:

> [A] cap-and-trade system can be more easily manipulated to allow additional emissions; if the permits become too pricey, regulators would likely sell or distribute more permits to keep the price 'reasonable'. Since the long-term signals from cap-and-trade are less powerful than a multi-year carbon tax, the behavioural

226

> changes (e.g. choice of the type of power plant) brought
> about by cap-and-trade could well turn out to be far
> fewer, as well. (2009: 2)

Such concerns are borne out by the existing record on carbon emissions trading. The global market grew to £126 billion last year, up from £63 billion in 2007, and nearly 12 times the value in 2005. This represented the value of a total of 4.8 billion tonnes of carbon dioxide, up 61 per cent from the 3 billion tonnes traded in 2007. However, the actual emissions cuts made and sold by UN-registered clean energy projects in developing countries fell by 30 per cent in 2008 to 389 million tonnes (Chestney and Szabo, 2009).

A tax on carbon

Contrary to the claims of cap and trade advocates, it can thus be countered that taxes are less likely to result in policy failure. Economic efficiency demands that those who create emissions should pay the costs, and taxes are the simplest way of forcing them to do so. Their advantages are many. They offer a broader scope for emissions reductions, as opposed to trading systems which can only be implemented among private firms or countries, and not among households and individual consumers. In this sense, they are the more democratic option, since they create greater coverage and are less susceptible to strategic lobbying for exceptions by firms or NGOs. Their universal guiding principle is distributive, since they simultaneously discriminate against polluters while allocating priority to the most vital cases of environmental need. They involve fewer administrative costs, are less complicated and more familiar to policymakers, and provide new avenues of generating revenue to tackle climate change for governments that are increasingly unwilling to incur political costs by expanding general taxation. Finally, they place a clear price on emissions for many years ahead, allowing for better long-term policy planning (see Sachs, 2009). Of course, there remains the substantial challenge of shifting taxation structures away from their primary focus on work and production towards a greater emphasis on pollution, externalities and consumption. It goes without saying that this will require a great effort, marked by short-term and long-term objectives, which could be weakened by new election results, changing coalitions and so on.

A new policy mix

In reality, the policy mix to address climate change is likely to contain multiple policy instruments. The prospect of large revenues from permit auctions has established significant political and economic interests in the creation and maintenance of markets for GHGs. Cap and trade also offers the potential for far greater levels of private sector funding than is the case for government-financed funds and schemes, and will create significant private sector flows from developed to developing countries, an absolute necessity for reaching a global deal. However, if policymakers are serious about putting a true price on carbon and other GHGs – which is essential if markets are to sort out efficient supply- and demand-side responses – then taxation will have to form a key element of policy as well, in order to ensure predictability of outcome, and the generation of new resources for the provision of urgent environmental goods.

Unfortunately, putting a price on all GHG emissions (whether through tradable permits or taxes) is not enough on its own to deliver the needed reductions. Existing market-based schemes, such as the EU ETS, or carbon taxation by individual European countries and US states, have so far failed to generate large-scale research into the development of breakthrough technologies. Such schemes might eventually result in a levelling-off or even a slight reduction of emissions, but will only stimulate a marginal diversification into alternative forms of energy such as solar and wind power. This is because private sector firms underinvest in research and development if they fear they will not be able to earn a decent profit on resulting product development. What is ultimately required is a fundamental overhaul of energy systems through transformative technologies that require a combination of factors to succeed – not only market incentives, but also applied scientific research, early high-cost investments, regulatory changes (e.g. building codes and practices), infrastructural development, information instruments (e.g. eco-labelling of energy appliances), and public acceptance.

To ensure flexibility and encourage innovation, regulations should be based on achieving particular results, rather than simply specifying the methods or technologies to be used to achieve those outcomes (OECD, 2007). Care needs to be taken in choosing instruments in a policy mix to ensure that they are complementary, avoid unnecessary overlap and are cost-effective. By setting too high a price or too tight a cap, policy will result in excess costs, while choosing policies that are too lenient will forgo the potential benefits of added, cost-effective mitigation measures, and risk the failure of meeting required targets.

The political elements of a democratic global deal

Climate change is a problem with global causes and consequences. A coordinated international effort is therefore required to achieve cost-effective and success-ful mitigation policies. However, the nature of the problem also means that international agreements will be difficult to reach, as Copenhagen in 2009 clearly showed. Countries and regions have very different inter-ests in achieving a solution, implying a highly contested distribution of costs and benefits. In addition, develop-ing countries, given their relatively small contribution to historical emissions, object to having their develop-ment impeded by restrictions. Finally, the challenges associated with enforcing a global solution may make some nations reluctant to participate, adding a source of uncertainty about how cost-effective the policies will be (CBO, 2005). However, despite the vigorous debate surrounding the type of policies required to combat climate change and how they should or should not be implemented, there is considerable overlap on what the political elements of a global deal should look like. At the most general level, most commentators agree that it should be broadly inclusive, multifaceted, state-centric and sustainable.

Participation

The key requirement is participation from all countries, and, most importantly, participation by the most powerful democracy in the world. The world has been waiting for the US to join the collective effort against climate change (Stiglitz and Stern, 2009). The integration of less developed states is also crucial, as already noted. Even if the developed states of the world were to cut their emissions to zero by 2050, without significant cuts in the rest of the world the overall goal of keeping a global rise in temperatures to under 2°C would be missed. Developing countries need to be convinced that they can simultaneously reduce their emissions and increase their growth rate by increasing their energy efficiency. They need, for instance, to eliminate distortions in their energy markets, such as large oil subsidies. But for most developing countries, the cheapest form of energy is coal (or other high-emission energy sources), and in those cases, there is a real trade-off. Money spent to reduce GHG emissions is money that could be invested or spent on education, healthcare or clean water. In such cases, developed countries, it can be argued, should pay for the incremental costs. However, as Victor et al. (2009) have pointed out, this is unlikely to happen – it is simply unrealistic to expect industrialized nations to contribute the tens or hundreds of billions of dollars needed for such a compensation scheme when official development assistance (including for wars in Iraq and Afghanistan) currently stands at around $100 billion for all purposes. Moreover, the countries that would get the most compensation, such as China, are now the West's most potent economic competitors.

Offset schemes and financial incentives

The alternative is some form of an offset scheme that allows industrialized nations to fund emissions reductions in developing nations while counting those reductions towards their own legal commitments. The idea is that this would require industrialized nations to pay a majority of the costs while also laying a foundation for the creation of a global emissions trading market. This was the aim behind the creation of the Clean Development Mechanism (CDM). However, although the CDM has, after a difficult start, been successful in creating a global market for GHGs, its design is fundamentally flawed and it has done very little to actually cut emissions or to assist host countries in achieving sustainable development (Pearson, 2007; Olsen, 2007; Muller, 2007).

Another important requirement will be the prevention of deforestation, which contributes 17 per cent of current carbon emissions, almost twice as much as transport (IPCC, 2007). Developing countries' tropical forests are an important source of carbon sequestration,

232

yet they are not provided with any compensation for these environmental services. Providing them with financial incentives will help to reduce emissions from forested lands and invest in low-carbon paths to sustainable development. In this regard, encouraging steps have been made in the implementation of the UN Fund for Reducing Emissions from Deforestation and Forest Degradation (UN-REDD). However, the establishment of a final framework for the transfer of funds is still some years away, with a final agreement only likely to come into effect after 2012. Moreover, there are serious concerns about the appropriate geographical scale of accounting and incentive mechanisms, monitoring, land tenure, elite capture of funds and the potential for fraud (Karousakis and Corfee-Morlot, 2007; Olander et al., 2009).

Participation and deliberation on a global scale are necessary, yet in their current forms, existing instruments of global environmental governance are ill-equipped to achieve results. What is required are representative institutions armed with the capacity and legitimacy needed to translate policy commitments into real world outcomes (see chapters 2 and 3). If a global deal is going to work, it must have an answer to the problem of governance, and embody an institutional structure that is accountable to a diversity of interests across the developed and developing world. Recourse to inclusive and broadly representative global decision-making channels is the most appropriate and effective way of doing this, and strengthening mechanisms of global governance will be key to constructing a global democratic response to the issue.

Democracy and the policy menu ahead

The challenge of tackling climate change will require the development of considerable institutional capacity and policy innovation. The goal of achieving this capacity, and the means to get there, will be undermined if countries of all stages of development are not directly involved in the shaping of solutions. Current policy development demonstrates this concern. The short-term path to effective environmental governance is to integrate a broader set of interests into existing multilateral governance capacity. The existing mandate of the GEF could be broadened in order to help coordinate and fund international environmental agreements and reflect the priorities of developing countries. Complementary to this, the UNEP could increase its status and responsibilities by becoming a specialized UN agency, with access to all the compulsory funding that this entails. The central challenge in the years ahead of compliance monitoring and enforcement could be facilitated through a formal international mechanism for settling environmental disputes through mediation and arbitration, similar to the World Bank's investment dispute body (Mabey, 2007). Enhancing the capacities and responsibilities of the GEF and the UNEP in this way would be a step towards the more consolidated and formal institutional capacity of a world environmental organization as a longer-term goal, driven perhaps by the G2 + 1 (the USA, China and the EU), but accountable to the G195.

In all these challenges, states remain key actors, as they hold the key to both domestic and international policymaking. The implementation of international agreements will be up to individual states – emissions trading and carbon pricing will require domestic legislation and technological advance will need state support to get off the ground (Giddens, 2009). However, state strategies at the domestic level should involve the creation of incentives, not overly tight regulation. Governments have an important role in 'editing' choice, but not in a way that precludes it altogether. This approach is represented in the form of what Giddens calls 'the ensuring state' (ibid.), the primary role of which is to help energize a diversity of groups to reach solutions to collective action problems. The state, so conceived, acts as a facilitator and enabler, rather than as a top-down agency. An ensuring state is one that has the capacity to produce definite outcomes. The principle goes even further: it also means a state that is responsible for monitoring public goals and for trying to make sure they are realized in a visible and legitimate fashion.

This will require a return to planning – not in the old sense of top-down hierarchies of control, but in a new sense of flexible regulation. This, in turn, will require finding ways to introduce regulation without undermining the entrepreneurialism and innovation upon which successful responses will depend. It will not be a straightforward process because planning must be reconciled with democratic freedoms. There will be push and pull between the political centre, regions and localities, which can only be resolved through deliberation and consultation. Most importantly, states will require a long-term vision that transcends the normal push and pull of partisan politics. This will not be easy to achieve.

Table 7.2: Summary of Governance and Policy Recommendations

Guiding principles: inclusiveness, political equality, deliberation, environmental sustainability, and economic effectiveness

	Governance	Policy
NATION-STATE	• broadening and deepening of the deliberative process • transformation of private preferences via a process of deliberation into positions that can withstand public scrutiny • continued involvement of citizens and civil society in the making and delivery of policy • leadership that confronts narrow interests, and sets out compelling scientific and economic cases for action	• taxation of carbon and other GHGs • just and equitable markets for carbon and other GHGs • applied scientific research • early high-cost investments • regulatory changes • infrastructural development • information instruments

| GLOBAL | • promotion of inclusive and broadly representative global decision-making channels
• assistance for developing countries to access necessary resources, capacity and technology for mitigation and adaptation
• broaden the existing mandate of the GEF
• increase the status and responsibility of the UNEP by upgrading it to a specialized UN agency | • develop effective offset schemes that allow industrialized nations to fund emissions reductions in developing nations.
• establishment of a formal international mechanism for settling environmental disputes through mediation and arbitration
• development of formal institutional capacity for a World Environmental Organization |

All this takes place in the context of a changing world order. The power structure on which the 1945 multilateral settlement was based is no longer intact, and the relative decline of the West and the rise of Asia raise fundamental questions about the premises of the 1945 multilateral order. Democracy and the international community now face a critical test. However, addressing the issue of climate change successfully holds out the prospect of reforging a rule-based politics, from the nation-state to the global level. Table 7.2 highlights the necessary steps to be taken along this road. By contrast, failure to meet the challenge could have deep and profound consequences, both for what people make of modern democratic politics and for the idea of rule-governed international politics. Under these conditions, the structural flaws of democracy could be said to have tragically trumped democratic agency and deliberative capacity.

Afterword

The twentieth century set down cosmopolitan stepping stones which create a tentative path to a more effective and accountable global politics. Since 1945, there has been a significant entrenchment of universal values concerning the equal dignity and worth of all human beings in international rules and law; the reconnection of international law and morality, as sovereignty is no longer merely cast as effective power but increasingly as legitimate authority defined in terms of the maintenance of human rights and democratic values; the establishment of new forms of governance systems, regional and global (however weak and incomplete); and the growing recognition that the global public good – whether conceived as financial stability, environmental protection, human security or the eradication of global poverty – requires coordinated multilateral action and multi-actor engagement if it is to be achieved in the long term. These developments need to be, and can be, built on.

The political space for the development of more effective and accountable global governance has to be made, and advances achieved, by the activities of all those forces that are engaged in the pursuit of greater coordination and accountability of the leading processes of globalization, the opening up of IGOs to key stakeholders and participants, the protection of human rights and fundamental freedoms, the creation of a low-carbon economy and sustainable development, and peaceful dispute settlement in leading geopolitical conflicts and civil wars. This is not a political project that starts from nowhere. It is, in fact, deeply rooted in the political world shaped and formed after the Holocaust, Stalinism, fascism and the Second World War. Moreover, it can be built on the many achievements of multilateralism (from the founding of the UN system to the development of the EU), international law (from the human rights regime to the establishment of the ICC) and the beginnings of multilayered governance (from the development of local government and cities and subnational regions to the dense web of international and transnational policymaking fora).

The boundaries between states, nations and societies can no longer claim the deep legal and moral significance they once had in the era of classic sovereignty; they can be judged, along with the communities they embody, by general, if not universal, standards. That is to say, they can be scrutinized in relation to standards which, in principle, apply to each person, each individual, who is held to be equally worthy of concern and respect. Concomitantly, shared membership in a political community, or spatial proximity, is not regarded as a sufficient source of moral privilege (Beitz, 1998, cf. 1979; Pogge, 1989, 1994a and Barry, 1999 and see below). Elements are in place not just for a liberal but for a cosmopolitan framework of democratic law.

The political and legal transformations (of the past 50 years especially) have, thus, gone some way towards circumscribing political power on a regional and global basis. Nonetheless, several major difficulties remain at the core of these tentative shifts. These difficulties need emphasizing before any unwarranted complacency slips into the analysis. In the first instance, any assessment of the cumulative impact of the legal and political changes must, of course, acknowledge their highly differentiated character, since they are not experienced uniformly by all states and regions. From the UK to Saudi Arabia, and from the USA to China, the extent, nature and form of the enmeshment of states in global legal and political structures clearly varies.

Second, while the liberal political order has gone some way towards taming the arrogance of 'princes' and 'princesses', and curbing some of their worst excesses, the spreading hold of the regime of liberal sovereignty has compounded the risks of arrogance in certain respects. This is so because in the transition from prince to prime minister or president, from unelected governors to elected governors, from the aristocratic few to the democratic many, political arrogance has been reinforced by the claim of the political elites to derive their support from that most virtuous source of power – the *demos*. Democratic princes can energetically pursue public policies – whether in security, trade, technology or welfare – because they feel, and to a degree are, mandated to do so. The border spill-over effects of their policies are not foremost on their minds, nor a core part of their political calculations. Thus, for example, some of the most significant risks of Western industrialization and energy use have been externalized across the planet. Liberal democratic America, geared to domestic elections and vociferous interest groups, has not weighed heavily the ramifications across borders of its choice of fuels, consumption levels or type of industrialization – George W. Bush's refusal after his election in 2001 to ratify the Kyoto agreement on greenhouse gas omissions is a case in point. Whether these choices will be significantly altered under President Obama remains to be seen.

Third, the problem of border spill-overs or externalities is compounded by a world marked increasingly by overlapping communities of fate – where the trajectories of each and every country are more tightly entwined than ever before. While democracy remains rooted in a fixed and bounded territorial conception of political community, contemporary regional and global forces disrupt any simple correspondence between national territory, sovereignty, political space and the democratic political community. These forces enable power and resources to flow across, over and around territorial boundaries, escaping mechanisms of democratic control. Questions about who should be accountable to whom, which socioeconomic processes should be regulated at what levels (local, national, regional, global), and on what basis, are left outside the sphere of liberal international thinking.

Fourth, while many pressing policy issues, from the regulation of financial markets to the management of genetic engineering, create challenges which transcend borders, existing intergovernmental organizations are insufficient to resolve these. Decision-making in leading IGOs, such as the World Bank and the IMF, is systematically skewed to dominant geopolitical and geoeconomic interests. Even when this is not the case, a crisis of legitimacy threatens these institutions. For the 'chains of delegation' from national states to multilateral rule-making bodies are too long, the basis of representation often unclear, and the mechanisms of accountability of the technical elites themselves who run the IGOs are weak or obscure (Keohane, 1998). Problems of transparency, accountability and democracy prevail at the global level. Whether 'princes' and 'princesses' rule in cities, states or multilateral bodies, their power will remain arbitrary unless tested and redeemed through accountability chains and democratic processes which embrace all those significantly affected by them.

Fifth, the security agenda bites into the scope and efficacy of the regime of liberal international sovereignty. Extensive questions have been raised since 9/11 about how counter-terrorist strategies are affecting human rights (Marks and Clapham, 2005: 347–9). Arrests and deportations in the US, UK and other countries highlight many problems, including new restrictions on freedom of speech and assembly, holding people incommunicado and/or for prolonged detention without charge, the ill-treatment of detainees, and degrading conditions of detention. In addition, the transfer of prisoners from Afghanistan and elsewhere to Guantánamo Bay illustrated numerous issues – again, holding people in harsh conditions without charge, and so on – in relation to international humanitarian law. More generally, human rights are now affected by a range of legislative, administrative and policy measures adopted in many countries in respect to the extension of the scope of surveillance, detention, immigration, deportation, among other things.

Accordingly, the political and legal transformations that have gone a long way to reshaping the interstate system since 1945 through new institutions of governance and law remain vulnerable and display a lack of both legitimacy and effectiveness in many core areas. Clear, effective and accountable decision-making is needed across a range of urgent global challenges; and, yet, the collective capacity for addressing these matters is in doubt. Nonetheless, this is an opportune moment to rethink global policy questions and objectives; given shifts in political and economic power across the world, it is highly unlikely that the multilateral order in its present shape and form will endure unchallenged in the years ahead. The dominant policy packages of the past three decades in economics and security have not delivered the goods and a learning opportunity beckons. In addition, significant institutional reform, for instance, in global financial governance, has been driven by policy failure and crises (see chapters 6 and 7). We need to build on the cosmopolitan steps of the last century and deepen the institutional hold of this agenda. Further steps in this direction remain within our grasp, however bleak the first decade of the twenty-first century has been in this regard. A cosmopolitan approach can serve to help clarify the basis of international law and buttress multilateral institutions, and ensure that the wisdom embedded in the universal principles and institutional advances of the post-1945 era is safeguarded, nurtured and advanced for future generations.

My understanding of cosmopolitanism in its key aspects is set out throughout this book. The eight principles elaborated in chapter 2 lay down the chief elements of the cosmopolitan moral universe, the basis for translating private activities into legitimate frameworks of collective action and the guiding orientations or priorities for public decision-making. The justifications for these principles lie in two fundamental metaprinciples: the principle of autonomy and the principle of impartialist reasoning. The first explicates an egalitarian conception of the person through the lens of citizenship, while the second places the test of reciprocity at the heart of discriminating between those political and ethical arguments that can be generalized and those that cannot. Having set out this framework, the book explores how, embedded in public democratic law, the eight principles can shape the institutional dimensions of contemporary life. Four dimensions are set out: the legal, the political, the economic and the cultural. Against this background, policy measures are explored which together provide an outline of the core ingredients of cosmopolitan politics, in the short and long term. The key areas of policy discussed include governance, security, economics, and the environment. Tables 1–3, at the end of this Afterword, summarize the key features of this approach.

The contemporary global order faces a number of powerful stress tests in the next few years. These tests will determine whether the achievements of the post-war multilateral settlement will be reforged to create a

new, more democratic, cosmopolitan order, or fragment
into geopolitical rivalries and regional blocs that would
make effective solutions to key global challenges far
more difficult. These stress tests include whether a
successful conclusion can be brought to the Doha
Trade Round, a satisfactory regulatory structure can
be imposed on global financial markets, a durable
agreement can be reached on the mitigation of – and
adaptation to – climate change, and a robust new
deal can be negotiated to renew the Nuclear Non-
Proliferation Treaty. At the time of writing, one cannot
be optimistic about success in any of these areas, and
yet a breakthrough in just one domain might provide a
new model of global politics going forward. The contemporary multi-actor, multilevel global system has out-
grown the geopolitical settlement of 1945, and there
needs to be decisive change in both its representative
and financial base if it is to be 'fit for purpose' in the
decades ahead. One cannot call a state a modern state
if it does not have an impartial system of representation
and a depersonalized taxation system, such that tax
does not depend on the voluntary contributions of the
rich. And yet neither of these modern features has been
present at the global level. A breakthrough in the global
politics of climate change or finance or trade or nuclear
weapons would create a significant learning opportunity
and space for the development of a more egalitarian,
representative, cosmopolitan politics.

A coalition of political groupings could emerge to
push these achievements further, comprising European
countries with strong liberal and social democratic traditions, liberal groups in the US polity which support

multilateralism and the rule of law in international affairs, developing countries struggling for fairer trade rules in the world economic order, the BASIC countries seeking to change the terms of negotiation between developed and developing nations, NGOs – from Amnesty International to Oxfam – campaigning for a more just, democratic and equitable world order, and transnational social movements contesting the nature and form of contemporary globalization and environmental politics. To the extent that the 2007 Bali discussions on a comprehensive 'Global Deal' on climate change were a success, it is attributable to EU leadership, positive action by key developing countries and continuing pressures by leading environmental INGOs. It is regrettable that the same forces could not have been more effective in Copenhagen in 2009.

Europe might have a special role in advancing the cause of more effective and accountable global governance. As the home of both social democracy and a historic experiment in governance beyond the state, Europe has direct experience in considering the appropriate designs for more effective and accountable suprastate governance. It offers novel ways of thinking about governance beyond the state which encourage a (relatively) more democratic – as opposed to more neo-liberal – vision of global governance. Moreover, Europe is in a strategic position (with strong links West and East, North and South) to build global constituencies for reform of the architecture and functioning of global governance. Through interregional dialogues, it has the potential to mobilize new cross-regional coalitions as a countervailing influence to those constituencies that oppose reform, including unilateralist forces in the US.

Of course, this is not to suggest that the EU can or should broker an anti-US coalition of transnational and international forces. On the contrary, it is crucial to recognize the complexity of US domestic politics and the existence of progressive social, political and economic forces seeking to advance a rather different kind of world order from that championed by the Republican right of the political spectrum. Despite its unilateralist inclinations in recent years, it is worth recalling that public opinion in the US (especially that of the younger generation) has been quite consistently in favour of the UN and multilateralism, and slightly more so than European publics (Norris, 2000). The 2008 US presidential campaign drew upon some of these cultural resources, although whether President Obama will become a catalyst of change in this regard is unclear at this time. Any European political strategy to promote a broad-based coalition for a new global governance arrangement must seek to enlist the support of these progressive forces within the US polity, while it must resist the siren voices within its own camp now calling with renewed energy for the exclusive re-emergence of national identities, ethnic purity and protectionism.

Although some of the interests of those groupings which might coalesce around a movement for such change would inevitably diverge on a wide range of issues, there is potentially an important overlapping sphere of concern among them for the strengthening of multilateralism, building new institutions for providing global public goods, regulating global financial markets, creating a new global trade regime that puts the poorest first, ameliorating urgent social injustices that kill thousands of men, women and children daily, and tackling climate change and other environmental problems. Of course, how far they can unite around these concerns – and can overcome fierce opposition from well-entrenched geopolitical and geoeconomic interests – remains to be seen. The stakes are very high, but so too are the potential gains for human security, development, democracy and social justice. Cosmopolitanism provides the means to deepen the hold of this agenda on our culture, politics and institutions.

Table 1: Cosmopolitan principles and justifications

Elements of the cosmopolitan moral universe
- equal worth and dignity
- active agency
- personal responsibility and accountability

Principles for translating private activities into legitimate frameworks of collective action
- consent
- deliberation and collective decision-making about public matters through voting procedures
- inclusiveness and subsidiarity

Guiding orientations for public decisions
- avoidance of serious harm
- sustainability

Metaprinciples of justification
- principle of autonomy
- principle of impartial reasoning

Table 2: Institutional dimensions of cosmopolitanism

Legal cosmopolitanism
- the entrenchment of public democratic law and a related charter of rights and obligations embracing political, social and economic power
- an interconnected global legal system, covering elements of criminal, human rights and environmental law
- submission to ICJ and ICC jurisdiction; creation of a new international human rights court, and an international environmental court

Political cosmopolitanism
- multilayered governance
- a network of democratic fora from the local to the global
- enhanced political regionalization
- establishment of effective, accountable, international human security forces on regional and global levels

Economic cosmopolitanism
- reframing market mechanisms and leading sites of economic power
- expanding the representative base of the IFIs to include developing countries and emerging markets
- global taxation mechanisms to fund global public goods
- distributive mechanisms to invest in the development of the capacity of the most economically vulnerable populations

Cultural cosmopolitanism
- recognition of increasing interconnectedness of political communities
- development of an understanding of overlapping communities of fate that require collective solutions – locally, nationally, regionally and globally
- the celebration of difference, diversity and hybridity while learning how to 'reason from the point of view of others' and mediate traditions.

Table 3: Directions of cosmopolitan politics

SHORT-TERM MEASURES
Governance
- reform of global governance: representative UN Security Council; establishment of Human Security Council; strengthened systems of representation at the global level; enhancement of national and regional governance infrastructures and capacities; enhancement of parliamentary scrutiny of development and foreign policy

Security
- strengthening of global humanitarian protection capacities
- implementation of the UN's MDGs
- strengthening of nuclear arms control
- tighter regulation of arms trade

Economy
- regulation of global markets: regulation of offshore financial centres; Tobin-style tax on financial transactions; strengthened Financial Stability Board and related supervisory bodies; voluntary codes of conduct for MNCs
- promoting development: abolition of debt of highly-indebted poor countries; meeting UN aid targets of 0.7 per cent GNP; fair trade rules; removal of EU and US subsidies on agriculture and textiles

Environment
- taxation of carbon and other GHGs
- regulation of markets for carbon and other GHGs and the development of effective carbon offset schemes
- development of information instruments
- establishment of a formal international mechanism for settling environmental disputes through mediation and arbitration

Table 3 (*Continued*)

Governance
- democratization of global governance; democratic UN second chamber; enhanced global public goods provision; development of global citizenship

Security
- permanent peacekeeping and humanitarian emergency forces
- regional security arrangements
- social exclusion and equity impact reviews of all global development and security policies

Economy
- taming global markets: world financial authority; global tax mechanisms; global competition authority
- market correcting: mandatory global labour and environmental standards; foreign investment codes and standards; codes of conduct for MNCs
- market promoting: privileged market access for poorer countries; convention on global labour mobility and migration

Environment
- incorporating the cost of carbon emissions and other environmentally damaging actions in the direct costs of products, commodities and services
- development of formal institutional capacity for a world environmental organization
- global jurisdiction for an environmental court
- shift to low carbon economy

Acknowledgements

A version of chapter 1 first appeared in *Contemporary Political Theory*, 1(1) (2002), under the title 'Globalization, Corporate Practice and Cosmopolitan Social Standards'. It appears here in a much amended and developed form.

An earlier version of chapter 2 previously appeared, under the same title, in G. Brock and H. Brighouse (eds), *The Political Philosophy of Cosmopolitanism*. Cambridge: Cambridge University Press, 2005.

Chapter 3 has been adapted from parts of 'Law of States, Law of Peoples: Three Models of Sovereignty', *Legal Theory*, 8(1) (2002), pp. 1–44.

Two sections of chapter 4 have been adapted from my previous writings. The first section draws on some material developed at much greater length in my 'Law of States, Law of Peoples', *Legal Theory*, 8(1) (2002). The second section draws on my 'Violence and Justice in a Global Age', and, with Mary Kaldor, on 'What Hope for the Future? Learning the Lessons of the Past'. Both these pieces were made available through OpenDemocracy.net. I would like to thank Mary Kaldor for allowing me to draw on our joint essay and to adapt some of the material for this book. Her work on old and new wars has been an especially important influence on me here. Furthermore, a version of the chapter has also appeared in *Constellations*, 9(1) (2002), pp. 74–88.

An earlier version of chapter 5 was first published in *New Political Economy*, 11(2), (2006), pp. 157–76.

A much revised version of chapter 6 will appear in Craig Calhoun (ed.), *Possible Futures*. New York: New York University Press, 2011.

Parts of chapter 7 appeared online, on *Policy Network: New Ideas for Progressive Politics*, on 12 January 2010, available at www.policy-network.net/events/events. aspx?id=3418.

Abbreviations

AIDS	acquired immune deficiency syndrome
APEC	Asia-Pacific Economic Cooperation
ARF	ASEAN Regional Forum
ASEAN	Association of South-East Asian Nations
BASIC	(or BASIC countries) Brazil, South Africa, India, China
CBO	Congressional Budget Office (USA)
CCPR	Convention on Civil and Political Rights
CDM	Clean Development Mechanism
CESCR	Convention on Economic, Social and Cultural Rights
CSD	Centre for Sustainable Development
ECOSOC	Economic and Social Council (UN)
EIA	Energy Information Administration (USA)
EMG	Environmental Management Group
EU ETS	European Union Emission Trading System
EU	European Union
FATF	Financial Action Task Force

Abbreviations

FDI	foreign direct investment
FSB	Financial Stability Board
G1	Group of One: United States of America
G2	Group of Two: United States plus China
G2+1	Group of Two plus one: G2 plus the EU
G20	Group of Twenty: see www.g20.org/about_what_is_g20.aspx
G24	Group of Twenty-Four: see www.g24.org/members.htm
G5	Group of Five: France, Germany, Japan, UK, US
G7	Group of Seven: G5 plus Canada and Italy
G8	Group of Eight: G7 plus Russia
GATT	(or GATT 1994) General Agreement on Tariffs and Trade
GDP	gross domestic product
GEF	Global Environment Facility
GHGs	greenhouse gases
GNP	gross national product
HIV	human immunodeficiency virus
IASB	International Accounting Standards Board
ICC	International Criminal Court
ICJ	International Court of Justice
IED	improvised explosive device
IFI	international financial institution
IGO	intergovernmental organization/international governmental organization
ILO	International Labour Organization
IMF	International Monetary Fund

INGO	international non-governmental organization
IOSCO	International Organization of Security Commissions
IPCC	International Panel on Climate Change
MDGs	Millennium Development Goals
MNC	multinational corporation/company
MPA	metaprinciple of autonomy
MPIR	metaprinciple of impartialist reasoning
NAFTA	North American Free Trade Agreement
NATO	North Atlantic Treaty Organization
NGO	non-governmental organization
NPT	(or NNPT) Nuclear Non-Proliferation Treaty
OECD	Organization for Economic Cooperation and Development
PBEC	Pacific Basin Economic Council
SIPRI	Stockholm International Peace Research Institute
TRIPS	Trade-Related Aspects of Intellectual Property Rights
UD	Universal Declaration of Human Rights
UK	United Kingdom
UN	United Nations
UNCTAD	United Nations Conference on Trade and Development
UNDP	United Nation Development Programme
UNEP	United Nations Environment Programme
UNESCO	United Nations Educational, Scientific and Cultural Organization
UNFCCC	United Nations Framework Convention on Climate Change

Abbreviations

UNICEF	United Nations Children's Fund
UN-REDD	United Nations Fund for Reducing Emissions for Deforestation and Forest Degradation
US/USA	United States/United States of America
WHO	World Health Organization
WTO	World Trade Organization

Notes

Chapter 1   Cosmopolitanism: Ideas, Realities and Deficits

1 Another way to put this point is to ask whether anyone would freely choose a 'principle of justice' which determined that people (present and/or future generations) suffer serious harm and disadvantage independently of their consent, such as, for instance, the 17 million children who die each year of diarrhoea. In the face of impartialist reasoning, this principle is wholly unconvincing. The impartialist emphasis on the necessity of taking account of the position of the other, of only regarding political outcomes as fair and reasonable if there are good reasons for holding that they would be equally acceptable to all parties, and of only treating the position of some socioeconomic groups as legitimate if they are acceptable to all people irrespective of where they come in the social hierarchy, does not provide grounds on which this principle could be accepted. And, yet, this is the principle of justice people are asked to accept, de facto, as a, if not the, principle of distribution in the global economic order.

2 There are many good reasons why cosmopolitan reasoning must be combined with cosmopolitan institutional design. However sound cosmopolitan reasoning might be, the full meaning of cosmopolitan principles cannot be specified independently of the conditions of their enactment. Different thinkers give priority to 'cosmopolitanism' but, even when they agree about its contemporary conceptual specificity, they often differ over its practical efficacy and implications. Differences about how to secure cosmopolitanism in legal, political and economic terms can reveal differences in how to interpret its meaning. The specification of a principle's 'condition of enactment' is a vital matter; for if a theory of the most appropriate form of cosmopolitanism is to be at all plausible, it must be concerned with both theoretical and practical issues, with philosophical as well as organizational and institutional questions. As I have put the point elsewhere, 'without this double focus, an arbitrary choice of principles and seemingly endless debates about them are encouraged' (Held, 2006a: 266). A consideration of principles, without an examination of the conditions for their realization, may generate a strong sense of virtue, but it will leave the actual meaning of such principles barely spelt out at all. A consideration of legal arrangements and political institutions, without reflecting upon the proper principles of their ordering, might, by contrast, lead to an understanding of their functioning, but it will barely help us to come to a judgement as to their appropriateness and desirability.

Chapter 2 Principles of Cosmopolitan Order

1 I would like to thank Gillian Brock for providing comments on this chapter. The section on cosmopolitan

principles draws on earlier work of mine (2002a, 2002b, 2004) but seeks to elaborate and extend this material in an argument about the scope and status of cosmopolitanism today.

2 The principle of active agency does not make any assumption about the extent of self-knowledge or reflexivity. Clearly, this varies and can be shaped by both unacknowledged conditions and unintended consequences of action (see Giddens, 1984). It does, however, assume that the course of agency is a course that includes choice and that agency itself is, in essence, defined by the capacity to act otherwise.

3 The obligations taken on in this context cannot, of course, all be fulfilled with the same types of initiative (personal, social or political) or at the same level (local, national or global). But whatever their mode of realization, all such efforts can be related to one common denominator: the concern to discharge obligations we take on by virtue of the claims we make for the recognition of personal responsibility-rights (cf. Raz, 1986: chs. 14–15).

4 Minorities clearly need to be protected in this process. The rights and obligations entailed by principles 4 and 5 have to be compatible with the protection of each person's equal interest in principles 1, 2 and 3 – an interest which follows from each person's recognition as being of equal worth, with an equal capacity to act and to account for their actions. Majorities ought not to be able to impose themselves arbitrarily upon others. Principles 4 and 5 have to be understood against the background specified by the first three principles; the latter frame the basis of their operation.

5 As Miller aptly wrote, 'an institution or practice is neutral when, as far as can reasonably be foreseen, it does not

favour any particular conception of the good at the expense of others' (1989: 7; see pp. 72–81).

6 I say 'first seven cosmopolitan principles' because the eighth, sustainability, has traditionally not been a core element of democratic thinking, although it ought to be (see chapter 7).

7 Another way to put the point is to say that the two metaprinciples constitute the minimal basis for political judgement: namely, an interpretation of the agents involved and a view of admissible reasons that bear on their joint undertakings. The metaprinciples specify how we should see agents when we see them as authors of norms and institutions that have a decisive impact on the public good. A comparison with Rousseau may illuminate the point further. Rousseau's understanding of the 'general will' involves the will of political agents when they constitute themselves as citizens (that is, as legislators not as private persons). Citizens abstract from their personal circumstances and from the type of institutions they would favour, in order to provide the best possible laws that would enhance the common good (see Held, 2006a: 43–9). In a parallel fashion, the metaprinciples describe the way in which agents, as citizens capable of deliberation, can be conceived as the authors of their own conception of the good while acknowledging limitation on the types of reasons they can give to each other in order to reach legitimate agreement. In other words, the metaprinciples represent the bounds of cosmopolitan political discourse, setting down a set of constraints which can be used to test the consistency and acceptability of our principles. The eight cosmopolitan principles can then be thought of as those which elaborate and best fit with those elements of public reason and political judgement. (I am indebted to Pietro Maffettone for discussion of these points.)

Chapter 5 Reframing Global Governance: Apocalypse Soon or Reform!

1 Against these mounting challenges to the post-war multi-lateral system, one might place the global outpouring of support for the campaign for tsunami relief. But six months after the tsunami, many countries had not fully paid their pledged support (the US had paid 43%, Canada 37%, Australia 20%, for example) and UN pleas for help in the Niger (where 2.5 million people faced starvation) and Malawi (where 5 million faced starvation) have been largely ignored (Byers, 2005: 4).

Chapter 6 Parallel Worlds: The Governance of Global Risks in Finance, Security, and the Environment

1 This chapter was written with Kevin Young, Fellow in Global Politics at the London School of Economics. The chapter is indebted to him at many levels, but above all to his outstanding knowledge of global finance and the challenge of global financial risk management. It has been edited and modified in some respects, with Kevin Young's permission, to fit into the flow of argument in this book.

2 For example, strong confidence in banks' own internal risk assessments was a cornerstone of both the Federal Reserve in the US and the Financial Services Authority in the UK, and this confidence was directly translated into the international regulatory standards for banking in the Basel II Capital Accord.

3 In the second half of 2008, the global economy slowed considerably, with GDP growth slowing from a 5% average between 2003 and 2007 to 2% in the second half of 2008, and international trade flows collapsed in the last

quarter of 2008, with world exports projected to decline in 2009 for the first time since the global recession of 1982. See World Bank (2009a: 25).

4 Rich countries in the OECD, for example, have little problem engaging in deficit financing, and large redistribution programmes, whereas the less developed countries are more constrained – not only because of the greater volatility and uncertainty of government revenue, but also due to weaker state capacities and the greater relative costs of capital flight associated with deficit financing.

5 The US accounts for the majority of the global increase – representing 58% of the global increase over the past 10 years, largely due to the wars in Iraq and Afghanistan, which have cost around a trillion dollars thus far. However, the US is far from the only country to pursue such a determined course of militarization. China and Russia have both nearly tripled their military expenditure, while other regional powers – such as Algeria, Brazil, India, Iran, Israel, South Korea and Saudi Arabia – have also made substantial contributions to the total increase (see SIPRI, 2009).

6 The effort to inject environmental sustainability criteria into international trade negotiations is a case in point. The creation of the WTO Committee on Trade and the Environment, and the Hong Kong Ministerial round of WTO negotiations, for example, saw some of the most extensive discussions on this matter to date. More recently, the WTO-UNEP collaboration on trade and the environment at the UNEP's Global Ministerial Environment Forum in Nairobi in February 2007 represents a further step in this direction.

7 This was the case, for example, in the ambitious proposals put forward by the EU, Japan, Norway and Switzerland

to include environmental issues in the Doha Ministerial Declaration during the Hong Kong round of WTO trade negotiations. Another example is the recent row over the use of the World Bank's Climate Investment funds in 2008, in which developing countries protested that allocation decisions be made by institutions with greater representation of developing countries.

8 One approach in this direction would be to steer the discourse of responsibility to the global commons from the geography of production to the geography of consumption. For example, while countries like China contribute a steadily increasing share of greenhouse gases into the atmosphere (though in per capita terms they are still far below many heavily industrialized states), many of the products being produced are destined for markets in Europe and the United States.

9 For example, the cumulative estimate of per-capita emissions for the United States and Britain's history has been estimated to be 1,100 tonnes of CO_2 per capita, but just 66 tonnes for China and 23 tonnes for India. The UNDP findings are based on data from World Resources Institute: see 'Climate Analysis Indicators Tool (CAIT)', available at www.wri.org/climate/project/description2.cfm?pld=93.

10 In this regard, the period following the Second World War established a series of cosmopolitan steps towards the delimitation of the nature and form of political community, sovereignty, and 'reasons of state' (see chapter 3).

11 For example, the IMF after the Second World War, the Basel Committee on Banking Supervision following the Herstaat banking crisis and, more recently, the creation of the Financial Stability Forum and the G20 forum following the East Asian financial crises of the late 1990s.

Chapter 7 Democracy, Climate Change and Global Governance

1 This chapter was written together with Angus Fane Hervey, a PhD candidate in the department of Government and Journal Manager of Global Policy at the London School of Economics. I would like to acknowledge his substantial contribution to this piece of writing. It would not have developed as it did without his key inputs, especially in regard to climate change policy.

2 This figure does not control for level of development and other variables. Nonetheless, it is a useful approximate indicator of emission levels during the period when the politics of climate change has become increasingly acute.

3 Midlarsky (1998) finds that democracies have a good record on land area protection, but not on deforestation, CO_2 emissions and soil erosion, while Didia (1997) holds that democratic countries in the tropics have lower deforestation rates, and Bhattarai & Hammig (2001) claim a similar result in Latin America and Africa. Li & Reuveny (2006) show a positive effect for democracy on emissions, deforestation, land degradation and water pollution, but Barrett and Graddy (2000) find that while political and civil freedoms mostly impact positively on air pollution, results for water pollution are mixed, and Torras & Boyce (1998) maintain that democracy is statistically insignificant for dissolved oxygen, fecal coliform and particulates emissions. Neumayer (2002) demonstrates that democracies sign more multilateral environmental treaties and comply more fully with international obligations, while Ward (2008) claims that liberal democracies generally promote sustainability in fossil fuel emissions, but only very weakly.

4 We would like to thank Michael Mason for his guidance through this maze of agents and agencies.

5 As Stern (2009: 104) points out, greater certainty about emissions levels comes with less certainty about prices. Unfortunately, there is always a trade-off – it is impossible to achieve both price and quantity certainty in an uncertain world. In this case, he suggests that price uncertainty is the lesser of the two evils.

References

Ackerman, B. (1994) Political Liberalisms. *Journal of Philosophy*, 91(7), pp. 364–86.

Annan, K. (2005) Three Crises and the Need for American Leadership. In A. Barnett et al., *Debating Globalization*, Cambridge: Polity.

Archibugi, D. (2009) *The Global Commonwealth of Citizens*. Princeton: Princeton University Press.

Archibugi, D. and Held, D. (eds) (1995) *Cosmopolitan Democracy: An Agenda for a New World Order*, Cambridge: Polity.

Archibugi, D., Held, D. and Köhler, M. (eds) (1998) *Re-imagining Political Community: Studies in Cosmopolitan Democracy*, Cambridge: Polity.

Arendt, H. (1961) The Crisis in Culture. In *Between Past and Future: Six Exercises in Political Thought*, New York: Viking Press, pp. 197–226.

Armstrong, K. (2001) The War We Should Fight, *Guardian* (13 October).

Baber, W. and Bartlet, R. (2009) *Global Democracy and Sustainable Jurisprudence*, Cambridge, MA: MIT Press.

Barnett, A., Held, D. and Henderson, C. (eds) (2005) *Debating Globalization*, Cambridge: Polity.

References

Barrett, S. and Graddy, K. (2000) Freedom, Growth, and the Environment, *Environment and Development Economics*, 5(4), pp. 433–56.

Barry, B. (1989) *Theories of Justice*, London: Harvester Wheatsheaf.

Barry, B. (1995) *Justice as Impartiality*, Oxford: Clarendon Press.

Barry, B. (1998a) International Society From a Cosmopolitan Perspective. In D. Mapel and T. Nardin (eds), *International Society: Diverse Ethical Perspectives*, Princeton: Princeton University Press, pp. 144–63.

Barry, B. (1998b) Something in the Disputation Not Unpleasant. In P. Kelly (ed.), *Impartiality, Neutrality and Justice: Re-thinking Brian Barry's Justice as Impartiality*, Edinburgh: Edinburgh University Press, pp. 186–257.

Barry, B. (1999) Statism and Nationalism: A Cosmopolitan Critique. In I. Shapiro and L. Brilmayer (eds), *Global Justice*, New York: New York University Press, pp. 12–66.

Bättig, M. and Bernauer, T. (2009) National Institutions and Global Public Goods: Are Democracies More Cooperative in Climate Change Policy?, *International Organization*, 63(2).

Beetham, D. (1999) *Democracy and Human Rights*, Cambridge: Polity.

Beitz, C. (1979) *Political Theory and International Relations*, Princeton: Princeton University Press.

Beitz, C. (1994) Cosmopolitan Liberalism and the States System. In C. Brown (ed.), *Political Restructuring in Europe: Ethical Perspectives*, London: Routledge, pp. 123–36.

Beitz, C. (1998) Philosophy of International Relations. In *Routledge Encyclopaedia of Philosophy*, London: Routledge, pp. 826–33.

References

Benhabib, S. (1992) *Situating the Self,* Cambridge: Polity.

Benhabib, S. (2000) Transformations of Citizenship: Dilemmas of Political Membership in the Global Era. Presented at the conference on globalization, Yale University, New Haven, 31 March – 2 April.

Bernauer, T. and Caduff, L. (2004) In Whose Interest? Pressure Group Politics, Economic Competition and Environmental Regulation, *Journal of Public Policy*, 24(1).

Betsill, M. and Corell, E. (2001) NGO Influence in International Environmental Negotiations: A Framework for Analysis, *Global Environmental Politics*, 1(4).

Bhattacharya, A. (2009) A Tangled Web, *Finance and Development* (March), pp. 40–3.

Bhattarai, M. and Hammig, M. (2001) Institutions and the Environmental Kuznets Curve for Deforestation: A Cross–country Analysis for Latin America, Africa and Asia, *World Development*, 29(6).

Biermann, F. and Pattberg, P. (2008) Global Environmental Governance: Taking Stock, Moving Forward, *Annual Review of Environment and Resources*, 33.

BIS (2007) Bank for International Settlements, *BIS 77th Annual Report* (24 June).

Blundell-Wignall, A., Atkinson, P. and Lee, S. H. (2008) The Current Financial Crisis: Causes and Policy Issues, *OECD Financial Market Trends*, 95(2).

Bohman, J. (1998) The Coming of Age of Deliberative Democracy, *Journal of Political Philosophy*, 6(4).

Bohman, J. and Lutz-Bachmann, M. (eds) (1997) *Perpetual Peace: Essays on Kant's Cosmopolitan Ideal*, Cambridge, MA: MIT Press.

Böhme, G. (2001) *Ethics in Context*, Cambridge: Polity.

Börzel, T. and Risse, T. (2005) Public Private Partnerships: Effective and Legitimate Tools for Transnational Governance? In E. Grande and L. Pauly (eds), *Complex*

References

Sovereignty. Reconstituting Political Authority in the Twenty-First Century, Toronto: University of Toronto Press.

Brimblecombe, P. (2005) The Globalization of Local Air Pollution, *Globalizations,* 2(3) (December), pp. 429–41.

Brown, C. (ed.) (1994) *Political Restructuring in Europe: Ethical Perspectives,* London: Routledge.

Brown, G. and Held, D. (eds) (2010) *The Cosmopolitanism Reader,* Cambridge: Polity.

Broz, J. (2008) Congressional Voting on Funding the International Financial Institutions, *Review of International Organizations,* 3(4) (December), pp. 351–74.

Broz, J. and Brewster Hawes, M. (2006) Congressional Politics of Financing the International Monetary Fund, *International Organization,* 60(2) (Spring), pp. 367–99.

Brunkhorst, H. (2005) *Solidarity: From Civic Friendship to a Global Legal Community.* Cambridge, MA: MIT Press.

Bueno de Mesquita, B., Smith, A., Siverson, R. and Morrow, J. (2003) *The Logic of Political Survival,* Cambridge, MA: MIT Press.

Bull, H. (1977) *The Anarchical Society,* London: Macmillan.

Burnheim, J. (1985) *Is Democracy Possible?,* Cambridge: Polity.

Byers, M. (2005) Are you a Global Citizen?, available at www.thetyee.ca/views/2005/10/05/globalcitizen/ (accessed June 2009).

Caney, S. (2001) Cosmopolitan Justice and Equalizing Opportunities. In T. Pogge (ed.), *Global Justice,* Oxford: Blackwell.

Cassese, A. (1988) *Violence and Law in the Modern Age,* Cambridge: Polity.

Castells, M. (1996) *The Rise of the Network Society,* Oxford: Blackwell.

References

CBO (2005) Uncertainty in Analyzing Climate Change: Policy Implications, *Report for the Congressional Budget Office of the Unites States.*

Chasek, P. and Rajamani, I. (2003) Steps Towards Enhanced Parity: Negotiating Capacity and Strategies of Developing Countries. In I. Kaul et al. (eds), *Providing Global Public Goods*, Oxford: Oxford University Press.

Chestney, N. and Szabo, M. (2009) Global Carbon Market Doubled in 2008, Cut Less CO2, *Reuters* (27 May).

Chinkin, C. (1998) International Law and Human Rights. In T. Evans (ed.), *Human Rights Fifty Years On*, Manchester: Manchester University Press, pp. 105–29.

Claessens, S., Underhill, G. R. D. and Zhang, X. (2008) The Political Economy of Basel II: The Costs for Poor Countries, *The World Economy*, 31(3), pp. 313–44.

Cohen, J. (ed.) (1996) *For Love of Country: Debating the Limits of Patriotism*, Boston: Beacon Press.

Cohen, J. (1999) Changing Paradigms of Citizenship and the Exclusiveness of the Demos, *International Sociology*, 14(3), pp. 245–68.

Conceição, P. (2003) Assessing the Provision Status of Global Public Goods. In I. Kaul et al. (eds), *Providing Global Public Goods*, Oxford: Oxford University Press.

Congleton, R. (1992) Political Institutions and Pollution Control, *Review of Economics and Statistics*, 74(3).

Crawford, J. (1995) Prospects for an International Criminal Court. In M. D. A. Freeman and R. Halson (eds), *Current Legal Problems 1995*, vol. 48, Part II: Collected Papers, Oxford: Oxford University Press.

Crawford, J. and Marks, S. (1998) The Global Democracy Deficit: An Essay on International Law and its Limits. In D. Archibugi, D. Held and M. Köhler (eds), *Re-imagining Political Community: Studies in Cosmopolitan Democracy*, Cambridge: Polity Press, pp. 72–90.

References

Dahl, R. A. (1989) *Democracy and its Critics*, New Haven: Yale University Press.

Davies, H. (2005) A Review of the Review, *Financial Markets, Institutions & Instruments*, 14(5), pp. 247–52.

Deacon, B. (2003) Global Social Governance Reform: From Institutions and Policies to Networks, Projects and Partnerships. In B. Deacon et al. (eds), *Global Social Governance Themes and Prospects*, Helsinki: Ministry for Foreign Affairs of Finland, Department for International Development Cooperation.

Desai, U. (1998) Environment, Economic Growth, and Government. In U. Desai (ed.), *Ecological Policy and Politics in Developing Countries*, Albany: State University of New York Press.

Didia, D. (1997) Democracies, Political Instability and Tropical Deforestation, *Global Environmental Change*, 7(1).

Dinstein, Y. (1993) Rules of War. In J. Krieger (ed.), *The Oxford Companion to Politics of the World*, Oxford: Oxford University Press.

Doyal, L. and Gough, I. (1991) *A Theory of Human Need*, London: Macmillan.

Dugard, J. (1997) Obstacles in the Way of an International Criminal Court, *Cambridge Law Journal*, 56(2), pp. 329–42.

The Economist (1998) A Survey of Human Rights (5 December).

The Economist (2009) An Astonishing Rebound (13 August).

EIA (2006) *International Energy Annual*, United States Energy Information Administration.

Eleftheriadis, P. (2001) The European Constitution and Cosmopolitan Ideals, *Columbia Journal of European Law*, 7(1), pp. 21–40.

References

Falk, R. (1995) *On Humane Governance*, Cambridge: Polity.

Falkner, R. (2007) *Business Power and Conflict in International Environmental Politics*, Basingstoke: Palgrave Macmillan.

Feinstein, L. (2005) *An Insider's Guide to UN Reform*, available at http://tpmcafe.talkingpointsmemo.com/2005/09/14/an_insiders_guide_to_un_reform/ (accessed July 2010).

Fernández-Armesto, F. (1995) *Millennium*, London: Bantam Press.

FSB (2009) Financial Stability Board Holds Inaugural Meeting in Basel, *Financial Stability Board Press Release, No. 28* (27 June), available at www.financialstabilityboard.org/press/pr_090627.pdf (accessed August 2009).

G24 (2009) Intergovernmental Group of Twenty-Four on International Monetary Affairs and Development, *Group of Twenty-Four Communiqué* (24 April).

Gadamer, H. G. (1975) *Truth and Method*, London: Sheed and Ward.

Germain, R. (2001) Global Financial Governance and the Problem of Inclusion, *Global Governance*, 7, pp. 411–26.

Germain, R. (2004) Globalising Accountability Within the International Organization of Credit: Financial Governance and the Public Sphere, *Global Society*, 18(3), pp. 217–42.

Giddens, A. (1984) *The Constitution of Society*, Cambridge: Polity.

Giddens, A. (1990) *The Consequences of Modernity*, Cambridge: Polity.

Giddens, A. (2009) *The Politics of Climate Change*, Cambridge: Polity.

Giddens, A. and Hutton, W. (2000) *On the Edge: Living with Global Capitalism*, London: Jonathan Cape.

Gingrich, N. and Mitchell, G. (2004) *The Task Force on the United Nations*, available at www.usip.org/un/report (accessed July 2009).

References

Goldblatt, D. et al. (1997) Economic Globalization and the Nation-State: Shifting Balances of Power, *Alternatives*, 22(3), pp. 269–87.

Goodin, R. (1992) *Green Political Theory*, Cambridge: Polity.

Grafton, R. Q. and Knowles, S. (2004) Social Capital and National Environmental Performance: A Cross-Sectional Analysis, *Journal of Environment and Development*, 13(4).

Griffith-Jones, S. and Persaud, A. (2008) *The Pro-Cyclical Impact of Basel II on Emerging Markets and Its Political Economy*, available at www.financialpolicy.org/financedev/persaud.pdf (accessed 2 December 2008).

Griffith-Jones, S. and Young, K. (2009) *Institutional Incentives and Geopolitical Representation in Global Financial Governance: Explaining the Puzzle of Regulatory Forbearance Before the Crisis*. Paper presented at the Task Force on Governance, Transparency and Accountability Meeting on National and International Financial Institutions, Columbia University (28 April).

Griffith-Jones, S., Ocampo, J. A. and Burke-Rude, S. (2008) Key Principles for Financial Reforms that G-20 Leaders Should Implement, *Initiative for Policy Dialogue Working Paper* (11 November).

Guardian (2009) Ships and Jets Are no Longer the Answer (18 September).

Habermas, J. (1973) *Wahrheitstheorien*. In H. Fahrenbach (ed.), *Wirchlichkeit und Reflexion*, Pfüllingen: Neske, pp. 211–65.

Habermas, J. (1988) *Theory and Practice*, Cambridge: Polity.

Habermas, J. (1996) *Between Facts and Norms: Contributions to a Discourse Theory of Law and Democracy*, Cambridge: Polity.

Habermas, J. (1999) Bestialität und Humanität, *Die Zeit* (18 April).

References

Hall, S. (1992) The Question of Cultural Identity. In S. Hall, D. Held and A. McGrew (eds), *Modernity and its Futures*, Cambridge: Polity.

Halliday, F. (1996) *Islam and the Myth of Confrontation*, London: I. B. Tauris.

Halliday, F. (2001) No Man is an Island, *Observer* (16 September).

Hardin, G. (1968) The Tragedy of the Commons, *Science*, 162, pp. 1243–8.

Hayek, F. (1976) *The Road to Serfdom*, London: Routledge.

Heater, D. (2002) *World Citizenship*, London: Continuum.

Heilbroner, R. (1974) *Inquiry Into the Human Prospect*, New York: Norton.

Held, D. (1995) *Democracy and the Global Order: From the Modern State to Cosmopolitan Governance*, Cambridge: Polity.

Held, D. (2002a) Globalization, Corporate Practice and Cosmopolitan Social Standards, *Contemporary Political Theory*, 1(1), pp. 59–78.

Held, D. (2002b) Law of States, Law of Peoples: Three Models of Sovereignty, *Legal Theory*, 8(1), pp. 1–44.

Held, D. (2003) *Cosmopolitanism: A Defence*, Cambridge: Polity.

Held, D. (2004) *Global Covenant: The Social Democratic Alternative to the Washington Consensus*, Cambridge: Polity.

Held, D. (2005). Principles of Cosmopolitan Order. In G. Brock and H. Brighouse (eds), *The Political Philosophy of Cosmopolitanism*. Cambridge: Cambridge University Press.

Held, D. (2006a) *Models of Democracy*, 3rd edn., Cambridge: Polity.

Held, D. (2006b) Reframing Global Governance: Apocalypse Soon or Reform!, *New Political Economy*, 11(2), pp. 157–76.

Held, D. and Kaldor, M. (2001) *What Hope for the Future?*, available at www.lse.ac.uk/depts/global/maryheld.htm (accessed 8 December 2008).

Held, D. and Kaya, A. (2007) *Global Inequality: Patterns and Explanations*, Cambridge: Polity.

Held, D. and McGrew, A. (eds) (2000) *The Global Transformation Reader*, Cambridge: Polity.

Held, D. and McGrew, A. (2002a) *Globalization/Anti-Globalization*, Cambridge: Polity.

Held, D. and McGrew, A. (eds) (2002b) *Governing Globalization: Power, Authority and Global Governance*, Cambridge: Polity.

Held, D. and McGrew, A. (2007a) *Globalization/Anti-Globalization: Beyond the Great Divide*, Cambridge: Polity.

Held, D. and McGrew, A. (eds) (2007b) *Globalization Theory: Approaches and Controversies*, Cambridge: Polity.

Held, D. and Moore, H. (eds) (2008) *Cultural Politics in a Global Age*, Oxford: Oneworld Publications.

Held, D. and Young, K. (2009) The Equivalence Principle. In O. Cramme and E. Jurado (eds), *Responses to the Global Crisis: Charting a Progressive Path*, London: Policy Network, pp. 37–9.

Held, D., McGrew, A., Goldblatt, D. and Perraton, J. (1999) *Global Transformations: Politics, Economics and Culture*, Cambridge: Polity.

Helleiner, E. and Momani, B. (2008) Slipping into Obscurity? Crisis and Reform at the IMF. In A. Alexandroff (ed.), *Can the World Be Governed? Possibilities for Effective Multilateralism*, Waterloo, Ontario: Wilfrid Laurier University Press.

Helleiner, E. and Pagliari, S. (2009) Crisis and the Reform of International Financial Regulation. In E. Helleiner, S.

References

Pagliari and H. Zimmermann (eds), *Global Finance in Crisis*, London: Routledge.

Helm, D. (2008) Climate-Change Policy: Why Has so Little Been Achieved?, *Oxford Review of Economic Policy*, 24(2).

Hettne, B. (1997) The Double Movement: Global Market Versus Regionalism. In R. W. Cox (ed.), *The New Realism: Perspectives on Multilateralism and World Order*, Tokyo: United Nations University Press.

Hill, T. (1987) The Importance of Autonomy. In E. Kittay and D. Meyers (eds), *Women and Moral Theory*, Towata, NJ: Rowman and Allanheld, pp. 129–38.

Hirst, P. and Thompson, G. (2002) The Future of Globalization, *Cooperation and Conflict*, 37(3), pp. 247–65.

Hoffmann, S. (2003) America Goes Backward, *New York Review of Books*, 50(10) (12 June), pp. 74–80.

Hoffmann, S. (2006) The Foreign Policy the US Needs, *New York Review of Books*, 53(10) (10 August), pp. 60–4.

Hoffmann, S., with Bozo, F. (2004) *Gulliver Unbound: The Imperial Temptation and the War in Iraq*, Lanham: Rowman and Littlefield.

Holden, B. (2002) *Democracy and Global Warming*, New York: Continuum.

Horstmann, A. (1976) Kosmopolit, Kosmopolitismus. In *Historisches Worterbuch der Philosphie*, Band 4, Basel: Schwabe, pp. 1156–68.

Human Security Centre (2005) *War and Peace in the 21st Century*, Human Security Report 2005, available at www.humansecurityreport.info (accessed 11 February 2006).

Hurrell, A. (1995) International Political Theory and the Global Environment. In K. Booth and S. Smith (eds), *International Relations Theory*, Cambridge: Polity, pp. 129–53.

278

References

Ikenberry, J. (2002) America's Imperial Ambition, *Foreign Affairs*, 81(5), pp. 44–60.

Ikenberry, J. (2005) A Weaker World, *Prospect*, 116 (November).

ILO (2009a) The Economic Crisis in Asia: It's About Real People, Real Jobs, *International Labour Organization Press Release* (26 June).

ILO (2009b) Migrant Working Girls, Victims of the Global Crisis, *International Labour Organization Press Release* (10 June).

IMF (2009) *World Economic Outlook: Crisis and Recovery*, Washington DC: International Monetary Fund.

Independent (the) (2009) The West 'Is Failing Afghanistan' says Nato Commander (1 September).

IPCC (2007) *Synthesis Report of the IPCC's Fourth Assessment Report*, International Panel on Climate Change.

Jancar-Webster, B. (1993) Eastern Europe and the Former Soviet Union. In S. Kamieniecki (ed.), *Environmental Politics in the International Arena: Movements, Parties, Organisations and Policy*, Albany: State University of New York Press.

Jones, A., LaFleur, V. and Purvis, N. (2009) Double Jeopardy: What the Climate Crisis Means for the Poor. In L. Brainard, A. Jones and N. Purvis (eds), *Climate Change and Global Poverty: A Billion Lives in the Balance*, Washington, DC: Brookings Institution Press.

Kahler, M. (2005) Defining Accountability Up: The Global Economic Multilaterals. In D. Held and M. Koenig-Archibugi (eds), *Global Governance and Public Accountability*, Oxford: Blackwell.

Kaldor, M. (1982) *The Baroque Arsenal*, New York: Hill & Wang.

Kaldor, M. (1998a) *New and Old Wars*, Cambridge: Polity.

References

Kaldor, M. (1998b) Reconceptualizing Organized Violence. In D. Archibugi, D. Held and M. Kohler (eds), *Re-imagining Political Community: Studies in Cosmopolitan Democracy*, Cambridge: Polity, pp. 91–112.

Kaldor, M. (2007) *Old and New Wars*, 2nd edn., Cambridge: Polity.

Kant, I. (1970) *Kant's Political Writings*, ed. and intro. by H. Reiss, Cambridge: Cambridge University Press.

Karousakis, K. and Corfee-Morlot, J. (2007) Financing Mechanisms to Reduce Emissions From Deforestation: Issues in Design and Implementation, *OECD/IEA Information Paper, Annex I, Expert Group on the UNFCCC*, Paris: OECD.

Kaul, I., Conceição, P., Le Goulven, K. and Mendoza, R. U. (eds) (2003) *Providing Global Public Goods*, Oxford: Oxford University Press.

Keck, M. and Sikkink, K. (1998) *Activists Beyond Borders: Advocacy Networks in International Politics*, Ithaca: Cornell University Press.

Kelly, P. (ed.) (1998) *Impartiality, Neutrality and Justice: Re-reading Brian Barry's Justice as Impartiality*, Edinburgh: Edinburgh University Press.

Keohane, R. O. (1995) Hobbes' Dilemma and Institutional Change in World Politics: Sovereignty in International Society. In H. Holm and G. Sorenson (eds), *Whose World Order?*, Boulder: Westview Press, pp. 165–86.

Keohane, R. O. (1998) International Institutions: Can Interdependence Work? *Foreign Policy* (Spring), pp. 82–96.

Keohane, R. O. (2001) Governance in a Partially Globalized World, *American Political Science Review*, Presidential Address, 95(1), pp. 1–13.

Keohane, R. O. (2003) Global Governance and Democratic Accountability. In D. Held and M. Koenig-Archibugi (eds),

References

Taming Globalization: Frontiers of Governance, Cambridge: Polity, pp. 130–59.

Keohane, R. O. and Raustiala, K. (2008) *Toward a Post-Kyoto Climate Change Architecture: A Political Analysis,* Discussion Paper 2008-01 (July), Cambridge, MA: Harvard Project on International Climate Agreements.

Khan, I. (2001) Terrorists Should be Tried in Court, *Guardian* (12 October).

King, D. A. (2004) Climate Change Science: Adapt, Mitigate, or Ignore?, *Science,* 303 (5655) (January), p. 176.

Kingsolver, B. (2001) A Pure, High Note of Anguish, *Los Angeles Times* (23 September).

Kirgis, F. (2001) *Terrorist Attacks on the World Trade Center and the Pentagon,* The American Society of International Law (September), available at www.asil.org/insights/insigh77.htm.

Kregel, J. (2006) From Monterrey to Basel: Who Rules the Banks?, *Social Watch,* pp. 26–8.

Kuper, A. (2000) Rawlsian Global Justice: Beyond *The Law of Peoples* to a Cosmopolitan Law of Persons, *Political Theory,* 28(5), pp. 640–74.

Leftwich, A. (2000) *States of Development,* Cambridge: Polity.

Li, Q. and Reuveny, R. (2006) Democracy and Environmental Degradation, *International Studies Quarterly,* 50(4).

Lim, W. (2008) The Demise of the Anglo-American Model of Capitalism, *Global Asia,* 3(4).

Linnér, B. O. and Jacob, M. (2003) From Stockholm to Kyoto and Beyond: A Review of the Globalization of Global Warming Policy and North–South Relations, *Globalizations,* 2(3) (December), pp. 403–15.

Lipietz, A. (1992) *Towards a New Economic Order,* Cambridge: Polity.

281

References

LSE (2008) Press Office Release, UK Launches Growth Centre to Tackle Global Effects of Credit Crunch (10 December), available at www.lse.ac.uk/collections/press AndInformationOffice/newsAndEvents/archives/2008/ IGClaunch.htm (accessed 15 December 2008).

Mabey, N. (2007) Sustainability and Foreign Policy. In D. Held and D. Mepham (eds), *Progressive Foreign Policy: New Directions for the UK*, Cambridge: Polity, pp. 99–114.

MacIntyre, A. (1981) *After Virtue*, London: Duckworth.

MacIntyre, A. (1988) *Whose Justice? Whose Rationality?*, London: Duckworth.

Mann, M. (1986) *The Sources of Social Power*, vol. 1, Cambridge: Cambridge University Press.

Mapel, D. and Nardin, T. (eds) (1998) *International Society: Diverse Ethical Perspectives*, Princeton: Princeton University Press.

Marks, S. and Clapham, A. (2005) *International Human Rights Lexicon*. Oxford: Oxford University Press.

Marshall, T. (1973) *Class, Citizenship and the Welfare State*, Westport, CT: Greenwood Press.

Mason, M. (2008) The Governance of Transnational Environmental Harm: Addressing New Modes of Accountability/Responsibility, *Global Environmental Politics*, 8(3).

McCarthy, T. (1991) *Ideals and Illusions*, Cambridge, MA: MIT Press.

McCarthy, T. (1999) On Reconciling Cosmopolitan Unity and National Diversity, *Public Culture*, 11(1), pp. 175–208.

McGrew, A. (2002) Between Two Worlds: Europe in a Globalizing Era, *Government and Opposition,* 37(3), pp. 343–58.

Meikle, J. (2005) Bill Gates Gives $258m to World Battle Against Malaria, *Guardian* (31 October).

References

Mendoza, R. V. (2003) The Multilateral Trade Regime: A Global Public Good for All?. In I. Kaul et al. (eds), *Providing Global Public Goods*, Oxford: Oxford University Press, pp. 455–83.

Meyrowitz, J. (1985) *No Sense of Place*, Oxford: Oxford University Press.

Midlarsky, M. (1998) Democracy and the Environment: An Empirical Assessment, *Journal of Peace Research*, 35(3).

Milanovic, B. (2002) *True World Income Distribution, 1988 and 1993*, available at www.blackwellpublishers.co.uk/specialarticles/ecoj50673.pdf.

Milanovic, B. (2005) *Worlds Apart: Measuring International and Global Inequality*, Princeton: Princeton University Press.

Miller, D. (1988) The Ethical Significance of Nationality, *Ethics*, 98(2), pp. 647–62.

Miller, D. (1989) *Market, State and Community: Theoretical Foundations of Market Socialism*, Oxford: Clarendon Press.

Miller, D. (1998) The Limits of Cosmopolitan Justice. In D. Mapel and T. Nardin (eds), *International Society: Diverse Ethical Perspectives*, Princeton: Princeton University Press, pp. 164–81.

Modelski, G. (1972), *Principles of World Politics*, New York: Free Press.

Moore, M. (2003) *A World Without Walls: Freedom, Development, Free Trade and Global Governance*, Cambridge: Cambridge University Press.

Muller, A. (2007) How to Make the Clean Development Mechanism Sustainable: The Potential of Rent Extraction, *Energy Policy*, 35(6).

Munton, R. (2003) Deliberative Democracy and Environmental Decision-Making. In F. Berkhout, M. Leach and I. Scoones

References

(eds), *Negotiating Environmental Change: New Perspectives From Social Science*, Cheltenham: Edward Elgar.

Murphy, C. (2000) Global Governance: Poorly Done and Poorly Understood, *International Affairs*, 76(4), pp. 789–803.

Neumayer, E. (2002) Do Democracies Exhibit Stronger International Environmental Commitment? A Cross-Country Analysis, *Journal of Peace Research*, 39(2).

New York Times (2009) *Asia's Recovery Highlights China's Ascendance* (23 August).

Norris, P. (2000) *A Virtuous Circle: Political Communications in Post-Industrial Democracies*, Cambridge: Cambridge University Press.

Nozick, R. (1974) *Anarchy, State and Utopia*, Oxford: Blackwell.

Nussbaum, M. C. (1996) Patriotism and Cosmopolitanism. In J. Cohen (ed.) *For Love of Country: Debating the Limits of Patriotism*, Boston: Beacon Press, pp. 3–17.

Nussbaum, M. C. (1997) Kant and Cosmopolitanism. In J. Bohman and M. Lutz-Bachmann (eds), *Perpetual Peace: Essays on Kant's Cosmopolitan Ideal*, Cambridge, MA: MIT Press, pp. 25–58.

Nye, J. S. and Donahue, J. D. (2000) *Governance in a Globalizing World*, Washington, DC: Brookings Institution Press.

Nyong, A. (2009) Climate Change Impacts in the Developing World: Implications for Sustainable Development. In L. Brainard, A. Jones and N. Purvis (eds), *Climate Change and Global Poverty: A Billion Lives in the Balance*, Washington, DC: Brookings Institution Press, pp. 43–64.

OECD (2007) Climate Change Policies, *OECD Policy Brief*, Organisation for Economic Cooperation and Development (August).

References

Offe, C. and Preuss, U. (1991) Democratic Institutions and Moral Resources. In D. Held (ed.), *Political Theory Today*, Cambridge: Polity.

Olander, L., Boyd, W., Lawlor, K., Myers Madeira, E. and Niles, J. (2009) International Forest Carbon and the Climate Change Challenge: Issues and Options, *Nicholas Institute for Environmental Policy Solutions Report*, Report No. 09-05.

Olsen, K. (2007) The Clean Development Mechanism's Contribution to Sustainable Development: A Review of the Literature, *Climatic Change*, 84.

Olson, M. (1982) *The Rise and Decline of Nations*, New Haven: Yale University Press.

O'Neill, O. (1990) Enlightenment as Autonomy: Kant's Vindication of Reason. In P. Hulme and L. Jordanova (eds), *The Enlightenment and Its Shadows*, London: Routledge, pp. 184–99.

O'Neill, O. (1991) Transnational Justice. In D. Held (ed.), *Political Theory Today*, Cambridge: Polity, pp. 276–304.

O'Neill, O. (2000) Agents of Justice, *Metaphilosophy*, 31(1&2), pp. 180–95.

Ophuls, W. (1977) *Ecology and the Politics of Scarcity*, San Francisco: Freeman.

Parekh, B. (2001) *Guardian* (interview) (11 October).

Payne, A. (2003) Globalization and Modes of Regionalist Governance. In D. Held and A. McGrew (eds), *The Global Transformations Reader*, Cambridge: Polity, pp. 213–22.

Payne, R. (1995) Freedom and the Environment, *Journal of Democracy*, 6(3).

Pearson, B. (2007) Market Failure: Why the Clean Development Mechanism Won't Promote Clean Development, *Journal of Cleaner Production*, 15(2).

Petraeus, D. (2010) Counterinsurgency Concepts: What We Learned in Iraq, *Global Policy*, 1(1), pp. 116–17.

References

Pocock, J. G. A. (1995) The Ideal of Citizenship Since Classical Times. In R. Beiner (ed.), *Theorizing Citizenship*, Albany: State University of New York Press.

Pogge, T. (1989) *Realizing Rawls*, Ithaca: Cornell University Press.

Pogge, T. (1994a) An Egalitarian Law of Peoples, *Philosophy and Public Affairs*, 23(3), pp. 195–224.

Pogge, T. (1994b) Cosmopolitanism and Sovereignty. In C. Brown (ed.), *Political Restructuring in Europe: Ethical Perspectives*, London: Routledge, pp. 89–122.

Pogge, T. (1999) Economic Justice and National Borders, *ReVision* (22 September).

Pogge, T. (2006) Why Inequality Matters. In D. Held and A. Kaya (eds), *Global Inequality: Patterns and Explanations*, Cambridge: Polity, pp. 132–47.

Pogge, T. (2007) Reframing Economic Security and Justice. In D. Held and A. McGrew (eds), *Globalization Theory: Approaches and Controversies*, Cambridge: Polity, pp. 207–24.

Porritt, J. (1984) *Seeing Green: The Politics of Ecology Explained*, Oxford: Blackwell.

Potter, D. et al. (eds) (1997) *Democratization*, Cambridge: Polity.

Prakash, A. and Potoski, M. (2006) *The Voluntary Environmentalists: Green Clubs, ISO 14001, and Voluntary Environmental Regulations*, Cambridge: Cambridge University Press.

Quah, D. (2008) Post-1990s East Asian Economic Growth, available online at http://econ.lse.ac.uk/staff/dquah/p/Post-1990s-eaeg-KDI-DQ.pdf (accessed January 2010).

Rapkin, D. and Strand, J. (2006) Reforming the IMF's Weighted Voting System, *The World Economy*, 29(3) (March), pp. 305–24.

References

Rawls, J. (1971) *A Theory of Justice*, Cambridge, MA: Harvard University Press.

Rawls, J. (1985) Justice as Fairness: Political not Metaphysical, *Philosophy of Public Affairs*, 14(3), pp. 223–51.

Raz, J. (1986) *The Morality of Freedom*, Oxford: Oxford University Press.

Rees, M. (2003) *Our Final Century*, New York: Arrow Books.

Reinhart, C. and Rogoff, K. (2008) Regulation Should Be International, *Financial Times* (18 November).

Rischard, J.-F. (2002) *High Noon*, New York: Basic Books.

Rodrik, D. (2005) Making Globalization Work for Development, Ralph Miliband Public Lecture, London School of Economics (18 November).

Rosenau, J. (1997) *Along the Domestic–Foreign Frontier*, Cambridge: Cambridge University Press.

Rosenau, J. (1998) Governance and Democracy in a Globalizing World. In D. Archibugi, D. Held and M. Köhler (eds), *Re-imagining Political Community: Studies in Cosmopolitan Democracy*, Cambridge: Polity, pp. 28–57.

Rosenau, J. N. (2002) Governance in a New Global Order. In D. Held and A. McGrew (eds), *Governing Globalization*, Cambridge: Polity, pp. 70–86.

Ruggie, J. (1993) Territoriality and Beyond: Problematizing Modernity in International Relations, *International Organization*, 47(1), pp. 139–74.

Ruggie, J. (2003) Taking Embedded Liberalism Global: the Corporate Connection. In D. Held and M. Koenig-Archibugi (eds), *Taming Globalization*, Cambridge: Polity, pp. 93–129.

Sachs, J. (2008) Keys to Climate Protection, *Scientific American Magazine* (April).

Sachs, J. (2009) Putting a Price on Carbon: An Emissions Cap or a Tax?, *Yale Global*, 360 (9 May).

287

References

Sardar, Z. (2001) My Fatwa on the Fanatics, *Guardian* (22 September).

Scanlon, T. M. (1998) *What We Owe to Each Other* Cambridge, MA: Belknap.

Scheffler, S. (1999) Conceptions of Cosmopolitanism, *Utilitas*, 11(3), pp. 255–76.

Schmidt, J. (1998) Civility, Enlightenment and Society: Conceptual Confusions and Kantian Remedies, *American Political Science Review*, 92(2), pp. 419–27.

Schumpeter, J. (1942) *Capitalism, Socialism, and Democracy*, New York: Harper.

Sen, A. (1985) The Moral Standing of the Market, *Social Philosophy and Policy*, 2(2), pp. 1–19.

Sen, A. (1992) *Inequality Re-examined*, Oxford: Clarendon Press.

Sen, A. (1996) Humanity and Citizenship. In Cohen, J. (ed.), *For Love of Country*, Boston: Beacon Press, pp. 111–18.

Sen, A. (1999) *Development as Freedom*, Oxford: Oxford University Press.

Singer, D. A. (2007) *Regulating Capital: Setting Standards for the International Financial System*, Ithaca: Cornell University Press.

SIPRI (2009) *SIPRI Yearbook 2009*, Stockholm International Peace Research Institute, Oxford: Oxford University Press.

SIPRI (2010) *SIPRI Multilateral Peace Operations Database*, Stockholm International Peace Research Institute, available at www.sipri.org/databases/pko (accessed January 2010).

Slaughter, A.-M. (2004) *A New World Order*, Princeton: Princeton University Press.

Solana, J. (2003) The Future of Transatlantic Relations, *Progressive Politics*, 2(2), available at www.policy-network.net/uploadedFiles/Publications/Publications/pp2.2%20 60-67_SOLANA.pdf.

References

Soros, G. (2006) *The Age of Fallibility: Consequences of the War on Terror*, New York: Public Affairs.

Stephens, T. (2009) *International Courts and Environmental Protection*, Cambridge: Cambridge University Press.

Stern, N. (2004) *The Stern Review on the Economics of Climate Change*, London: HM Treasury, Government of the United Kingdom.

Stern, N. (2006) *The Economics of Climate Change: The Stern Review,* Cambridge: Cambridge University Press.

Stern, N. (2009) *A Blueprint For a Safer Planet*, London: The Bodley Head.

Stern, N. and Tubiana, L. (2008) *A Progressive Global Deal on Climate Change*, Paper Presentation (5 April), available at http://documents.scribd.com/docs/mo91frl 3sskk5a2q7i9.pdf (accessed 15 December).

Stevis, D. (2005) The Globalizations of the Environment, *Globalizations*, 2(3) (December), pp. 323–33.

Stiglitz, J. (2007) *Making Globalization Work*, London: Penguin.

Stiglitz, J. and Stern, N. (2009) Obama's Chance to Lead a Green Recovery, *Financial Times* (2 March).

Tan, K. (1998) Liberal Toleration in the Law of Peoples, *Ethics*, 108(2), pp. 276–95.

Thompson, G. (2000) Economic Globalization? In D. Held (ed.), *A Globalizing World?*, London: Routledge.

Torras, M. and Boyce, J. (1998) Income, Inequality, and Pollution: An Assessment of the Environmental Kuznets Curve, *Ecological Economics*, 25(2).

Tully, J. (1995) *Strange Multiplicity: Constitutionalism in an Age of Diversity*, Cambridge: Cambridge University Press.

UN (1988) *Human Rights: A Compilation of International Instruments*, New York: United Nations.

References

UN High-level Panel (2005) *A More Secure World,* available at www.un.org/secureworld/.

UN System Chief Executives Board for Coordination (2008) *Acting on Climate Change: The UN System Delivering as One,* New York: United Nations.

Underhill, G. R. D. and Zhang, X. (2008) Setting the Rules: Private Power, Political Underpinnings, and Legitimacy in Global Monetary and Financial Governance, *International Affairs,* 84(3), pp. 535–54.

UNDP (1997) *Human Development Report 1997,* UN Development Programme, New York: Oxford University Press.

UNDP (1999) *Globalization with a Human Face: Human Development Report 1999,* UN Development Programme, New York: Oxford University Press.

UNDP (2005) *Human Development Report 2005.* New York: UNDP; also available at www.hdr.undp.org/report5/global/2005.

UNDP (2008) *Human Development Report 2007/8,* UN Development Programme, New York: Oxford University Press.

Victor, D., Morgan, G., Apt, J., Steinbruner, J. and Ricke, K. (2009) The Geoengineering Option: A Last Resort Against Global Warming?, *Foreign Affairs* (March/April).

Vincent, J. (1992) Modernity and Universal Human Rights. In A. McGrew and P. Lewis (eds), *Global Politics,* Cambridge: Polity.

Wade, R. (2006) Should We Worry About Income Inequality? In D. Held and A. Kaya (eds), *Global Inequality: Patterns and Explanations,* Cambridge: Polity, pp. 104–31.

Waldron, J. (1992) Minority Cultures and the Cosmopolitan Alternative, *University of Michigan Journal of Law Reform,* 25, pp. 751–93.

References

Waldron, J. (2000) What is Cosmopolitan? *Journal of Political Philosophy*, 8(2), pp. 227–43.

Walzer M. (1983) *Spheres of Justice: A Defence of Pluralism and Equality*, Oxford: Martin Robertson.

Ward, H. (2008) Liberal Democracy and Sustainability, *Environmental Politics*, 17(3).

Weale, A. (1998) From Contracts to Pluralism? In P. Kelly (ed.), *Impartiality, Neutrality and Justice: Re-reading Brian Barry's Justice as Impartiality*, Edinburgh: Edinburgh University Press, pp. 9–34.

Weller, M. (1997) The Reality of the Emerging Universal Constitutional Order: Putting the Pieces Together, *Cambridge Review of International Affairs*, 10(2) (Winter/Spring), pp. 40–63.

Wolf, M. (2004) *Why Globalization Works*, New Haven: Yale University Press.

World Bank (2009a) *Global Monitoring Report 2009: A Development Emergency*, Washington, DC: The IBRD/World Bank.

World Bank (2009b) New Risks From Global Crisis Create Development Emergency, Say World Bank, IMF, *World Bank Press Release* (24 April), available at http://go.worldbank.org/6UJ27933Z0 (accessed July 2009).

Young, H. (2001) It May Not Be PC to Say, *Guardian* (9 October).

Index

accountability 5
  climate change and 25
  cosmopolitan principle 39, 71,
    103
  global governance 162
  human rights commitment 55
  IGOs 178
  partial democracies 52
  states and climate change 217
Ackerman, Bruce 44, 129
advocacy networks 35
Afghanistan 139
  cost of war 10
  military action in 132, 155–6
  security agenda and 243
  strategy in 9, 11
Africa
  global financial crisis 193–5
  UN soldiers abuse in 158
agency
  economic 108–10
  impartialist reasoning 91
  metaprinciple of autonomy 83
  moral perspectives 76–7
  principle of cosmopolitanism 69,
    70
  social justice and 73
  see also self-determination

Amnesty International 57,
    250
Annan, Kofi 147
anti-globalization protest 61
Archibugi, Daniele 178
Arendt, Hannah 90
Argentina 215
Asia
  economic growth of 2–3,
    238
  regional governance 33
  unemployment in 194
Asia-Pacific Economic Cooperation
    (APEC) 33
Association of South-East Asian
    Nations (ASEAN) 33
Australia 206, 215
autonomy
  impartialist reasoning 89
  life chances and 126–7
  metaprinciple of 82–5, 91

Bali conference 199, 250–1
Balkans 171
Bank for International
    Settlements 189, 190, 192
Barry, B. 44, 148
  impartialist reasoning 85

292

Index

Basel Committee on Banking
    Supervision 189, 190, 191–2,
    206
Bättig, M. 213
Beijing Conference on Women 114
Beitz, C. 44
Belgium 216
Bernauer, T. 213
Bin Laden, Osama 138, 139
biomedical technology 145
Bosnia 121
BP 32
Brazil
    banking increase 192
    carbon emissions 215
    emergence of 116
    governance roles 204, 206
    growth of 160
Bretton-Woods institutions
    see International Monetary Fund;
    World Bank
Bush, George W. 155, 159
    Doctrine of 197
    Kyoto agreement 242
    'war on terror' 130–1, 132
business and corporations 27, 32–3
    as agents of justice 59–60
    global governance 34–5
    social democracy 167–9

Cairo Conference on Population
    Control 114
Canada 214
capacity problem 24, 186–7,
    202–3
    environmental
    governance 199–200
Centre for Sustainable
    Development 221–2
Chemical Weapons
    Convention 159–60
China 183
    banking increase 192
    benefits from globalization 6

carbon footprint 202, 214
    economic growth of 2–3, 116,
    152–3, 160, 171
    governance roles 204, 206
    military needs 10
    military spending 196–7
citizens and citizenship 245
    active 105
    cosmopolitan 23
    multilevel 179–80
    obligations of 120
    reason and 40
    universal 43
    world 101, 180
civil society
    global 150
    Kantian cosmopolitanism 41–2
    transnational 31–3, 114
civilians
    violence against 124, 131, 133–5
Clean Development
    Mechanism 200, 232
climate change 217–19
    authoritarianism and 211
    cap and trade system 225–7,
    228, 230
    costs of 201
    democracy and 24–5
    emissions 213, 214–16
    global action 209
    global governance 198, 200–2,
    203–4, 220–4
    incentive and tax
    policies 224–30, 232–3
    lack of progress on 143–4
    measures towards 248, 249
    participation 231–2
    policymaking 234–8
    politics of agreements 230–3
    research and evidence 211–13
    short-termism 209
    state democracy and 208,
    209–14, 217–19
    transformative technologies 229

Index

coercion and deception 87, 107
colonialism and imperialism
  Kant rejects 43
Commission for Sustainable
  Development 199
communication
  cosmopolitan dialogue 42
  global interconnectedness 111
  speed of 29
communications technology 149
communities of fate 36, 73, 242
  all-inclusive
    decision-making 176–7
  citizenship 180
  overlapping 102, 106, 118–19
  universal 92
conflict resolution 25
conscientious objection 120
consent
  principle of cosmopolitanism 69,
    71
consumerism
  post-Cold War 150
Convention on Certain
  Conventional Weapons 159
Convention on Civil and Political
  Rights 51
Convention on Offences and
  Certain Other Acts Committed
  on Board Aircraft 123
Copenhagen Conference on Climate
  Change 114, 200, 204, 230
cosmopolitan law 21, 92, 247
  democratic public law 104
  framework of 99–103
  global legal system 105
  institutions of 103–5
cosmopolitanism
  classical 15, 39–41, 68
  concepts of 67–9
  contemporary 21–2, 44–50,
    68–9
  cultural institutions 110–12
  defining x–xi, 25, 49–50

economic institutions 58, 107–10
egalitarian individualism 44–5
elements of 15
embedded in states 50
global institutions and 57–8
impartialist reasoning 46–8
institutionalizing 62–3
justification 81–2
Kantian 15, 41–3, 68, 98–9
layered 16, 21, 80–1
measures towards 248–9
membership 51–2
order 20–1
political 112–16, 239–41
principles of 20, 69–75, 97–8,
  245
reciprocal recognition 45–6
reframing the market 60–6
resolution of issues 102–3
terrorism and 141–2
thick or thin 77–80
crime
  global police force 178
  international law and 55
  transnational issues 38–9
culture
  cosmopolitan ideals and 55–6,
    247
  identity 89
  institutions of
    cosmopolitanism 110–12
  networks of 29
  specificity 21
Czech Republic 216

decision-making 245
  beyond borders 172–3
  collective 15–16, 72, 76, 246
  consent 71
  exclusion and marginalization 5
  impartial reasoning 85–91
  principle of cosmopolitanism 69
  representation and power 162–5
  self-referring 24, 210

Index

stakeholders and 175
territory and borders 36
democracy 20, 23
　all-inclusive 173–7
　avenues of voice 166
　climate change and 24–5, 234–8
　concept of ix
　cosmopolitan law and 103
　dialogue of 76–7
　disjunctures with
　　globalization 35–9
　global economics 27
　global governance 147–8
　globalization and x
　impartialist reasoning 86
　international agreements 51–2
　Islam and 140
　layered cosmopolitanism 80
　legitimacy of 17–20
　multilayered xii
　networks of fora 107
　partial 52
　of the people 241–2
　post-Cold War 150
　short-termism 24, 209, 217–19
　states and climate change 208,
　　209–14, 217–19
　territorial conception of 36
　terrorist attacks and 128–31
　voting systems 53
　weak multilateralism 210–11
democratic public law 25, 245
　defined 17
　metaprinciple of autonomy
　　82–5
developing countries
　climate change and 201
　economic cosmopolitanism 110
　global financial crisis 193–5
　impartialist reasoning 89
　international representation
　　163
　reframing the market 65–6
　space for 169

difference and diversity 19, 25, 76,
　112
　globalization dramatizes 93
　human rights and 70
　hybrid cultures 111–12
　of legal structures 241
discourse
　ethical 16–17
　sectional interests 53
diversity and difference xi
Doha Trade Round 159, 181, 228,
　246, 265

economics
　compared agendas 181–2
　cosmopolitan institutions 107–10
　cosmopolitan reframing 60–6,
　　247, 248, 249
　emerging countries 116, 171
　environmental 5, 224–7, 236–7
　externalities 242
　fairness and 62
　liberalizing approach 151–3
　multilateral institutions 159
　political intervention 108–10
　power and 64–5, 126–8
　regional regulation 60
　replacing Washington
　　Consensus 165–6
　rethinking policy 244
　short-termism 217–19
　shortcomings of liberalism 5–7
　social democratic 166–72,
　　181–2
　sustainable development 74
　transborder issues and 242–3
　Washington Consensus 5,
　　12–14, 23, 115, 150–7, 171,
　　181–2
　weakness of capitalism 7
　world financial flows 30
education 22, 144–5
　economic liberalism and 6
　effect of financial crisis 194

Index

egalitarian individualism 15, 54–5
  cosmopolitan principle 44–5, 49,
    69–70, 77
egalitarianism
  basic value of 95
  cosmopolitan law 104
  environmental policy 236–7
  impartialist reasoning 88
  layered cosmopolitanism 80–1
  metaprinciple of autonomy 83
  multilevel citizenship 179–80
  thick cosmopolitanism 77–9
Egypt 139, 215
employment
  see labour
Enlightenment thought 68, 140
environment 24
  codes of conduct 55
  collective decisions 4, 16
  cost of inaction 148
  degradation of 150
  externalities 154
  framework for policy 75
  global court for 105
  global governance 198–202,
    203–4
  intensifying impacts 198
  international agreements 24–5
  measure to
    cosmopolitanism 248, 249
  overlapping communities 106
  problem of externalities 5
  reframing market and 62
  resource distribution 89
  social democracy 166, 167–8
  sustainability 155
  taxes and 169
  transnational issues 38–9
  see also climate change
Environment Management
  Group 199, 221–2
ethics
  see moral and ethical
    perspectives

ethnicity and nationality 89
European Union
  building global
    constituencies 250–2
  concept of 180
  Emission Trading System 226,
    229
  global affairs 116
  historical context 94
  layers of law 125
  pooled sovereignty 113–14
  power and economics 126
  regional governance 33
  Social Chapter 61, 114, 167
  weakened governance of 34,
    157, 158–9

finance and financial institutions 24
  fragmented and weak 189–95
  global governance 188–95, 202,
    203–7
  military spending 196–7
  networks of 29
  for public goods 164
  regulation 7
  transnational issues 38–9
  see also financial global crisis
Financial Action Task Force 32,
  189
financial global crisis 184–5, 188,
  192–5
  analysis of current 23–4
  Asian economies and 3
  economic liberalism and 6
  effect on international
    trade 29–30
  impact of 12–13
  structural weakness of 7
Financial Stability (Forum)
  Board 189, 190, 204–5
France 158
  banking decline 192
  carbon emissions 215
  military spending 10, 196

Index

freedom
  of movement 53
  terrorist attacks and 128–31

Gates, Bill 161
Germany 192, 214
Giddens, Anthony 235
Gingrich, Newt 171
Global Alliance for Vaccines and
  Immunizations 33
Global Environment Facility 199,
  200, 222, 234, 237
global governance 20, 23, 54
  boundaries 162
  building constituencies 250–2
  capacity problem 186–7
  climate change 220–4
  cost of inaction 148
  democracy 147–8
  division of labour 160–1
  foundations of 94–5
  inertia of 161–2
  measure to
    cosmopolitanism 248, 249
  multilayered 31–3, 107, 177–83
  paradox of our times 4
  policy processes 33
  power imbalances 162–5
  problem-solving 185–6
  regional 23
  replacing Washington
    Consensus 165–6
  responsibility 187–8
  social justice 147
  solidarity 146–7
  support for sovereignty 57–8
  surface trends 157–60
  transnational issues 38–9
  see also international
    governmental organizations
    (IGOs); nation-states;
    sovereignty
global order 20
  cooperative efforts 13–14

core values 102
cosmopolitan conception
  of 100–2
paradox of our times 23
Global Water Partnership 33
globalization
  countries benefiting by 152
  defining ix–x, 28–31
  democracy and x
  disjunctures with
    democracy 35–9
  dramatizes difference 93
  interconnectedness 110–12,
    149–50, 185–6
  international law and justice
    119
  multilayered xii
  political space 30–1
  production and 30
  spatial 28–9
  stretching and intensifying
    20
  trade and capital flows 153–4
governance
  multilateralism 24
Greece 216
Greenpeace 31, 57
Group (G8, etc) countries 159
  climate change policy 234
  decision-making process 2
  global financial
    governance 204–6
  powerful states 13
  recession and 3
Guantánamo Bay 243
Guardian newspaper 138

Habermas, Jürgen
  ideal speech situation 46, 85
  public sphere 49
  world citizenship 101, 180
Hague Convention for the
  Suppression of Unlawful
  Seizure of Aircraft 123

Index

Hall, Stuart 111
Halliday, Fred 139
Hamza, Imam 138
harm avoidance 48–9, 246
  impartialist reasoning 89
  principle of cosmopolitanism 69,
    73–4
  responsibility to protect 171
Hayek, F. 61
health and illness 22
  climate change and 201
  cost of inaction 148
  economic liberalism and 6
  HIV/AIDS 31, 32, 161
  lack of progress in 144
  malaria 161–2
  transnational issues 38–9
Hill, T. 46–7, 85
Hobbes, Thomas 134, 156
hospitality 92, 98–9
housing 22
human rights
  central to international law 54–6
  diversity and 70
  global social democracy 167–8
  international agreements 21, 22,
    51–2
  Islam and 140
  political legitimacy and 18–19
  preventing abuse of 122
  reframing market and 63
  states and 124–6
  strengthening conventions 178
humankind
  common heritage of 56–7
  common problems and fate 19
  fate of xi
  in harmony 40
  historical perspective of 93–5,
    240
  as a single moral realm 44–5
  sustaining 4
  terrorist attacks and 128–31
  threats to 142

Iceland 193
identity
  fluidity of 111–12
  nation-states and 102
Ikenberry, John 157
impartialist reasoning
  metaprinciple of (MPIR) 15,
    16–17, 82, 85–91
  principle of 46–8, 54–5
  as a social activity 90–1
inclusion
  all-inclusive democracy 173–7
  climate change and 25
  decision-making 72
  environmental policy 235–8
  global governance and 5
  principle of cosmopolitanism 69,
    72–3
  reciprocal recognition 45
  see also participation
India 183
  benefits from globalization 6,
    152
  carbon footprint 202, 214
  emergence of 116, 160, 171
  governance roles 204, 206
Indonesia 215
inequality 53
  justice issues 135
  law and life chances 126–8
  national life chances 6
  see also poverty
interest groups
  climate change and 210
  discourse and 53
International Accounting Standards
  Board 32, 189, 190
International Association of
  Insurance Supervisors
  189
International Bill of Human
  Rights 51, 54–5, 55
International Chamber of
  Commerce 32

Index

International Court of Justice 105, 247
Environmental Chamber 199, 223
International Criminal Court 55, 247
cosmopolitan law and 105
defining crimes against humanity 124
effectiveness of 121–2
historical context 94
terrorism and 119
international governmental organizations (IGOs) 1–2
accountability and responsibility 178
autonomy from states 221
changing global power 34
codes of conduct 55
for cosmopolitan law 103–5
division of labour 160–1
economics 159, 243
environmental agreements 199
no clear division of labour 186–7
opening up 240
supports sovereignty 57
voting systems and accountability 53
International Labour Organization (ILO)
standards of 63
international law 21
collective agreed frameworks 75
coordinating areas of law 167
crimes against humanity 120–1
developing human rulebook 4
global legal system 105
human rights central to 54–5
human rights courts 178
inequality and 126–8
layers of 125
limits on multilateralism 8–9

reframing market system and 61–6
rejects moral particularlism 21
against terrorism 133–7
transformation of 119–26
International Monetary Fund 1, 2, 190
competing priorities 161
counter-productive results 6
decision-making power 191
global financial crisis 193
global governance 205
liberal economic approach 151
International Organization of Securities Commissions 189, 206
international trade
see globalization; market system; trade
Iran 139, 214
Iraq war 21, 155–6, 216
cost of 10
'surge' in 12
UN and 157–8
US security agenda 8, 9
use of white phosphorus in 160
Islam
cosmopolitanism and 22
Iraqi sectarianism 156
terrorism and 133, 137–41
Israel 134
Italy 214

Japan
banking decline 192
carbon emissions 214
power and economics 126
jobs
see labour
Jordan 139
justice
business and 59–60
global terrorism and 134
see also law

Index

Kaldor, Mary 133
Kant, Immanuel
  cosmopolitanism 21, 41–3
  critical reason 52
  interconnectedness 118
  membership 51
  public use of reason 68
  rejects colonialism 43
  universal community 92, 98–9
  violent abrogation of law 136–7
Kaul, Inge 163–4
Kazakhstan 215
Keohane, Bob 173–4
Khan, Imran 134
King, Sir David 143
Kingsolver, Barbara 117, 129
Kirgis, Frederic 124
Kosovo 121
Kyoto Protocol 199, 242

labour 22
  child 168, 194
  market system and 63–5
  trade unions 168
law
  diversity of structures 241
  violent abrogation of 136–7
  see also cosmopolitan law;
    democratic public law;
    international law
Lebanon 139
Liberia 171
life chances 89
local affiliations 15, 19

McChrystal, General Stanley 11
Make Poverty History 31
Malaysia 215
Mandela, Nelson 183
marginalization
  see inclusion
market system
  globalization and 5–7, 27, 150,
    151

inequalities 135
  reframing 20, 61–6, 110
  social factors and 5–6
  volatility of 128
Marshall, T. 83
metaprinciple of autonomy
    (MPA) 16–17
metaprinciple of impartialist
    reasoning (MPIR) 15, 16–17,
    82, 85–91
Mexico 192
  carbon emissions 214
  governance roles 206
Meyrowitz, J. 111
migration
  EU and 158–9
  pressure of 150
  refugees and asylum
    seekers 53–4
military
  arms control agreements 159–60
  defensive needs 10–11
  global law enforcement 178
  global spending 9–10
  obligations of citizens 120
  paramilitaries 122–3
  'Revolution in Military
    Affairs' 131–2
  spending 196–7
  see also warfare
Millennium Development
    Goals 144–5, 147, 194
Miller, D.
  thick and thin
    cosmopolitanism 77, 78–9
minorities
  decision-making 72
Mitchell, George 171
Monterrey Consensus 192
Moore, Mike 161
moral and ethical perspectives 25
  common framework for 19
  cosmopolitan elements 246
  cosmopolitan principles 74–5

Index

dialogue of 76–7
Islam and 140
market and inequalities 135
moral imperialism 87
neutrality 80–1
Nurmberg principles 120–1
particularism 21
reasoning 85–6, 88
situational complexity 80
universal standards 64
value pluralism 81
worth 41

nation-states
borders of 36
changing sovereignty 96–7
classic and liberal
    sovereignty 106
collaboration on problems 4
competition between 4
cosmpolitanism and 50
democracy beyond
    borders 172–3
'ensuring' 235
financial regulation 190–1
and global governance 31–3
human rights and 55, 124–6
inequalities 6
layered governance 177–8
non-state consultation 162–5
other forms of governance
    113
paradox of our times 23
paramilitaries 122–3
power over UN 58
reframing the market 65
territorial sovereignty 99–100,
    122, 167
transnational issues 38–9
'war' on terrorism 131
'withering away' 100–2
nationalism 50, 93, 102
natural disasters
compared to terrorism 117–18

need
    amelioration of 48–9
    categories of 174–5
    levels of vulnerability 73–4
    neglect of 88
Netherlands 158, 215
Nigeria 216
non-governmental organizations
    (NGOs)
    autonomy 221
    global governance 31–3, 35
    social democratic support 250–1
    support sovereignty 57
North American Free Trade
    Agreement (NAFTA) 62, 114,
    167
    power and economics 126
North Atlantic Treaty Organization
    (NATO) 8
    arms control agreements 159
    post-Cold War 195
    strategy in Afghanistan 11
    weakened governance 157
Nuclear Non-Proliferation
    Treaty 125, 246
Nuremberg principles 120–1, 134
Nussbaum, Martha 40

Obama, Barack 160, 242, 252
Offe, C. 217–18
O'Neill, O.
    moral imperialism 87
Organization for Economic
    Co-operation and Development
    (OECD)
    climate change
        governance 222–3
    Environment Directorate 199
Organization of Security
    Commissions 32
Oxfam 250

Pacific Basin Economic Council 33
Pakistan 216

Index

Palestine 134, 139
Panitchpakdi, Supachai 194
paradox of our times 220
  global governance 143–6
Parekh, Bhikhu 138–9
participation
  cosmopolitan society 42–3
Petraeus, General David 12
pluralism
  political cosmopolitanism 81
  values 81
Pogge, Thomas 44, 145
Poland 215
policy-making
  collective problems 31
  see also decision-making
politics
  capacity to rule 37
  changing global power 33–4
  changing sovereignty 96–7
  collective decision-making 15–16
  common framework for 19
  compared agendas 181–2
  cosmopolitan 105–7, 239–41, 247
  economic intervention 108–10
  effectiveness 23
  globalized space of 30–1
  impartialist reasoning 88
  interconnectedness 110–12
  of international agreement 230–3
  legitimacy of 99
  liberal sovereignty 100
  metaprinciple of autonomy 82–5
  principle of consent 71
  short-termism 209
  situational complexity 80
  standards of 48–9
poverty
  cost of inaction 148
  global financial crisis 193–5
  Millennium Goals 144–5
  reduction programmes 167

social democracy 166
  transfer of resources 110
power
  complexity of 53
  cosmopolitanism 25
  diffusion of x
  fairness and 62
  global changes 33–4
  impartialist reasoning 89, 91
  legitimacy of 99
  networks of 37
  supports for sovereignty 57–8
Poznań conference 199
prejudice 89
Preuss, U. 217–18
public agencies 34
public goods
  coordinated action 239
  economic liberalism 6
  global 186, 206–7
  multilateral action for 37–8
public participation
  economic interest and 66
  the general will 76
  layered cosmopolitanism 80
  reasoning 50, 68, 71, 88
  reciprocal recognition 45

al-Qaeda 139

Rawls, John 82, 85
  citizens and decision-making 18
reasoning
  of citizens 40
  critical 52
  market-driven 53
  moral and ethical perspectives 85
  public use of 50, 68, 71, 88
  thin cosmopolitanism 78–9
  see also impartialist reasoning
reciprocal recognition 15, 17, 54–5
  principle of 45–6
regional governance 107

Index

regulation
  collective agreement 75
  compared agendas 181–2
  cosmopolitan framework 39
  environmental policy 235–8
responsibility
  cosmopolitan principles 69, 71,
    75
  global governance 187–8
  IGOs 178
  institutions 160–1
  layered cosmopolitanism 80
  problem of 24
Richards, General Sir David 11
rights and obligations
  universalism 50–1
Rio Conference on the
  Environment 1, 114
risk 24
Romania 216
Rushdie, Salman 112
Russia
  in Afghanistan 132
  carbon emissions 214
  governance roles 206
  military expenditure 10
  Soviet Cold War 8, 195
Rwanda 121

Sachs, J. 226–7
Sardar, Ziauddin 137
Saudi Arabia 215
Save the Children 57
Scheffler, S. 78
security 24
  accountable 107
  Bush Doctrine 197
  Cold War era 7–8
  difficulties of 243–4
  global governance 195–8, 202–3
  Human Security agenda 166–72,
    182–3
  measure to cosmopolitanism
    248, 249

new global covenant 170
Washington agenda 14, 23, 115,
  150–1, 171, 182–3
self-determination 25
  economics and 58, 108–10
  international agreements
    51–2
  life chances and 126–7
  metaprinciple of autonomy 83
  national or human 93–4
  territory and 36
  see also agency; democracy
Seneca (the Younger), Lucius
  Annaeus 40
service sectors 30
Sierra Leone 171
Singapore 216
social contexts
  economic investments 109
  if disadvantage 136
  impartial reasoning and 90–1
  pluralism 81
  reframing market and 62–6
  status 89
social democracy
  comparison of agendas 181–2
  framework of
    governance 166–72
social justice 20, 23, 155
  global economics 27
  global governance 147
  impartialist reasoning 86, 91
  market system and 61
  principle of cosmopolitanism
    73
South Africa 214
South Korea 206, 214
sovereignty
  changes of 96–7
  classic and liberal 18–19,
    99–100, 106, 125
  cosmopolitan 94, 99, 100–3
  international support for 57
  legitimate authority 239

Index

sovereignty (cont.)
    from the people 241–2
    social democracy 167
    of states 122
Spain 215
stakeholders
    closer to decision-makers 175
    consultation with 168
    decision-making processes 164
    global public goods 207
    self-referring decision 210
states
    see nation-states
Stern, N. 225
Stockholm International Peace
    Research Institute 9–10, 11
Stoicism 15, 40, 68
subsidiarity
    principle of cosmopolitanism 69,
        72–3
sustainability 16, 246
    global environmental
        agreements 25
    human life and xi
    principle of cosmopolitanism 69,
        74

Taiwan 215
Tan, K. 81
taxes
    economic cosmopolitanism 109
    environmental 224, 227–8, 236
    global mechanisms 110
    impartial representation 250–1
    Tobin 65, 169, 248
territory and borders 36
    arbitrary 41
    cosmopolitan principles 55–6, 84
    decision-making beyond 164–5
    democracy beyond
        borders 172–3
    nation over human 93–4
    origins 21–2
    overcoming 111

sovereignty 99–100
spatial globalization 28–9
spilling over borders 242
transborder interaction x
units of decision-making 72
terrorism
    aircraft hijackings 123
    cosmopolitanism and 141–2
    fighting against 130–3
    implications of 22
    Islam and 137–41
    possible weapons of 145
    rule of law and 133–7
    security agenda 8–9, 243–4
    Sept 11th 21, 117–19, 123,
        128–31, 136, 138–9, 155
    war on terror 130–1, 132,
        135–6, 155
Thailand 215
Torture Convention 55
trade 29–30
    see also globalization; market
        system
trade unions 63
transnational issues
    shift to rights and duties 56
    sovereignty over 106–7
transport systems
    economic liberalism and 6
    speed of 29
Turkey 215
Tutu, Archbishop Desmond 201

Uganda 171
Ukraine 215
United Arab Emirates 216
United Kingdom
    carbon emissions 214
    military spending 196
    reaction against terrorism 133
United Nations
    Charter of 21, 70
    Declaration of Human
        Rights 142